I0763125

Flora Culture

This book is dedicated to Jane, Grant, and Penny

To repair the world, we'll need to understand not only what is broken, but also how it was broken.

—BANU SUBRAMANIAM

Flora Culture

How Flowers Shape Our World

Christin Geall

New York · Paris · London · Milan

Contents

Introduction

After my book *Cultivated: The Elements of Floral Style* came out in 2020, I felt I'd reached a crest in my thinking, akin to that point of having climbed a hill only to see a mountain looming on the horizon. That mountain was sustainability, a very slippery word, so it made for a long, slow climb.

As I muddled along, I noticed others too were thinking about their relationships to flowers, plants, and gardens. They were asking: where did their flowers really come from? Why did they choose to grow what they did? Why did they buy certain flowers to express emotions? And why did everything—including gardens, floral art, and flowers—suddenly seem politicized? To borrow from Maddy Smith, gardening and florals aren't just about the present, they connect us to our past and encourage us to look toward the future. But was it necessary to challenge our relationship to plants so deeply?

Yes.

We are dependent upon flowers. Flowers are paramount to the survival of all species, including our own. Our love of flowers and desire to be close to them has, across cultures and for millennia, created both landscapes and livelihoods. My quest to understand how we might live with them in greater harmony is the reason I wrote this new book.

As it was developing, I gave this book the working title *A Cultivated Manifesto*, which sounds pretty radical, but manifestos aim to articulate visions, alter thought, effect change, and marry the personal to the political. Things need to change in horticulture and floristry to accommodate present realities—both scientific and cultural—and our desire, our very love of plants and flowers, is shaping our world in ways not many of us fully understand.

Flora Culture is intended help you navigate this new landscape. The book is designed as an abecedarium, which is a fun word for a collection of alphabetically arranged material—in this case, short essays on topics drawn from art, design, botany, history, biopolitics, and social science. It's a collage of ideas, some provocative, some edifying and entertaining, and you don't need to read the essays in order. You might find one topic unfolds the way a flower opens, revealing increasing complexity the closer you look. Or a caption might spur you to flip to another page. Do what you like. The ABC structure gave me a frame. You can decide on your aperture.

Most gardening and floral books aim to inspire a sense of wonder and reverence for the beauty of nature. That's my goal here too, but I count people as a part of nature, so you will also find the faces of flower lovers and growers in these pages. My explicit goal was to highlight an international array of plants and people, partly to subvert the Eurocentrism that dominates so many floral books published today and to expand the range of the conversations we have about plants. While this introduction isn't the place to thank the people that appear in this book (see the acknowledgments) it is the place to say that about half of the pictures I captured myself; the remainder came from far more professional photographers.

At one point in the development of this book, my publisher looked at some sample pages and said, "I thought this book was about floral design." It's not, ultimately, but I'm grateful to Rizzoli for giving me the space to create a new vision of a floral book, one that challenges us to be wiser designers, gardeners, and flower lovers. Call it a manifesto if you like.

A spring collection of modern cultivars from my garden.

Aesthetics

The Power of Art

1

There's an old adage in journalism to follow the money, and in the cut-flower industry you can't help notice how much money there actually is: the global trade exceeds $8 billion a year.

How do you deconstruct that? With the price paid to farmers or the price at the supermarket? With trade deals or agricultural policies? Do you start with the World Bank or a grower-owned co-op? Or do you look at the numbers not as dollars but as signifiers of value?

Let's start with the world's top twenty commercial cut flowers. I bet you can guess most of them—roses, carnations, gerbera daisies, lilies, tulips, daffodils, and chrysanthemums. Their sales align with holidays and flowery rituals: Valentine's Day, Easter, Thanksgiving, Christmas. The others on the list are fillers—the plants we don't always see but apparently want in commercial bouquets: hypericum, statice, and solidago.

Are these flowers so ubiquitous because they're prettier or easier to grow than others? No. Roses alone make up 41 percent of the global flower trade, and if you've ever tried to grow a blemish-free rose with a two-foot-long stem, you'd know that's a very tough row to hoe.

Tastes dictate what's grown, and in the case of commercial roses, people seem to value a flower more for its appearance and meaning than its scent. Another case of demand creating a market: tulips. It takes a tulip farmer two to three years to create a salable bulb and a flower farmer a handful of months before harvesting one single flower. (The bulb will never bloom again because it's more efficient economically to toss the whole plant, post-harvest, on the compost heap.)

What we see changes what we know. What we know changes what we see.

—JEAN PIAGET

So why has so much horticultural effort gone into these flowers? Culture. We value these plants. We keep choosing the same blooms again and again. Why?

The market provides a limited range of options for one thing, but to paraphrase the French sociologist Pierre Bourdieu, there's an economic incentive for the dominant class to confer meaning and status on objects it already owns or has access to. You're likely thinking: *I don't own tulips or roses. What is he talking about?* But consider the history of Western art, the works held in museums, and the flowers we see represented there: roses, tulips, sunflowers, etc. When I first read that quote by Bourdieu my entire perspective on flowers shifted. The Victorian language of flowers, wherein specific flowers held symbolic meanings, looked like a quirky way to promote British blooms and values at the height of its empire. Peonies in China, once solely an extravagance of the aristocracy, today represent good fortune (and cost a lot). The tulip mania of seventeenth-century Holland, when rare virus-ridden "broken" tulips cost the equivalent of a tradesman's annual earnings, fits with Bourdieu's view that the more highly an object is valued culturally, the more you can charge for it.

Perhaps you live in the global north, in an ex-colony, or in a country that once derived wealth from colonies overseas. What flowers do you have access to? What flowers do you promote? How might that confer meaning or bolster value?

The ubiquity of the top twenty flowers in the global market, whether grown locally or not, says more about us than we would like to admit. Namely, that we're leaning into a homogenization of design and implicitly devaluing the diversity of plants and floral styles possible on this earth.

One single stem of Kenyan baby's breath sold in the UK has a carbon footprint greater than a Dutch- or even Kenyan-grown rose—topping out at more than three tons of CO_2 emissions per stem. That's a sad truth, but the sadder one is that baby's breath, though considered plebeian, is made into "clouds" of high art for global brands—thereby accruing aesthetic and economic value, and so the cycle of demand repeats. Today more garlands of baby's breath and roses are traded in Kuala Lumpur than local flowers.

I think it's important for us to ask what effect our flower choices might have and how the art we create from flowers carries meaning. Aesthetics undoubtedly have power—that $8 billion of trade in flowers shapes landscapes and livelihoods the world over. So consider: how do you judge flowers? Does your culture value some colors or flowers more than others? Do you look at a ceiling dripping with orchids as a signal of spending and therefore prestige?

Consider how culture and class may be shaping your aesthetics. What values might be conveyed by field-to-vase artisanal works? Landedness? The privileges of space and the time to forage and grow, or simply the luxury of choice?

There is no firm right or wrong in aesthetics, only reverberations and repercussions. We all have prejudices, botanical or otherwise. This isn't inherently bad, but the global market for cut flowers has narrowed artistic practice and excluded areas of expertise and knowledge. And that's a tremendous loss to us all.

1 *Vase of Flowers (Pink Background)*, Odilon Redon, 1906.

Anthropocene

Feral Ecologies

1

In my lifetime, I've been educated to believe that biodiversity is sacrosanct. Granted I've lived much of my life on the raw edge of Western expansionism: on Lekwungen land on the northwest coast of Canada, where "wilderness" was often a part of daily life and its disappearance both visible and visceral.

In 1992, the very first United Nations Convention on Biodiversity took shape at the Earth Summit in Rio de Janeiro, Brazil. I'd just entered a new environmental studies program on the Salish Sea and recall the collective excitement: we felt certain that Indigenous people would have a voice in shaping the future, and though we didn't have this term at the time, we felt that traditional ecological knowledge (TEK) would be not only incorporated into ideas around land management, but that the little things—the bats, bees, fungi, and flowers—would count.

And they did, literally, get counted. Researchers went out to identify and quantify what was left of the world's diversity: its languages, species, and lifeways. In retrospect, I see that era as a kind of neo-Enlightenment; we still believed Western science might save us if we could just gather enough evidence to argue our case. It hasn't.

> Ours is the geological epoch not of humanity, but of capital.
>
> —ANDREAS MALM

Currently, one-third of the world is composed of novel ecosystems, places where the landscape is so altered by humans that the idea of going back to a natural state is no longer imaginable. We live in "feral ecologies" surrounded by "anthrofloras." How to make sense of feral ecologies in a more-than-human-world? Visit the Feral Atlas online, a humanities project out of Stanford University. Plants resistant to herbicides? One result of human actions. Domestic cats decimating bird populations the world over? Wetlands choked with invasive species? Wildfires? Flooding? Stronger and more frequent hurricanes? The list could go on and on. Feral means wild not in a wilderness sense but rather as things gone awry or out of control. In feral ecosystems, flux is constant.

We have a new word to mark this era: Anthropocene.

We're all a part of the *anthro* but what about the *cene*? In the 1830s, when geology came into its own as a discipline, scientists needed a way to demarcate geologic time. They struck upon the Greek suffix -cene, which means new or recent, in order to split the sixty-six million-year Cenozoic period (in which we've had mammals on earth) into more salient chunks. Researchers have used different indicators as tools for understanding the changes of the Anthropocene. These include global population, CO_2 emissions, water use, ozone depletion, species extinctions, economic growth (GDP), and temperature. Graphs depicting these indices between 1750 and 2000 show a marked trajectory. The rapid ecological changes since the industrial revolution (aka the Great Acceleration) set us on a J-curve of temperature increase and species introductions. From about the time I started university with the wind of the Earth Summit at my back, "the world has lost . . . about a billion acres of forest."[1]

Is it all bad news? Largely. And those who contribute the least toward climate change—the poor—suffer most of all.

Yet, some thinkers are noting how other organisms are thriving in this human-dominated world.[2] The Puerto Rican ecologist Ariel Lugo has noticed that on abandoned plantations, species diversity has increased from that of native forests. He argues that invasive and naturalized species help colonize disturbed land and create conditions where native species can grow. He refers to disturbance (whether by hurricane, fire, human forces, or otherwise) as "inducers of biotic creativity."[3] Changing species composition in ecosystems, as Lugo notes, is often "highly upsetting to conservation groups," but in Puerto Rico—urbanized, almost entirely altered by invasive species, people, and climatic events—invasive African bees are pollinating endemic, endangered plants.

In the Anthropocene, change is constant.

2

1 *Developing Carriageway Situation*, 2025, from the Super Nature series by Australian photographer Daniel Shipp. Shipp's inspiration derived from the eighteenth-century romanticization of "brooding landscapes" and "exotic flora."

2 *Bismarckia nobilis* in Gardens by the Bay, Singapore.

1

1 *Empire* by Feifei Zhou from the Feral Atlas. It "shows a process of land- and waterscape modification from an imperial surveyor's point of view. We invite viewers to imagine themselves standing on top of a hill, looking down to the landscape that starts with an interplantation between peasants' farms and colonial crops, gradually merges into intensified large-scale colonial plantation and water management projects in the middle, and finally arrives at the metropole, close to the shore."

2 *Species Royalty*, a collage I collaborated on with Ana Myerscough in 2024.

Appropriation

Sensitivity in Design

I quote others . . . the better to express myself.

—MICHEL DE MONTAIGNE

The Tropenmuseum in Amsterdam no longer exists—well, not under that name. *Tropen* means tropical. What, I had wondered, was a tropical museum doing in Amsterdam? And if it wasn't a botanical garden, how did it come to be one of the largest museums in the city?

The story goes back to 1864 and the founding of the Koloniaal-museum, when plants and artifacts were collected from overseas territories and colonies owned by the Dutch. Later, in the 1920s, at a grand, new location, more ethnographic material was added from around the world. Then the Germans took over the building during the war, and afterward the museum's name changed again—to the Indies Institute. When Indonesia sought its independence from the Netherlands, the Institute helped prepare Dutch soldiers to fight their former colonial subjects. After Indonesia's independence in 1945, the name Tropenmuseum was chosen. I visited in 2022, the last year the Tropen-museum held that name; the museum was in the process of decolonizing, having returned hundreds of items to Indonesia. In 2023, the museum rebranded again, joining other regional museums under the banner or Wereldmuseum, or World Museum.

One of the goals of postcolonial interpretation is to rethink words, distinctions, and categories, and encourage new conversations. When I visited, a display on appropriation challenged viewers to consider: what culture is yours? In a diverse and mobile world that can be a tough question to answer, so the museum did not. Rather the exhibit encouraged visitors to form their own opinions by posing questions such as, "When is sharing a form of stealing?"

Cultural appreciation involves respect for cultural signs and symbols. It also means creating works with the knowledge, consent, and inclusion of the group in question. Cultural appropriation is different—and stems from the traditional meaning of the word, to take and make use of without the authority or right to do so.

This might look like anything from Armenian American Kim Kardashian's cornrows (aka her Bo West look, which was in reference to the white actress Bo Derek's use of the Black hairstyle in the movie *10*), to brands like Gucci wrapping a white male model in a Sikh turban, or Victoria's Secret using white runway models dressed variously (and partially and inaccurately of course) with a Chinese dragon and a Lakota-style feather warbonnet.

Cultural appropriation usually follows from a history of exploitation of one group to the benefit of another, so consider: are you co-opting elements of another culture and trivializing it? Are you doing so for profit? Floral designers making leis might consider how their work is sensitive to culture and history. Many instances of non-Indigenous designers using Indigenous motifs without consent led to the creation of the Indian Arts and Crafts Act in the United States. Fines are severe.

As the Deh'cho Dene and Métis Cree artist and writer Coral Madge notes: "The designs and techniques used in Indigenous art and craft are living . . . When we homogenize Indigenous designs or rely on stereotype, we lose this inheritance."[4]

A further form of appropriation needs mentioning: that of one species appro-priating the guise or image of another and benefiting materially at the expense of that species. This idea comes from fashion, whereby a levy or species royalty might be paid toward leopard conservation by designers selling clothing show-casing the image of the animal's spots. Great idea: perhaps the next time you see a palm tree on a shirt, imagine the impact that a species royalty might have upon palm conservation.

2

Arid

What Is a Succulent?

Water and temperature are limiting factors in species diversity, so deserts generally host fewer species than tropical rainforests and temperate deciduous woodlands. Savannas have more species than deserts and tundra fewer. Of course, deserts differ the world over, but one thing they all have are succulents.

What technically is a succulent? Horticulturists and botanists might differ on which plants they characterize as such, but most agree that technically succulents include any plant that stores water in stems, roots, or leaves. Yuccas store water in their roots. Pachypodiums and many cactus-like euphorbias (e.g., Canary Island spurge) store water in their stems, while the familiar houseplant kalanchoe and agave (of tequila fame) store water in their thickened leaves.

So is succulent the right term to use when speaking of aloes, cacti, or quirky tropical euphorbias like crown-of-thorns? Yes. Simply stated, a cactus is a succulent, but a succulent isn't necessarily a cactus. Almost all cacti originate in the Americas.

> I have always found people, places, and plants on the edge more fascinating. It is the edge that moves one forward.
>
> —TOMÁS ATENCIO

The Desert Botanic Garden in Phoenix, Arizona, houses one of the best collections of succulents in the world. Protecting more than four hundred endangered species and displaying more than four thousand living plants, the garden is built of spires and spines, angles and textures. Deserts present extremes of drought, heat, and cold, so desert plants also look extreme: a thick fleshy treelike trunk with tiny leaves (*Fouquieria*), a plant that looks like a rock (*Lithops*), a brittle bare bush burst into delicate bloom (*Calliandra*).

For the record, an air plant (a type of bromeliad in the genus *Tillandsia*) is not a succulent though it looks like one. A succulent requires soil. Air plants do not, as they are epiphytes.

Some bromeliads store water too—you can often see it pooled in the center of the plant. Interestingly, aloes sometimes use this technique as well, so both are technically succulents.

Aloes grow all over the world now, but their natural range is limited to Africa and the Middle East. In the 1920s, aloe farms in southern France and Spain supplied cut flowers to Paris and London. Like many succulent flowers, the blooms have a great vase life.

Despite succulents offering stunning flowers, their flowering schedules and life cycles make them hard to monetize. One example is the century plant, aka agave. Some varieties bloom after eight years, others take eighty. And no matter when the flower appears, the plant will die after the effort of flowering. However agaves have two reproductive strategies beyond the hope of seeds: little vegetative growths at the base (like bromeliads, they produce pups) and bulbils, which form on the flower stalk. When the stalk senesces and bends to earth, these bulbils will root in soil.

The Mexican designer Dafne Tovar regularly uses living succulents in her work. Of potted rhipsalis (*R. quellebambenis*), she notes, "Using one very interesting element creates a feeling both precise and elevated. The visual impact is big, and with clay pots, the energy is really grounded too." She added, "Plus, the plants go on to the next event, so there's no waste."

2

1 Desert Botanical Garden, Phoenix, Arizona.

2 George Washington Carver with his painting *Yucca and Cactus*. Carver was a plant scientist, artist, and agronomist born into slavery in Mississippi, c. 1861. Carver's work on food crops led to a revitalization of agriculture in the American South (after cotton had depleted the soil). His work on peanuts and soybeans improved the lives of black families. In 1941, *Time* magazine called him America's "Black Leonardo."

Armature

Botanical Structures

> # The purpose of art is to convey the truth of the thing, not to be the truth itself.
>
> —KATE ATKINSON

Recently, I was doing a demonstration on the lawn of a library, arranging flowers in a big urn for a crowd. One woman who was late to arrive piped up, "What do you have in there?" She meant the undercarriage, the structural elements of the design concealed in the vessel. What was I using? Foam? She said she was an architect, that she wanted to understand how I was achieving such height and offsetting weight.

"An armature," I replied hoping for a shared language of design.

Armature has two meanings for plant people—one biological, one cultural. In botany, armature refers to elements of a plant's defense against predators, such as spikes, thorns, teeth, or sharp or serrated edges. While plants can defend themselves through chemical means, they also use mechanical armatures to ward off browsing beasts. Think of the tough crown of a pineapple or acacias with spines longer than their leaves. (Giraffes have extra tough lips and highly mobile tongues, allowing them to work around the acacia's armature.)

In sculpture, an armature refers to any kind of frame built to support other materials. Standing sculptures of clay or plaster that cannot support themselves require armatures. Similarly, in floral design an armature might be built of sticks, wood, wire, or any number of natural or industrial products, but the essential role is the same: to support the elements of the design. Some armatures are left exposed making them integral to our appreciation of the design; others are concealed by flowers and plants.

If the architect had arrived earlier, she would have understood my pre-plastic strategies (not sticks and stones, rather reusable chicken wire and a pin frog), but her question about foam was a good one. In the 1950s a type of armature came into fashion known as floral foam. Technically, it would probably like to be known as a medium on par with soil, but it's far from that. Floral foam is a plastic made from formaldehyde and phenolic foam, rendering it both nonbiodegradable and toxic to humans (see Microplastics, which almost all plastics turn into).

Floral foam is one of those industrial products like bisphenol A (BPA), a kind of soft plastic, that initially may have seemed like a good idea, but history has proven it to be decidedly not. The Royal Horticultural Society in the United Kingdom banned floral foam from all its shows in 2021. As of now, no government has yet banned it, but we can hope (and lobby).

Today numerous companies are innovating with biologicals to reinvent foam. Some may be marketed as compostable while not elaborating on the fact that "compostable" doesn't mean the product can be tossed in a bin with your food scraps and become soil. Rather the material is industrially compostable. Such plastics need high temperatures and specialized facilities, which few municipalities have. I tend to agree with Rita Feldmann of the Sustainable Floristry Network, who concluded that "we need flowers decoupled from industrial materials."[5] Basketry could save us all yet.

2

1 Hawaiian-grown flowers supported by an armature.

2 Endangered *Melocactus intortus* above Nelson's Dockyard, Antigua.

Aroids

Favored Flowers

> It's a really horrible feeling knowing that an obsession could lead to, potentially, the destruction of something you genuinely love.
>
> —MATT ORCHARD

What comes to mind when you read this word: *Amorphophallus*? A lovely big dick? That's pretty much where my mind went despite the Greek *amorphos*, meaning shapeless or deformed, which I suppose the spadix of the titan arum flower may be if you're seeking a particularly human penile comparison. The spadix of this arum looks vaguely like a pale green, giant, waxy candle without a wick. It rises from an elegant, ruched collar (the spathe), which is tinted dried-blood red on the inside and green on the out.

I've never seen this arum in person—the largest unbranched inflorescence in the world (the largest inflorescence goes to a palm)—but if I had I probably wouldn't be writing about what the plant looks like in bloom; I'd be remarking on its scent. Feces, cheese, old socks, a tantalizing buffet for flesh-eating carrion beetles and flies, which pollinate the plant and are drawn to the tiny flowers nestled at the base of the spadix, right above its, um, saclike base.

Not all arums smell foul—it depends on where their pollinators lay their eggs. A fly whose larvae love rotting fruit will visit an arum that smells like the same. If you're a flower and need a dung-loving midge, it behooves you to smell like feces. Faced with a scarab beetle that lays its eggs in carrion? Try rotting flesh.

I'm hinting toward coevolution here, but back to aroids: what wonders this plant family gives us! More than four thousand species, including philodendrons, colocasias, calla lilies, peace lilies, pathos, anthuriums, and monsteras. From macrame plant hangers to Sumatran jungles, from English lords-and-ladies to skunk cabbages and scarlet anthuriums, we have long been enraptured by aroids and arums.

Beyond scent, aroids have coevolved with other creatures for mutual benefit. One such example is the arum reed frog, which hangs out in the white folds of calla lilies (*Zantedeschia aethiopica*) in South Africa. The tiny frogs change color to match the pale yellow spadix, tuck their bright orange toes under their bodies, and wait for pollinating insects to slip down the slick tip of the spadix, eating what they can catch.

Botanists are still discovering new species of aroids. As researcher and doctoral student Marco Vinicio Cedeño Fonseca (pictured on the following page with an undescribed species of giant anthurium from Colombia) explained, "New species result from botanical exploration, taxonomic revision, and ecological studies. Integrated studies—looking at taxonomy, ecology, biogeography and at the molecular level, also help us to explain why a plant is a new species."[6] The centers for aroid diversity today (*Philodendron* and *Anthurium* are the biggest genera), Marco told me, are the tropical Andes. "However, in the case of *Monstera* it is the Talamanca mountain range" of Costa Rica.

Collectors have long coveted the arum family, and as with so many plants, the rarer a plant is, the more people want it. In the Victorian era, German plant collector Wilhelm Kalbreyer discovered the king anthurium, *Anthurium veitchii*, a giant with six-foot leaves. The spadix of this flower generates its own heat. Titillating to say the least. Apparently, "when the wife of American shipping magnate Charles Morgan suddenly died in the summer of 1885 and left her heirs two thousand exotic plants to sell at auction in New York City, her flaming red anthuriums drew bids of up to $110 per plant."[7] That's close to $4,000 today.

I asked Marco about collectors as he's often out in the field, walking through cloud forests in rubber boots, scaling hillsides tangled in foliage. Did he feel they were supporting conservation initiatives or has the trade in rare species had the opposite effect? He said, "This is a good question. Some of them are always supporting the projects. However, there are many people illegally collecting plants in the wild, which is directly negative for the species due to the reduction of the natural populations."

Through Marco I learned of Art Into Acres, which protects land and lifeways around the world. Using the backing of museums, galleries, and artists, the initiative is stewarding more than thirty million acres of tropical and boreal forests. As the founder Haley Mellin noted, "One of the commitments that I've found with biodiversity and betadiversity conservation is that it's not aesthetic conservation. It's not: 'This place is beautiful I'm going to conserve it.' It's: 'This place is necessary.'"[8]

1 John Lewis Childs catalog, 1898.

2 Aroid researcher and doctoral student Marco Vinicio Cedeño Fonseca with an undescribed species of giant *Anthurium* from Colombia.

3 Charles Jaftha at his flower farm in Cape Town, South Africa.

4 Workers at Green Point Nurseries near Hilo, Hawaii.

3

4

Auction

The Price of Desire

I'm kneeling, face-to-face with a paphiopedilum. Its pouty lip glistens. Lines etched on petals and sepals lure my eyes to a clitoral staminode shining yellow. I think of the hoverflies who might pollinate the flower and why I'm in Japan, crouched before dawn ogling an orchid. "I've been a predator of beauty all my life," the poet Brian Brett once wrote. "And beauty has many faces." This orchid is one tiny face in a building that houses millions.

> In this world
> We walk on the
> roof of hell,
> Gazing at flowers.
>
> —KOBAYASHI ISSA

The Ota flower market moves about 2.5 million stems a day. Sitting between the port of Tokyo and Haneda Airport, it spans over ninety-five acres, trading in seafood, fruits, vegetables, and flowers.

I meet Ryoji Kato, executive officer, manager of president office of the Ota Floriculture Auction Company, and ask him about the paphiopedilums on display near his office, each thin stem hung with a minuscule label. The flowers are exceptional, new varieties from Japanese breeders, he says. I think about scale and proportion, how in this vast complex, a tiny flower holds sway.

"Japan grows about forty thousand different types of flowers for commercial purposes. Ota trades about twenty thousand types of plants over a year," he tells me.

Ryoji is obviously precise, but also kind and generous with his time. We walk past another display highlighting more work of local growers—*kokedamas* of dwarf sakura trees, years old and barely a foot high—before he escorts me to the auction, explaining what I'll see. I take in a vast room of steeply tiered seats. Eight huge monitors are mounted on one wall below which about thirty men stand ready, boxes of flowers stacked behind them. (At Ota and the world's largest floral auction at Aalsmeer in the Netherlands, which trades about forty-six million flowers a day, there is also an image market, an auction room where flowers don't physically appear, rather their likenesses do on a screen, along with grower information, name, type, and quantity.) About a hundred buyers mill into the stalled seats, greet colleagues, and settle behind narrow desks fitted with monitors.

A traditional auction usually involves people bidding against one another, driving up the price of a cherished item. Buyers drop out of the bidding as the price increases until eventually the item sells to the highest bidder. The auctioneer is incentivized to work the crowd—in the art world, commission is usually 10 percent of the hammer price.

Flower auctions don't work this way, in part because there are so many flowers and also because numerous buyers want a share of the lot. Plus, it would take far too long to auction buckets of flowers on a massive scale every day, so the Dutch inverted the auction system in 1902. Now the auctioneer sets a minimum price and starts the bidding at the highest price. The price drops on the clock, and the buyers hit a button when the price is right. In this way, those who are willing to pay more get earlier access to blooms and multiple buyers can usually get a portion of the lot.

Japan converted to the Dutch auction system in 1990, Ryoji tells me, and it's a good thing he orients me because suddenly the bell sounds and everything happens fast.

The line of men working the flowers bow deeply to the buyers. Rising, they grab bunches and hold branches aloft. Boxes zoom along in front of them, their arms flying up and down, keeping pace. Six little auctions take place simultaneously in the one room. My eyes flick to the riveted buyers. The price clocks tick, boxes flip open, flowers disappear on conveyor belts, and the stream of merchandise seems to never end.

In the Netherlands, about 80 percent of the flowers and plants bought at auction go abroad. Exporters and wholesalers work Ota as well, but not many—about 99 percent of its flowers stay in Japan. When I remark on this fact, Ryoji pulls his shoulders back and smiles. "We have practiced floral design for over twelve thousand years."

He leads me to the distribution halls where electric (and ethylene-free—see the entry on Ripe) forklifts zip around organizing shipments on trolleys. It's like looking into a Richard Scarry book: a busytown of people, steel, plastic, concrete, and plants. A shopping area for the public abuts this zone, and Ryoji leaves me there, my eyes lured by ruffled pansies and fuzzy clovers—long-stemmed varieties I've yet to see in the trade. I can barely carry on a conversation; I'm deep-sea diving into bunches of flowers, holding my breath in joy. I hold my hands together in thanks as we say goodbye.

1 An albino variety of *Paphiopedilum fairrieanum* at the Ota Floriculture Auction in Tokyo. The display next to the auction entrance features Japanese-grown flowers. This *Paphiopedilum* is endangered in the wild, growing only in the Indian Himalayas and Bhutan.

Bedding

Carpets of Color

Have you ever seen a word spelled out in flowers? A floral clock? Or an animal built of begonias? These horticultural feats may seem dated, but they endure today—on traffic islands, at airports, in amusement parks, cemeteries, and public and private gardens. The style, initially flat, was known as carpet bedding, referencing the gardens planted to look like carpets when viewed from on high out the windows of grand French châteaux. (You could also say that the plants wove themselves together into carpets, rather than merely resembling them.)

In the West, intricate garden designs had been around since Tudor knot garden times, but bedding as we know it today—the massing of quick-growing plants into decorative seasonal displays—began in the mid-1800s when, as Noel Kingsbury notes, "gardening came of age as a mass-market hobby in the newly industrialized countries." As with any analysis of a change in culture or style, it's useful to ask both how the change was possible and why it happened. Just because something is possible doesn't mean it will happen of course. The conditions must be right.

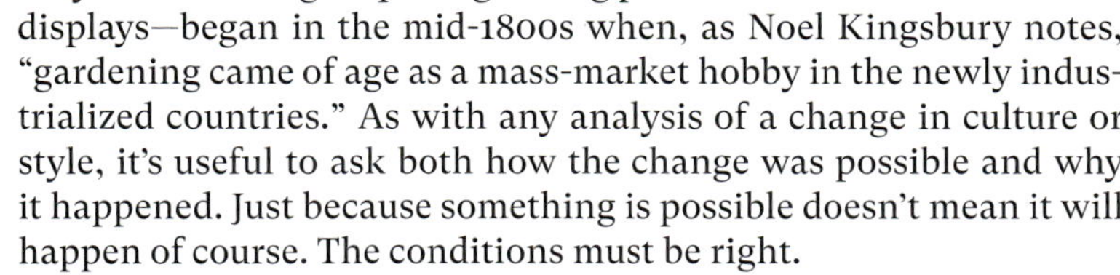

In my mind, two things made carpet bedding possible. First, the influx of new species. For centuries, botanists had collected useful plants abroad (see Bioprospecting), but by the mid-1800s huge profits could be made on plants that had horticultural potential. Today's bedding plants—a dazzling array of pelargoniums, petunias, marigolds, dahlias, begonias, calceolarias, impatiens, verbenas, and coleus—were all relatively new introductions in the mid-nineteenth century, and breeders competed to find new species overseas (and to breed an endless array of new varieties from them back in Europe and America).

Once acquired though, how did these tender species survive the temperatures of the global north? They didn't entirely have to. The climate hadn't shifted, but the technological environment where plants grew had. The industrial revolution supplied glass and iron, so it became possible grow tender plants en masse.

This production of semitropical and half-hardy plants for summer bedding was not only possible for the first time in history, it was also lucrative—explorers did deals with breeders, breeders did deals with nurseries, and nurseries brought a steady stream of new plants to the market very much as they do today. Garden plants and bedding plants generated over $3.5 billion in the United States in 2023.[9]

Embedded in our own rapidly changing technological age, it's interesting to contemplate the changes of the nineteenth century: the development of the telegraph, the steam engine, steamships, railroads. All of these innovations changed people's relationships to flowers and plants. As Judith Taylor notes, "Greenhouses, Wardian cases, and even seed catalogues... inspired a sense that global distances were being radically compressed."[10]

That's a lot to pack into a flower bed: empire, commerce, and industry. But carpet bedding feels like the perfect style of horticulture for the dawning of our industrial age. It was highly consumptive, mass-marketable, and disposable. Whereas Tudor gardeners might have clipped perennial species into shape, carpet bedding style used tender plants for a summer show, a one-off spectacle of all that was new, including the plants. When the show was over, the plants were ripped out of the ground or left to be killed by frost until spring, when the cycle started again. At the turn of the twentieth century, the style reached new heights when the American Alice Rothschild had a large three-dimensional living basket built at her estate in England. Such sculptures, built with wire frames, soil, and recently internal irrigation, are often tightly packed and color-filled—masses to please the masses.

That's not a snobbish sentiment solely—and I think here we come to the *why* of carpet bedding. In the nineteenth century, the population of Europe doubled and grew by a whopping 1,400 percent in the

Spring 1898
John A. Salzer Seed Co.
La Crosse Wis.
FLOWERS OF PARADISE.
Imagination paints for us the Garden of Eden—Paradise—as a veritable bower of flowers and blossoms, of ferns and vines, of fragrant masses of blooming glories. We have endeavored to reproduce them in our
"FLOWERS OF PARADISE"
Drawn from every nation, every country and clime, in endless sorts and countless varieties and numberless shapes, forms, sizes and colors.
A package of above Flowers of Paradise is given free of all cost with each order for 40 cents or more, from this catalogue. See also further description inside of front cover. Price per pkg. 25 cents, 3 pkgs. 50 cents.

United States. Growth begat growth, and in the burgeoning cities, few urbanites had access to outdoor space. City parks, squares, boulevards, and gardens became sources of civic pride. Horticultural feats, be they a giant floral sundial or a petite, packable and basket-bound begonia, were prized. As suburbs developed, people gained access to small garden spaces to grow their own fashionable flowers and foreign plants, which now originated from all over the world. As Taylor notes, "By the middle of the nineteenth century, a gardener sitting at home in Britain or the United States could place a single order for seeds that originated in South America, Asia, Europe, and Australia."[11]

The saddest thing I can imagine is to get used to luxury.

—CHARLIE CHAPLIN

Of course, to every stylistic horticultural action there's a reaction. Frederick Law Olmsted called carpet bedding "childish, vulgar, flaunting,"[12] and in England, two influential gardeners stand out in rebellion to the carpet bedding style: William Robinson and Gertrude Jekyll. Robinson had worked as a gardener in the London park system and came to eschew the massed bedding of exotics. He became a journalist and writer, authoring *The Wild Garden* in 1870 and *The English Flower Garden* in 1883. Jekyll, a prodigious writer (fourteen books and more than one thousand articles), garden designer (more than four hundred), and plant collector herself, denounced snobbery toward familiar flower varieties in her book *Annuals & Biennials*, suggesting "a valuable annual should not be neglected because it is so common and easy to grow and because it was so much overdone in monotonous lines in the old bedding days . . . . If the plant was misused it was not the fault of the plant but that of the general acceptance of a poor sort of gardening."[13] Robinson and Jekyll articulated many of the ideas temperate gardeners uphold about flower gardens today, including that perennials should be mixed with annuals in herbaceous borders in order to sustain displays over multiple seasons.

1 Promotional postcard from Vetterle and Reinelt, a longstanding tuberous begonia nursery in Capitola, California. Customers were welcome to browse the more than one million plants on display.

2 Catalog of plants and seeds from John A. Salzer Seed Company, 1898.

3 Postcard of coronation bed from Wolverhampton, England, 1912.

3

1

Bioprospecting

The World in Your Garden

A hundred and twenty years ago, Ball Horticulture was a cut-flower farm in Chicago. Today the company holds 40 percent of the US market for bedding and potted plants. As a multinational, Ball bioprospects, but before we get to that drama, let's set the stage: the UN Development Program defines bioprospecting as "the systematic search for biochemical and genetic information in nature in order to develop commercially valuable products for pharmaceutical, agricultural, cosmetic and other purposes." Simplified, bioprospecting is the investigation of living things for commercial gain.

From rubber to shea butter, from tulips to tomatoes, humans have long traveled to acquire plants (and the knowledge of what to do with them). This pursuit means there are more than four hundred million plants stored in herbaria, with more tropical plant specimens in the global north than in the south.

Cases in point: Sir Joseph Banks's florilegium, a document illustrating the collection of specimens acquired on his Pacific voyage of 1768–1771 with Captain James Cook, was published in thirty-four parts to accommodate 738 plants. The English botanist J. D. Hooker returned from India with 150,000 specimens. Were they bioprospecting? Yes. Were these collections developed thanks to the unacknowledged labor and knowledge of local guides? Yes. Were the collections made in the context of expanding imperialist economies? Entirely.

Consider the familiar story of breadfruit. Banks first ate it on his Pacific voyage with Captain Cook in 1769. The trees are related to jackfruit and fig and produce carbohydrate-rich fruits. Banks thought breadfruit, easily propagated and a reliable producer, might feed slaves inexpensively in the West Indies. On his return to England, he helped organize an expedition to Tahiti to procure the trees. Enter William Bligh, the infamous captain of the *Bounty*, who set out with half-barrel casks for planting up the trees, canvas covers for protection, and a gardener for tending them. (Yes, there was a mutiny on the *Bounty*, but Bligh did eventually succeed in delivering the trees.)

Just to be clear, bioprospecting is not trade. It's not Captain Cook handing nails to Hawaiians in exchange for food. It's not the Ottomans allowing the Venetians to trade salt or seeds for silk. In the age of Western expansionism, bioprospecting expeditions were regarded as a vital imperial tool. As Mary Kuhn notes, these trips allowed colonial powers in Europe to catalog potentially useful plants around the globe.[14]

When is bioprospecting outright stealing? Between 1843 and 1846, the Scotsman Robert Fortune, on behalf of the Horticultural Society of London (later the RHS), disguised himself as an Asian merchant in order to collect plants outside of the strictly controlled trading ports established by the Chinese. He smuggled out the now familiar ornamentals *Anemone huphensis* var. *japonica*, *Jasminum nudiflorum*, *Mahonia japonica*, and *Weigela florida*. Another English commercial bioprospector, William John Burchell, collected forty thousand specimens, two thousand types of seeds, and almost three hundred bulbs in South Africa between 1810 and 1815.[15] Apparently he lived in a wagon with his plunder. His father was a nurseryman in London, and the plants he collected were destined to be bred for the trade. Today Britons grow about fourteen thousand nonnative species and over fifty thousand varieties and cultivars of plants.

We can trace the United States' billion-dollar soy industry to the genetic material sourced from 4,500 soybean samples gathered on a 1929 seed expedition to Korea, Manchuria, and Japan (whose people have received little in return, save a seed bank they can draw from). The contemporary scientist Dr. Vandana Shiva, who saw indigenous crop varieties snatched by corporations from India, describes biopiracy as "biological theft; illegal collection of indigenous plants by corporations who patent them for their own use."[16]

> Fashion is the leading edge of planned obsolescence.
>
> —JONATHAN STERNE

The World of Flowers

EMBLAZONED WITH BEAUTY, this floral map shows the origins of 117 of man's favorite flowers. As people began to move from one part of the world to another, they carried plants with them. Explorers, conquerors, and adventurers returned to their homelands with flowers from far-off places. Colonists carried seeds and bulbs to the New World. Some have done so well in their adopted regions that their beginnings are seldom remembered. Holland's tulip is a native of Turkey; the "French" marigold arrived in Europe with the return of the conquistadors from Mexico. To trace these blossoms to their source, GEOGRAPHIC artist Ned Seidler consulted Dr. Mildred E. Mathias, Professor of Botany at the University of California at Los Angeles.

1 *Arctosis* spp. in the Karoo, South Africa.

2 *A Map of the Dispersion of Flowers Around the Earth*, Ned Seidler, *National Geographic*, 1968.

Not only does biopiracy speak to the exploitation of plant resources, it also acknowledges the theft of intellectual property. Collecting landraces or interviewing healers about medicinal plants and then using those plants for patented drugs without acknowledging the intellectual property holder and compensating them has haunted the history of botany.

It wasn't until 1992, with the UN Convention on Biological Diversity, that low-income countries were finally able to assert their sovereign rights over their biological resources, and it was a short five years later that Ball Horticulture entered into an agreement with the National Botanical Institute of South Africa to explore that country's rich botanical heritage for profit. And what a heritage it is—South Africa has more than twenty thousand species of plants. Of course, many of the country's flowers had already been pirated—by the colonizing Dutch, and later the English. Gladioli, scented geraniums, freesias, ice plants, agapanthus, and countless other ornamental plants from South Africa were in wide cultivation by the time Ball showed up on the scene.

In 1999, Ball went to South Africa with a modern bioprospecting win-win deal:[17] we give you money, you search for plants, you give us plants that could be interesting, and if we make money from commercializing those plants, we'll give you a royalty, less any money we advanced you for the research of finding them (I don't want to tell you how much this sounds like writing).

Following the rules of the Convention on Biological Diversity, South Africa granted Ball access to their botanical resources with this idea of benefit sharing, but the royalties turned out to be paltry; *Plectranthus* and *Arctotis* generated some money initially, but after the research costs were deducted and other deliverables fell short of everyone's hopes, South African growers and the public decried the deal, generating headlines like "South Africa's Floral Heritage Sold to US Company." The deal, as far as I can tell, remains in force today.[18] As one commentator put it, in Namaqualand, a remote region of the country close to the Namibian border awash both in rare succulents and spectacular drought-tolerant flowers (which blew my botanical mind), the deal stifled floricultural opportunities for Namaqualanders to bring their own species to market. The fallout led to a national biodiversity act being passed, a wider recognition of the importance of the country's flora, and a global awareness of the complexities of modern bioprospecting for flowers.

South African genetic material is estimated to contribute one to two billion dollars to the global trade in plants and flowers (roughly estimated at about fifteen billion). That's around ten percent. Does the country profit? No.

Today Ball owns Burpee Seeds, Darwin Perennials, PanAmerican Seed in the US, Blooming Passion in China, Outback Plants in Australia, BiGi Seeds in Italy, and countless other companies including a South African one distributing bulbs, plants, and seeds to home gardeners and nurseries. Ball grows flowers everywhere from Costa Rica to California, Vietnam, Japan, Chile, the Netherlands, and Mexico.[19] Want to grow gerbera daisies (South African) on a massive scale? You'll likely buy seed from Ball. Shopping for dahlias (Mexican) or callas (South African) at Costco or stuffing a basket with petunias in England? You're likely buying from Ball. They're everywhere.

In 2010, largely in response to drug-hunting and agricultural seed-grabs from the global south, the UN Convention on Biological Diversity passed the Nagoya Protocol to protect the holders of traditional knowledge in respect to genetic resources. The goal of the protocol is "fair and equitable sharing of benefits arising from their utilization."[20] Today some advocates of bioprospecting suggest that species-rich, low-income nations could use the money from corporate payouts to fund plant and land conservation projects, which—in the context of bioprospecting—sounds like the north using the south again, putting resources in a bank they can draw on without paying much interest.

3 Spring vygies in Namaqualand, South Africa. Namaqualand is a sparsely populated biodiversity hotspot long subject to bioprospecting.

Botanical

On Travel

> He that would eat of love must eat it where it hangs.
>
> —EDNA ST. VINCENT MILLAY

In the Marianne North Gallery at Kew Gardens in London, 832 botanical paintings hang frame-kissing-frame in two vaulted rooms, both almost visible at once. Agaves, orchids, cacti, palms, spices, fruits, and flowers from India, Australia, South Africa, Japan, the Seychelles, Borneo, Chile, and America are splayed out before you. It's a lot to take in, like being with a lover who gives too much, too soon, and despite being enraptured, you somehow feel diminished by their largesse.

North paid for the gallery's construction and opened it to the public in 1882. I first visited 104 years later, when I was a young intern in the alpine department at Kew. North's paintings didn't resonate with me then; while I'd painted Canadian wildflowers for some one-off conservation work, I wasn't into what I then would have called tropical flowers. I likely couldn't contextualize her work either as the rub between botanical illustration and colonization didn't have the friction it does for me now. The gallery spoke to me, yes, but I had no idea what to say back.

When North was a young woman, before she set off abroad to paint, she attended England's first Great Exhibition at the Crystal Palace. Britain's colonies—India, Canada, Australia, the West Indies, etc.—were all represented. As Richard Mabey notes: "Nothing was more encouraging to an aggressively expansive and optimistic people than the ceaseless parade of new resources and natural marvels that its explorers and entrepreneurs were bringing home from the colonies." While world's fairs highlighted imperial conquests—animal, vegetable, or human—economic botanists went on the hunt for foods, medicines, resources, and products to feed the factories of the global north. Marianne North was not among them. She stands apart for many reasons but primarily for being a woman. Still, she was a part of her time, a time when the affluent and educated went abroad on study tours, archaeological digs, painting trips, and collecting expeditions, and through them colonization, capitalism, individualism, and globalization spread.

North's gallery—the busy Victorian all of it—the paintings, the architecture, the colors, tiles, gilt, and the 265 species of exotic wood, framed piece-by-piece as wainscoting, is more reminiscent of a cabinet of curiosities than a gallery. The serried paintings are numbered with corresponding cards lower down in the gallery, so your head bobs up and down if you choose to read. In Australia, the tag of a lush floral still life simply reads, "Wild Flowers of the Blue Mountains, New South Wales." What looks like three species is laconically described as "Brazilian orchids." There are not solely plant portraits, but also landscapes and scenes of villages, portals, ruins, gates, and islands. The paintings sing, but the text beguiles: "Chilean ground orchids and other flowers" reads a floriferous #18, while #441 says, "Green-flowered Ixia, and other Cape Singularities." It's easy to wonder, but hard to learn.

North was fifty-two when she opened the gallery, precisely the age I am when I can afford to sit with her work for a long time. I go to the gallery six times during a visit to London to see my son and hole up in a flat in Kew to write. I'm working on this book, without quite yet knowing the shape of it, so instead of wandering the glasshouses or writing, I spend my mornings reading about North. Eventually I want to know how she created such a vast body of work by my age. How could she, a nineteenth-century woman, have traveled alone in Borneo? And India and Africa? How did she eschew marriage, children? Focus so intently on her craft? I sit in the gallery thinking, "it's research," when maybe what I'm looking for is the answer to the question of how her passion and commitment might guide me in the next chapter of my life.

That answer is not in her autobiography. It's tamely titled *Recollections of a Happy Life* and serves more as a travelogue than a memoir. The opening page stolidly traces her lineage. In the first hundred words she lists eight prestigious male names. It's an honest start, I suppose, these markers of privilege. North had means; she did not work for a wage. Who, in her position or of her gender back then would, or even could? Her father was a member of Parliament. When he died and she resolved to paint plants and travel, she knew well the social fabric of empire and pulled the many strings accorded to her class. She had been introduced by her father to Sir William Hooker, the first official director of Kew; later his son Joseph, also a director of Kew Gardens, would approve her donation of the gallery. Her autobiography details how on her travels she used letters of introduction like tickets to ride—in rutted roads on colonial governors' buggies, up rivers, over mountains—to places where she might get a bed and maid, or rent a house, or slum it on a camp cot in a barn. By today's standards she was, by turns, incredibly brave and bewildering. She barely batted an eyelash at slavery, writing in 1894 (more than sixty years after the UK's Slavery Abolition Act): "It is a mistake to suppose that slaves are not well treated; I have seen them petted as we pet animals, and they usually went about grinning and singing." Not to diminish the horror of those words, but the Great Exhibition may have had an effect. To borrow from Michael Brooks: "The exposition's human and material displays educated visitors about . . . their colonial subjects' lifestyles in an idyllic and picturesque manner, devoid of any notion of resistance, conflict, pacification or violence." North considered herself civilized, and her nation considered itself a civilizing force. In Brazil, she was questioned how it is she could afford to travel and paint flowers. "Did the Government pay my expenses?" she wrote. No, she did, but so odd was her independent, womanly path and so broad the reach of colonial science, that it wasn't such a strange question to have been asked.

My favorite grandmother had a safari room with brass tables, animal skins, and grass wallpaper where she hung a small, framed map of the world. She pushed colored pins into this map to record her travels. With matching thread, she connected cities and countries so that patterns stretched across the hemispheres. One thin yellow line went up the Yangtze. Blue thread strung together the Falklands, and green triangles fell across the Black Sea. Europe dazzled me with its web of pins, while New Zealand and Australia were connected in a taut white line stretching to and from Hawaii. In Africa, she had one color for Egypt and Morocco, another for Kenya, South Africa, and the Seychelles. The Galapagos she wove into a small nest of purple, mirroring the pale blue clouds of thread floating above the Caribbean. In one corner of the world, she strung out a legend with the threads, each color labeled with a year.

When I was learning to color the countries of the world in school, I'd sit at my desk gnawing a rainbow of colored pencils, straining to remember what shade went where, to somehow match my legend to my Granny's. I could not, and a part of me now cannot, but the ethos of travel-as-edification still burns in my veins.

Looking back at my younger intern self, I'm guessing I saw North's work and figured, with twenty-something aplomb, I could do something similar with my life: travel, garden, make art, and write. But I didn't have enough money or focus or gumption then, and so I did not do something similar with my life. I had a baby shortly after leaving Kew and found my way into grad school. And with that child now settled not far from the garden, I wondered about tourism, and the value and harm in it.

2

I read Jamaica Kincaid. "Every native would like to find a way out, every native would like a rest, every native would like a tour. But some natives—most natives in the world—cannot go anywhere. They are too poor. They are too poor to go anywhere. They are too poor to escape the reality of their lives; and they are too poor to live properly in the place they live, which is the very place you, the tourist, want to go—so when the natives see you, the tourist, they envy you, they envy your ability to leave your own banality and boredom, they envy your ability to turn their own banality and boredom into a source of pleasure for yourself."[21] According to the United Nations World Tourism Organization's World Tourism Barometer, in 1950, two hundred thousand people arrived in Asia and the Pacific. In 1980, twenty-three million. In 2018, 343 million.

When North arrived in Jamaica, her first tropical country, she wrote, "I was in a state of ecstasy, and hardly knew what to paint first."

In the nineteenth century, botanists went abroad to collect, sketch, and press plants. The style they used—taxonomic, line drawn—could be reproduced lithographically, watercolored, and later in the century, reproduced by chromolithography. Interest in plants grew from these books, and botany, topmost among all the sciences, was considered an acceptable subject for women. North also saw the early days of mass-produced hothouse-grown plants, carpet bedding of tropical plants, a fern craze, and an orchid craze, all fueled by botanical exploration and exploitation in the global south.

But North was not a collector or botanist. She was a painter working in oil. She also worked by ecological associations, so in the gallery section marked "Jamaica," *Leonotis nepetifolia* (an African species) flames orange while a hummingbird sails past. In Borneo, the white stars of a *Crinum* (that would come to be named for her) fill the frame, and you're sated with just that one image until you glimpse the same plant growing in the stream behind. Her pictures give the what but also hint at the who, why, and where.

Some suggest this was North's desire—to show the connections between living things. Her era was also Darwin's, and she knew of his work. They eventually met in 1880. Unfettered by conventional employment and outside the academy, North painted what she saw. Victorian botanists were deconstructing seed from leaf, prying things apart, and if not fully objectifying nature, then at the very least stripping the subjective from it. North did the opposite, painted the people in the garden, the child carrying the fruit, and the bird with a plant's seed.

Over that week of sitting with North's work, I came to see how I was viewing it as an older woman, through a fractured lens of history, politics, and identity, while in my heart of hearts, I admired her clarity of focus. Her words, "after a month of perfect quiet and incessant painting," sounded like peace. I too wanted to deep-see, to do my work and have my identity fall away. Instead, I checked my privilege at almost every intersection of thought, and rightly so too. But there are so many thoughts, so many intersections, and some days, it felt like too much. North's paintings made me want to lose myself when I felt that I lived in an era that required that self to be constantly, indefatigably present.

"The way we see things is affected by what we know or what we believe," John Berger once wrote. You visit a gallery, bring a new set of issues to it, and you see something new. That's how art works. It's you and the art, and the art isn't changing—you are.

3

1 *Green-flowered Ixia and other Cape Singularities*, Marianne North. Painted near Ceres in South Africa, the image features *Ixia viridiflora* (green-flowered Ixia), *Pelargonium triste* (leaf and flowers), *Ixia speciosa* (red), *Watsonia* (pink), *Cyrtanthus* (orange), *Helichrysum* (white), with *Leucospermum* and *Helipterum eximium* below. North painted 110 pictures in South Africa over a nine-month trip between 1882 and 1883.

2 The Marianne North gallery at the Royal Botanic Gardens, Kew, England.

3 A reproduction of an engraving of Marianne North that appeared in *The Illustrated London News*, 1883.

Breeding

Flowers and Fashion

1

In 2015, at a nursery in South Korea owned by Hyuk Jin Lee, the popular African houseplant Zanzibar gem (*Zamioculcas*) developed a black leaf on an otherwise green plant. Realizing the potential of the mutation, Lee propagated the dark leaf through leaf cuttings and over years, ensured the color was stable before seeking a patent for his new cultivar, which he named 'Dowon.' To reach the global market, Hyuk Jin Lee granted the propagation rights to Costa Farms in the United States, who then developed the trademark name Raven™ for marketing purposes.

Flower breeders and plant enthusiasts look out for sports, such as a flower with radically different petal colors or a leaf that suddenly variegates or changes color. In all living things, a genetic mix-up can lead to a mutation. A plant may change its morphology or appearance, as was the case with white currants suddenly appearing on a portion of a red currant plant or the nectarine, which was first a sport of a peach tree. While the characteristics that led to the development of a sport may not sexually reproduce to type (for example, if you had planted that first nectarine pit in the hopes of growing more, you'd likely get peaches), horticulturists are able to vegetatively reproduce sports by taking cuttings or through tissue culture.

Why? There's money in the miracle. Plant breeders only have a handful of methods to create new flowers. Like Lee, they might discover a natural mutation or induce an artificial mutation (radiation can be used), or happen upon a cross-pollination, or deliberately cross-pollinate, or select within an existing population over time, or combine these methods however they can.

> The fact that some choice is good doesn't necessarily mean that more choice is better.
>
> —BARRY SCHWARTZ

Breeder's rights are granted only if the plant variety is new, distinct, uniform, and stable. In many countries a breeder can protect their rights through patents, but generally the breeder doesn't make money until the plant is licensed—think Proven Winners in the United States or Emsflower in Europe. Corporations like Costa Farms figure out how to produce the plant en masse, market it, and sell it. They report their sales to the breeder, who then earns a licensing fee per plant sold. Breeders might earn 25 percent of the retail price of a one-gallon perennial in the US market.

Now picture the plant section of a big box store or a florist's shop—there's not a ton of diversity in the types of plants available, but often there's choice when it comes to color or size. Why? Swapping out old colors for new ones is one of the ways to catch a customer's eye.[22] According to Dr. Rick Grazzini of GardenGenetics, "Brands approach the color wheel a bit like a lazy Susan: by spinning the disk and doling out new color palette options over time, they can pique the consumer's interest again and again with a lively update to a reliable mainstay."[23]

As Coco Chanel once quipped, "Fashion is made to become unfashionable," and this is entirely true for flowers and plants. According to Royal FloraHolland, every year between 1,200 and 1,500 new varieties of flowers and plants are created in the Netherlands. Japanese breeders also introduce between two thousand and three thousand new varieties every year. From petunias to dahlias to callas to verbenas, ornamental horticulture is built on the business of breeding.

But what's available? Ironically, both too much and not enough. To quote Mike Rimland reflecting on what we see in garden centers: "To date, there are about 100 different genera with thousands of varieties that make up the core annual side. On the indoor side, there are about 20 different genera with hundreds of varieties that encompass the core of the business."[24]

Haven't we all had enough?

2

1 July blooms from my garden.

2 Theodore L. Mead first visited Florida in 1869. He became an avid horticulturist near Oviedo, breeding crinums, gladioli, orchids, amaryllis, caladiums, and daylilies. He is pictured here with his "Mead Type Amaryllis" hybrids.

Bromeliads

Iconic Plants

> Knowledge is like a garden: if it is not cultivated, it cannot be harvested.
>
> —GUINEAN PROVERB

Spectacularly beautiful, brilliantly designed to survive periods of drought, easy to grow, and many with robust showy flowers in white, scarlet, orange, yellow, blue, and magenta, the bromeliad family gives us tiny air plants and the Queen of the Andes, a fifty-foot-tall plant known as Puya. Most bromeliads are succulents, but they may not look it. Many grow in trees as epiphytes, and some root into the earth. There are about 3,700 species in the Bromeliacae family, and all are endemic to the Americas save one African species, *Pitcarnia feliciana*, which scientists suggest has lived in West Africa for ten million years, the first seeds of which likely traveled in a bird over the Atlantic. More species are discovered every day.

Iconic and ancient, pineapples are bromeliads, with robust leaves that grow in a rosette. The domestication of the fruit likely originated in Brazil and Paraguay and happened thousands of years ago, so no one really knows precisely, but the Guarani name for the pineapple, *ananas*, means "excellent fruit" and is the genus name for pineapple, *Ananas comosus*. The cultivation of pineapple drifted into the Caribbean with the Taíno people, then leaped to India and the Philippines from the New World empires of Portugal and Spain.

When Christopher Columbus returned to Spain with a pineapple, royalty went mad for the fruit (it even has a crown—which is the botanical term for the tuft of leaves spouting from the top), and the wealthy classes followed the fad, eventually growing pineapples in hothouses and presenting them as tokens of good taste. Need to impress dinner guests? Rent-a-pineapple for a table centerpiece. Truly, a rental trade in pineapples as signifiers of status meant the fruit wasn't eaten as much as admired in eighteenth-century Europe. Simultaneously the pineapple became an architectural detail appearing as door knockers and on railings, churches, and facades. In early America, Caribbean pineapples traveled with rum, molasses, and enslaved people to the colonies, where the fruit became associated with hospitality.

While pineapples became memes, cultural signifiers of wealth, generosity, and conviviality, it was the fruit's skin that made it such a sophisticated and robust traveler. Pineapples need only about two inches of rain a month to thrive (not much in tropical regions) and have a thick waxy cuticle to withstand heat and reduce water loss. Each leaf is shaped into a trough to capture moisture that might blow in or fall upon it.

Now consider the outside of a pineapple. All the shaggy bits on the fruit are remnants of the flower bracts. The individual flowers, once pollinated, fuse together into a fruit. This makes the pineapple a syncarp, a compound fruit much like figs, breadfruit, custard apples, and mulberries. The strategy of joining together to produce a large tasty fruit helps to ensure the dispersal of seeds.

Many bromeliads are used in landscaping in warm climates today. The genera *Aechmea* and *Guzmania* have spectacular long-lasting flowers and striking leaves, thrive in hot temperatures, climb trees, spread across hillsides, tolerate poor soils, and store water. Bromeliads with flowers that rise up from (or bloom in) water storage tanks die after flowering. They're monocarpic, as are pineapples, living one sweet life but leaving vegetative offsets (sometimes called pups) behind.

Do bromeliads make good cut flowers? Absolutely. They last for weeks if treated well. Why aren't they in the trade, save the odd mini pineapple? The life span of the plant: one and done, despite the gift of pups. Should they be used more in design? One hundred percent for those who have access to them.

Bromeliads also make good houseplants with the interesting attribute of releasing oxygen at night (most plants emit water vapor and oxygen during the day when they are photosynthesizing). Why are bromeliads different? Like cacti, bromeliads need to keep their stomata closed during hot days to reduce water loss. The cool of the evening offers them protection to breathe. If you struggle with sleep, consider a bounty of bromeliads and a humidifier, which offers benefits to you both.

2

3

4

1 Aechmea blooms can hold out of water for days.

2 David Shiigi and his daughter breed new varieties of Guzmanias, Aechmeas, and other bromeliads in Hawaii.

3 Chantal Mayeling Garcia Romero with a collection of perennial flowers and foliages at the Hermitage, Nevis.

4 Pineapple varieties, published in *The Gardeners' Chronicle*, 1874.

5 From *Metamorphosis Insectorum Surinamensium* by Maria Sibylla Merian, 1705.

5

Bulb

Underground Wonders

Recently the Virginia Cooperative Extension, perhaps trying to get ahead of climate change or diversify the floral palette of American growers, issued a bulletin encouraging growers to "Sell Cut Flowers from Perennial Summer-Flowering Bulbs."[25] If spring-planted and mulched in winter, the author argued, numerous options were available to growers. You can almost hear the "innovate!" plea in the writer's voice: "Many flower crops are sensitive to day length. Crops that bloom during long days such as larkspur, yarrow, peonies and gypsophila cannot be made to bloom after the summer equinox on June 21st . . . [and] growers offer the same inventory of sunflowers, zinnias, celosia and gladiolas. . . . "

His suggestions: Try alstroemeria, ixia, ornithogalum, amarcrinum (a cross of amaryllis and Crinum), crocosmia, crinum, hymenocallis, nerine, tuberose, and calla lilies instead. Many of these are South African, and all are geophytes.

A geophyte (literally earth-plant or ground-plant) is a terrestrial plant that has an underground storage system. Tuberose comes from a tuber, calla from a rhizome, nerine from a bulb, and crocosmia from a corm. Many plants have storage organs underground, but to be a geophyte you must have a perennating bud too (think of an eye on a dahlia tuber or ginger root). Geophytes often hail from places with short, intense growing seasons, such as alpine regions and arid climates. They take advantage of seasonal rainfall, leafing out when times are good and storing moisture and energy as carbohydrates. After this, a period of dormancy lasts until the conditions are favorable for flowering. Then seeds disperse until the next cycle of rain initiates germination. Many geophytes take years to flower from seed, needing to slowly build up underground reserves.

For some gardeners, bulbs are a hard sell. As one California grower of native geophytes noted, "Geophytes combine the evanescence of an annual with the maintenance requirements of a perennial. In practical terms, this means that, although temporarily vanished, they continue to take up valuable garden real estate that could otherwise be used for plants that you can, you know, actually *see*."[26]

Ten percent of Greece's flora are geophytes, and South Africa has the richest geophyte flora in the world, with about two thousand flowering bulb species. One plant they now share in common is naked ladies (March lilies in South Africa), which bloom in September from parched earth in Greece. These are the true amaryllis (*Amaryllis belladonna*) native to South Africa, candy pink and naturalized in warm regions around the world. What many people call amaryllis are not—they're hippeastrums.

Many bulbs, corms, and tubers are perennial and reproduce in situ (if you deadhead or remove the seeds the plant will devote more energy to bulb production), so while the investment is greater than a packet of seeds, geophytes increase in number over time if provided with the right growing conditions.

Despite their association with xeric landscapes, some geophytes are adapted to floods and others live along stream banks (iris) or even in water (crinum and taro). If soil erodes around a geophyte or a rock is in the way, the plant is cable of moving. What? Yes! By alternately swelling and shrinking its roots, a geophyte can miraculously pull itself through soil.[27]

1

The idea of waiting for something makes it more exciting.

—ANDY WARHOL

1 South African photographer Kyle Goetsch captured these Sandhof lilies (*Crinum paludosum*); they bloom every few years in Namibia when six to twelve inches of rain accumulate in what are normally dry lakebeds. The flowers bloom for just over a week.

2

2

4

3

2 Tulipieres were designed to showcase novelty flowers in the homes of European elites in the seventeenth and eighteenth centuries. This is a small modern reproduction of traditional Delftware.

3 Taylors Bulbs, Chelsea Flower Show, 2025.

4 A postage stamp from Uzbekistan, showing the foxtail lily *Eremurus korolkowii*. Central Asia has the highest concentration of foxtail lilies (*Eremurus*). The plant is adapted to grasslands and semi-deserts.

5 *Cyanella alba* ssp. *flavascens* only grows in and around the Biedouw Valley, South Africa. The peach flowers, *Moraea miniata*, are called *tulp* in Afrikaans, which means "tulip" in Dutch. The purple flower is *Gladiolus venustus*.

6 Jenks Farmer holding one of his *Crinums* at his farm in South Carolina.

7 Tulips for sale at the October bloemenmarkt in Utrecht.

8 *Amaryllis belladonna* in the home of Gordon Watson in Tangier, Morocco.

5

6

7

8

Chromophobia

The Fear of Color

After my last book came out sporting an orange cover, I began to wear orange, peach, and coral, tossing a flaming scarf around my neck to perk me up, and bought a paprika handbag and another in tangerine. Color-lover Alexander Theroux has this to say of the orange tithonia, or the Mexican sunflower: "It is a fire-drake so tropically dense, so sulphurously ripe, so madly glorious, that in the daring and almost insolent boldness of its pure orange fulgor, it could actually be burning."[28]

> **To me, color is a sense in itself.**
>
> —JADÉ FADOJUTIMI

No chromophobia there. But some people do have a real fear of certain colors. Xanthophobia is a fear of yellow, and erythrophobia is a fear of red. For these people, color can initiate a hormonal and terrifying response. Today treatment can involve video simulations, acclimating people to their fear by moving from a spot of discomforting color to virtually standing in a room surrounded by a hue.

The artist David Batchelor once visited an almost pure white home of an art collector. The experience spurred him to write a book on the subject of chromophobia in which he argued, "in the West, since Antiquity, color has been systematically marginalized, reviled, diminished, and degraded . . . ."[29] A bold statement but understandable, particularly when earlier, the German thinker Johann Wolfgang von Goethe wrote in his influential *Theory of Colors*, published in 1810, that "savage nations, uneducated people, and children have a great predilection for vivid colors."[30]

Consider the implications, both socially and aesthetically. Surely we're biased toward some colors and against others depending on both culture and biology. But color itself? Line and form, as Kassia St. Clair writes in *The Secret Lives of Color*, were "the true glories of art," in Western culture. "Color was seen as a distraction."[31]

Thankfully things have changed to some degree, but it's hard not to think how many strip floral design down to make it art. Take a simple vine, make it a line, twist it into a form, and hang it from the ceiling. We assert line and form, placing our work on stark white plinths in galleries in the attempt to move from designer to artist. This dominance of line and form, Batchelor says, makes us think of color as something we fill spaces with—be that a blank wall, a shirt, or even a floral arrangement. We know the shape of things and add color, just as we did in primary school, by coloring in space.

There is another way: "The impassioned colorist invents his form for his color," said Charles Blanc after considering the Chinese mastery of color.[32]

In writing my last book I wasn't prepared for the complexities of color, scientifically and psychologically, and thus expounded over thirty-eight pages on the subject without thinking enough about the cultural connotations of color.

Batchelor is bolder. He writes, "Color is made out to be the property of some 'foreign' body—usually the feminine, the oriental, the primitive, the infantile, the vulgar, the queer or the pathological . . . color is relegated to the realm of the superficial, the supplementary, the inessential or the cosmetic."[33] First comes architecture, then interiors, then the vase of bodacious blooms on the table.

My advice: never judge another culture's use of color. To use "garish" is gauche. As the painter Wassily Kandinsky said in *Concerning the Spiritual in Art*, "Color is a power which directly influences the soul."

2

1 Pride Month flowers from my garden in British Columbia.

2 Artificial flowers in Nicaragua. While the country grows flowers for export, the average farmworker's wage is often less than $2,000 per annum.

Climate

Beyond Weather

1

A long time ago, I sailed on a schooner from Lisbon to St. Barts. The Atlantic crossing from the Canaries took thirty-two days, and I mention that time because while I was technically more interested in constellations, plastics, and flagellating creatures than I was in the weather, every day of that voyage I celebrated the wind that would get me back to land.

And what an easy wind it was—the same trade wind that had blown those first European caravels to the Caribbean. Born in what is called the Intertropical Convergence Zone, these trade winds form when warm air rises near the equator and other air moves in to fill that void. It's simple convection. Add the spin of our planet and you get clockwise trade winds in the northern hemisphere and counter-clockwise trades south of the equator. (The area around the equator often doesn't have much wind at all, hence the doldrums.) If we add moisture to this scenario, we can build out the idea of climate as it relates to the plants in this book. Moisture evaporates quickly at the equator, forming clouds, rainfall, and rainbows, which dazzle by the day. All that dynamism and moisture can spiral into cyclones and hurricanes, making tropical regions some of the wettest places on earth.

The tropics are the most botanically diverse places on earth, containing about 30 percent of the world's known species of plants. The Kew scientist Alexandre Antonelli recently put it into perspective for me: The British Isles are home to 3,100 seed plants; tropical Africa 56,000; Southeast Asia and Australia 50,000; and the North and South American tropics 118,000.[34]

> On the last day of the world I would want to plant a tree.
>
> —W. S. MERWIN

But not all tropics are what we might consider "tropical." So we should technically define where these regions are: between the Tropics of Cancer and Capricorn.

Generally three types of biomes exist in this region: tropical rainforest; tropical seasonal forest and savanna, which experience less rainfall; and finally subtropical desert. Each of these environments is easy to picture, perhaps even iconic. You might imagine a lush rainforest hung with vines and epiphytic orchids in Malaysia or a giraffe nibbling an acacia on Kenya's grassy savannas or a subtropical desert of saguaro cacti, arms outstretched, in the American Southwest.

Subtropical forests cover vast regions of Australia, Latin and South America, Central Africa, and Southeast Asia. Tree felling for wood extraction and agriculture have altered many of these ecosystems irreversibly; it's estimated that every year humans create fifty thousand square miles of new desert.

In terms of biodiversity, many of us are familiar with biodiversity powerhouse the Brazilian Amazon (home to fifteen thousand different tree species), but Indonesia, Colombia, China, Peru, Mexico, Australia, Ecuador, India, and the United States are also in the top ten of the most biodiverse countries in the world, in that order. Obviously, the size of those countries matters. If biodiversity is correlated to land area by density, a different picture emerges: Trinidad and Tobago is number one, followed by other small tropical countries such as Brunei, Gambia, El Salvador, Rwanda, Jamaica, Belize, and Costa Rica.[35]

In Rwanda, only 11 percent of the country's tree cover is found in forests, but in carbon terms the country is still highly vegetated, which matters for climate change mitigation and biodiversity. As researcher Maurice Mugabowindekwe notes: "The country has a rich landscape variation including savannas, woodlands, sub-humid and humid forests, shrubland, agro-ecosystem mosaics, and urban tree ecosystems which are representative of most tropical countries."[36] Rwanda, Jamaica, and Trinidad and Tobago have relatively high population densities. These are not countries of wilderness; stewardship saves lives—and not just our own.

2

1 Wildflower bloom, Biedouw Valley, South Africa.

2 Photographer Peter Caton documents the South Sudanese communities who, he writes, "may represent the world's first permanent mass displacement due to climate change." An estimated 6.4 million people in South Sudan are at risk of starvation. Through a series titled Unyielding Floods, Caton reports on the devastation of natural disaster, food insecurity, and loss of dignified living. Caton shares the words of Nyachuana Lok, pictured: "I am destroying this flooded house so I can make a house in a dry place for my children."

Cold Chain

Plants on the Move

1

Please ensure your seat beat is fastened. There could be some psychic turbulence.

Chances are you've flown with flowers. British Airways, American, Lufthansa, Emirates, KLM, and countless other airlines ship flowers around the world in what's known as the cold chain: refrigerated infrastructure used to transport and store perishable goods. The minute a rose is cut, it has to rely on stored sugars. The goal of the global floral industry is to get that rose to the consumer within twenty-four to forty-eight hours. One way of slowing the rate of respiration (when a plant exhales carbon dioxide and water) is to chill it. Every flower is different in terms of its tolerance for cold and its ability to hold. For example, a carnation held out of water near freezing can last four months in cold storage. A carnation held in water, just four weeks.[37] A cymbidium might last a month in the chain, a gloriosa lily a week. If the cold chain is interrupted and a bloom reaches room temperature, a flower can lose up to 40 percent of its vase life.

> **In most climates seasonality has such an obvious connection with growth and rest that it is hardly necessary to elaborate on the idea that to interfere with nature is to invite disaster.**
>
> —JACK GOODY

In a global industry worth about $58 billion, margins and margins of error matter. Ecuador has long been the leading exporter of cut flowers to Russia, which might give you an indicator of how long and insane cold chains can be in a globalized economy. The UK imports about 90 percent of its flowers, and the number of flowers traveling daily by air is staggering. A cargo 747 can hold 1.65 million roses, or about one hundred tons (one hundred thousand kilograms). Every week about four hundred tons of flowers leave Nairobi with that number jumping 55 percent prior to Valentine's Day. (1-800-Flowers in the United States delivered about fourteen million roses on Valentine's Day in 2020.)[38]

The Netherlands imports botanicals from approximately sixty countries through Schiphol Airport before either redistributing them abroad or selling them on to European markets. Tracking cold chains can reveal economic power and control. In Nungari Mwangi's article "Propertied Proletarians? The Kenyan Cut-Flower Industry," he notes: "Absurdly, Nigeria currently imports Kenyan flowers via a convoluted trade route from Holland or the UK—perpetuating the neocolonial hegemony of Europe as the hub of trade."[39]

Miami receives about twenty-two million flowers a day. Dallas receives twelve tons of flowers per week from Colombia alone. One means of controlling the cold chain is to conglomerate. Many companies have vertically integrated, such as Wafex, which "provides a steady pipeline of new varieties, grown under license all year-round," and offers "breeding, production, bouquet making, importing, exporting, wholesaling, and on-line sales and fulfillment direct to the consumer."[40]

Needless to say, the world's cold chains (whether for food or flowers) run on petroleum. Shipping flowers by sea is one way of decarbonizing, with some estimates suggesting a carbon savings of 80 percent compared to air travel.

We can also look to various characteristics in flowers and make better choices (see Footprint). We can try to break the chain.

2

1 *Flowers for Lisa #1, 2014* by Abelardo Morell.

2 Ota Floriculture Auction, Tokyo.

1

Colonial

Commonwealth Couture

In 1953, Constance Spry was commissioned to flower Queen Elizabeth II's coronation. What flowers does one use for a coronation? With the date set for early June, what could be grown?

Ten acres of flowers were grown for the Queen's coronation by royal gardeners after Spry had asserted her schemes, including phlox, verbenas, and salvias. But those acres of blooms weren't enough, and thus royal parks had to pony up. Wisley was snipped, the Commonwealth was tapped, and Connie's own garden raided along with those of her friends. At the last minute, Italy came to the rescue with a gift of red flowers.

According to Sue Shephard, author of *The Surprising Life of Constance Spry*, Elizabeth Windsor's gown was embroidered with jewels designed to resemble the following plants: "The lotus flower for Ceylon and India, mimosa for Australia, wheat and jute for Pakistan, the protea for South Africa, fern for New Zealand, shamrock for Ireland, leek for Wales and rose for England."[41] Canada was among the Commonwealth countries too—symbolized by a maple leaf. As Shephard writes: "the government's wish was for the new Queen to be a beacon of hope for a future of optimism and post-imperialist unity."[42]

Featuring flowers of former colonies on Elizabeth's gown served to recognize the newly emerging Commonwealth of Nations who held allegiance to the Crown. Meghan Markle would carry forward this tradition for her wedding to the Duke of Sussex in 2018. Her sixteen-foot veil featured fifty-three flowers of the Commonwealth (there are fifty-six member states today). Those flowers and plants included the following.[43]

ASIA:
Bangladesh – white water lily (*Nymphaea nouchali*)
Brunei Darussalam – simpor (*Dillenia suffruticosa*)
India – Indian lotus (*Nelumbo nucifera*)
Malaysia – bunga raya hibiscus (*Hibiscus x rosa-sinensis*)
Pakistan – jasmine (*Jasminum officinale*)
Singapore – Miss Joaquim Orchid (*Vanda* Miss Joaquim)
Sri Lanka – blue water lily (*Nymphaea nouchali*)

CARIBBEAN & AMERICAS:
Antigua and Barbuda – agave (*Agave karatto*)
Bahamas – yellow elder (*Tecoma stans*)
Barbados – the pride of Barbados (*Caesalpinia pulcherrima*)
Belize – black orchid (*Encyclia cochleata*)
Canada – bunchberry (*Cornus canadensis*)
Dominica – Carib wood (*Sabinea carinalis*)
Grenada – bougainvillea (*Bougainvillea*)
Guyana – Victoria regia water lily (*Victoria amazonica*)
Jamaica – lignum vitae (*Guiacum officinale*)

2

Saint Lucia – rose and marguerite (*Gomphrena*)
Saint Kitts and Nevis – royal poinciana (*Delonix regia*)
Saint Vincent and the Grenadines – Soufrière tree (*Spachea perforata*)
Trinidad and Tobago – chaconia (*Warszewiczia coccinea*)

EUROPE:
Cyprus – cyclamen (*Cyclamen cyprium*)
Malta – Maltese centaury (*Cheirolophus crassifolius*)

AFRICA:
Botswana – ear of sorghum and cat's claw (*Uncaria tomentosa*)
Cameroon – red stinkwood (*Prunus africana*)
Gambia – white variety orchid (genus unconfirmed)
Ghana – caladium (*Caladium*)
Kenya – tropical orchid (genus unconfirmed)
Lesotho – spiral aloe (*Aloe polyphylla*)
Malawi – white lotus (*Nymphaea lotus*)
Mauritius – boucle d'oreille (*Ruizia boutoniana*)
Mozambique – maroon bell bean (*Markhamia zanzibarica*)
Namibia – welwitschia (*Welwitschia mirabilis*)
Nigeria – yellow trumpet (*Costus spectabilis*)
Rwanda – torch lily (*Kniphofia uvaria*)
Seychelles – tropic bird orchid (*Angraecum eburneum*)
Sierra Leone – scadoxus (*Scadoxus cinnabarinus*)
South Africa – king protea (*Protea cynaroides*)
Swaziland – fire heath (*Erica cerinthoides*)
Uganda – desert rose (*Adenium obesum*)
United Republic of Tanzania – African violet (*Saintpaulia*)
Zambia – bougainvillea (*Bougainvillea*)

3

UNITED KINGDOM:
England – rose (*Rosa*)
Wales – daffodil (*Narcissus*)
Northern Ireland – flax flower (*Linum usitatissimum*)
Scotland – thistle (*Onopordum acanthium*)

PACIFIC:
Australia – golden wattle (*Acacia pycnantha*)
Fiji – tagimoucia (*Medinilla waterhousei*)
Kiribati – Starbuck Island daisy (*Bidens kiribatiensis*)
Nauru – tamanu (*Calophyllum inophyllum*)
New Zealand – kowhai (*Sophora microphylla*)
Papua – Sepik blue orchid (*Dendrobium lasianthera*)
Samoa – teuila (*Alpinia purpurata*)
Solomon Islands – kwara'ae (*Hibiscus*)
Tonga – heilala (*Garcinia sessilis*)
Tuvalu – plumeria (*Plumeria*)
Vanuatu – anthurium (*Anthurium*)

> You can be up to your boobies in white satin, with gardenias in your hair and no sugar cane for miles, but you can still be working on a plantation.
>
> —BILLIE HOLIDAY

4

1 Queen Elizabeth II in her coronation gown designed by British couturier Sir Norman Hartnell.

2 *The Devilfish in Egyptian Waters*, 1888. Cartoon of the satirical John Bull of England likely by the Austrian-born American cartoonist and political commentator Joseph Keppler.

3 Golden Rock Inn on Nevis, built around the remnants of a nineteenth-century sugar plantation.

4 Empire Marketing Board poster, Edgar Ainsworth, 1931.

5 Empire Marketing Board poster, Edward McKnight Kauffer, c. 1926–1934.

6 Empire Marketing Board poster, Spencer G. Pryse, 1927.

5

6

Corm

Banana Republics

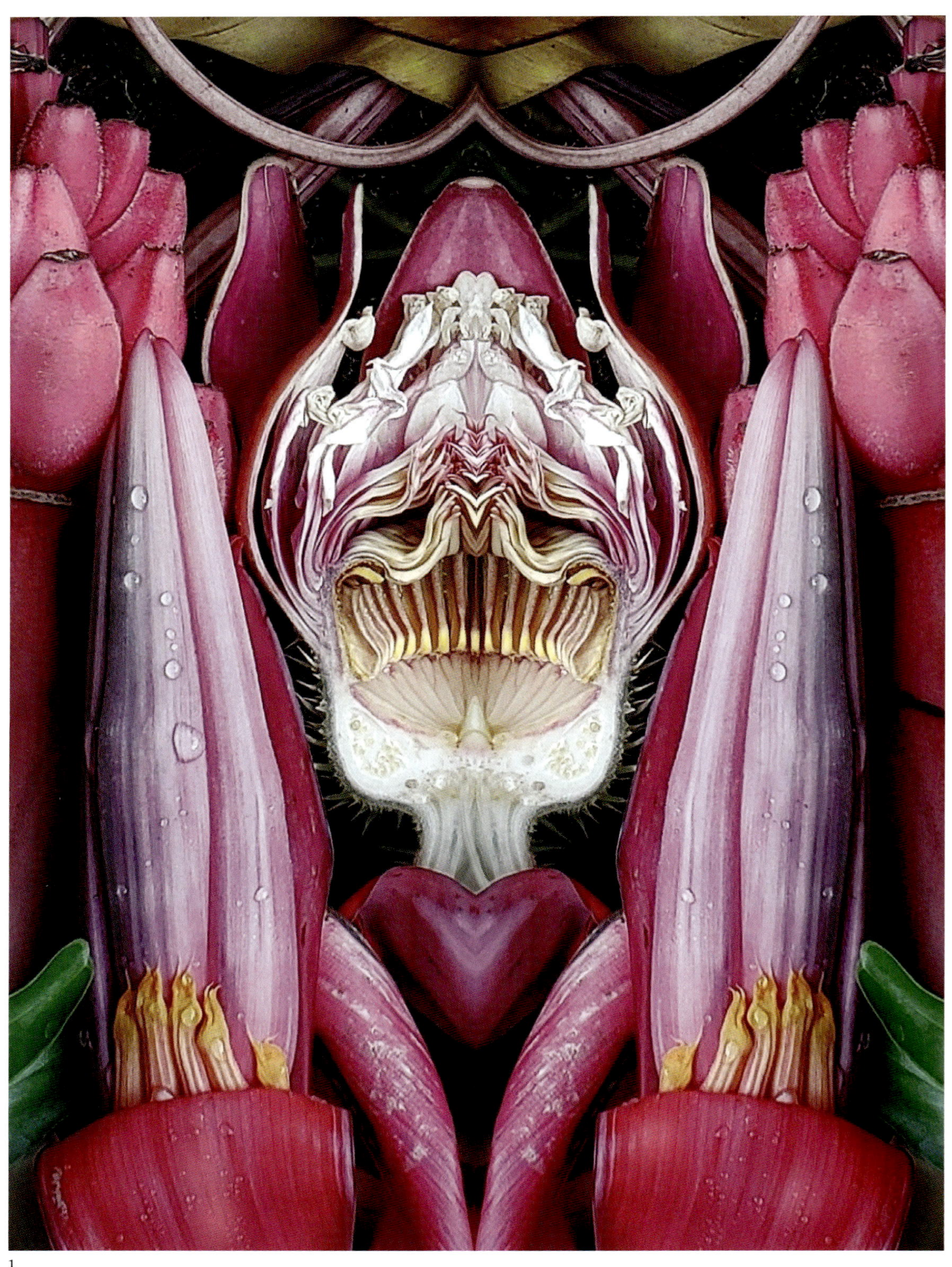

What do an anemone and a banana have in common? They both grow from corms. Thus a banana isn't a tree but a herbaceous plant, and the banana is the largest herbaceous flowering plant in the world.

The world loves bananas; we eat about a hundred billion a year. There are more than a thousand varieties of banana, even if one, the Cavendish, has become ubiquitous in the West. Rwandans eat the most—about five bananas per person per day, though many of these are the variety Kayinja and brewed, cooked, or juiced.

About seven thousand years ago, wild bananas were cultivated in New Guinea (there were approximately seven thousand tribal groups in New Guinea at the time, and almost as many today, so forgive me for not naming the groups). The plant went first to the Philippines, then later Sri Lanka, and arrived in Africa about five thousand years ago.[44] The banana traveled because it was so eminently useful—as a starchy food, food wrap, medicine, fermented beverage, and fiber (in the twelfth century the Japanese used banana in the weaving of kimonos). Bananas also offer shade to understory crops, making them valued agroforestry plants. According to the UN's Food and Agriculture Organization, approximately 1.2 billion people depend on agroforestry systems—mainly in tropical regions.

Science has taught me that everything is more complicated than we first assume, and that being able to derive happiness from discovery is the recipe for a beautiful life.

—HOPE JAHREN

The banana's global importance underscores its myriad of forms. There are red bananas, ice cream bananas, apple bananas, pink and scarlet bananas, hardy bananas, ornamental bananas, dwarf bananas, and some that function as foliage plants, and others that deliver pounds of fruit. In Micronesia, bananas are orange, almost mango-like. The Democratic Republic of the Congo has the highest diversity of plantain varieties. (Compared to bananas, plantains are starchier, and have lower sugar and thicker skins. Globally we consume far more plantains than bananas.)

Banana flowers as we know them are actually an assemblage of sex organs and bracts. The bracts are a beautiful dusky rusty red or maroon. These can be peeled back to reveal the florets. The calyces and pistils can be discarded when eating the blooms, though entire banana flowers are eaten throughout Southeast Asia. Whole, they have a texture reminiscent of artichokes if you serve the bracts and blooms together.

Cultivated bananas have lost the ability to reproduce sexually. How does the plant then make fruit? The answer is by parthenocarpy, which is a naturally occurring mutation in some plants (and an adaptation) that makes fruits like eggplants and pineapples seedless. Parthenocarpy can be induced artificially or occur naturally. In the case of cultivated bananas, the male flowers are sterile. The female flowers respond to a growth hormone and produce fruit without fertilization.

At times in my life I've been embarrassed to have bananas in the house. Nothing against the fruit of course, but in Canada they signified variously a kind of climate change denialism and support for American banana republics. What's a banana republic? A country caught in the grip of plantation-model economics, wherein food is produced for export by underpaid workers ruled by elites. Chiquita, once the United Fruit Company, was the target of O. Henry's critique when he coined the term in 1904 referencing the United States' involvement with oligarchic governments in Guatemala and Honduras.

Someone please make an arrangement out of that.

2

1 *Victoria cruziana*, *Musa velutina*, *colocasia*, and *philodendron* in the garden of Billy Van Bakker.

2 Collaborative work by Hamish Powell and This Humid House.

3 A poster by Víctor Interiano, an artist born in El Salvador and now based in Los Angeles.

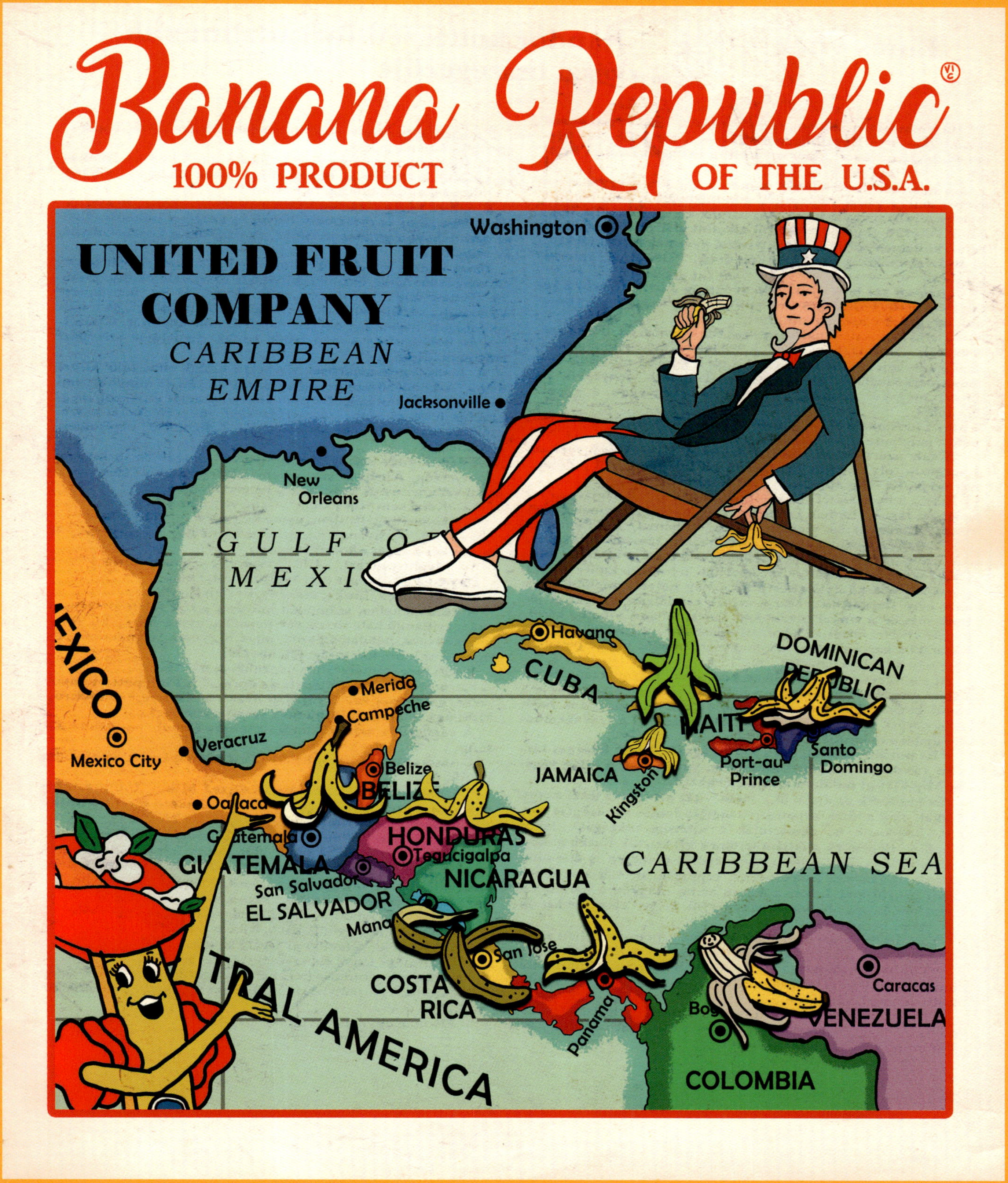

Banana

100% PRODUCT OF THE U.S.A.

UNITED FRUIT COMPANY

CARIBBEAN EMPIRE

Washington
Jacksonville
New Orleans
GULF OF MEXICO
MEXICO
Mexico City
Veracruz
Oaxaca
Merida
Campeche
Belize
BELIZE
Guatemala
GUATEMALA
San Salvador
EL SALVADOR
HONDURAS
Tegucigalpa
NICARAGUA
Managua
COSTA RICA
San Jose
Panama
CENTRAL AMERICA
Havana
CUBA
JAMAICA
Kingston
HAITI
Port-au-Prince
DOMINICAN REPUBLIC
Santo Domingo
CARIBBEAN SEA
Bogota
COLOMBIA
Caracas
VENEZUELA

Cultivar

Conformity and Complexity

What kind of avocado is that? Have you ever asked that question? For most of my life, I've seen two varieties—a smooth bright green one and a smaller rough-skinned version. Back when David Fairchild traveled the world at the end of the nineteenth century seeking new food crops to diversify the farmlands and palates of America on behalf of the US Department of Agriculture, he encountered alligator pears in Jamaica, Venezuela, and finally Chile, where he bit into the creamiest, tastiest, and, given his radar was attuned to the needs of his nation, most frost-hardy variety of all.

Originating in central Mexico, the word avocado comes from the Aztec word for testicle, given the fruits droop from trees in pairs. Most modern commercial varieties derive from the species *Persea americana*. After the US introduction and local breeding, one avocado was selected for its productivity. As Daniel Stone writes in *The Food Explorer: The True Adventures of the Globe-Trotting Botanist Who Transformed What America Eats*: "On the afternoon of August 27th, 1935, a full thirty-six years after Fairchild collected the Chilean ancestor avocado, and ten thousand years after humans first domesticated the fruit, the man (Hass) applied for a patent. . . ."

The ascendancy of the Hass avocado reminds us that the crops we consume have been tailored not only to the senses, but also their workability: How long do they crop for? How resistant are they to disease? How well do they tolerate refrigeration? There is no question that trade-offs are made along the way. In food we might sacrifice flavor for rigor; in flowers, vase life is too often given priority over scent. For a plant to become profitable these days, it must have the characteristics a globalized consumer culture requires and desires: the ability to ripen post-harvest, pack well, tolerate chilling, and resist bruising.

Thousands of years ago Chinese gardeners selected roses and peonies in which a genetic mutation had occurred—the flowers' stamens had converted to petals. These doubles had fuller, larger flowers, but without sexual organs, they couldn't reproduce by seed. Today carnations, camellias, ranunculi, and many other flowers are often sterile, reliant upon humans to reproduce.

We refer to these horticultural varieties of plants that have developed through human interaction and selection as cultivars or cultigens. Cultigen is the broader term, with a cultivar referring to a "cultivated variety." The International Code of Nomenclature for Cultivated Plants (ICNCP) regulates the naming system for these plants. When you see a genus name followed by an epithet held in single quotes, such as *Anthurium* 'New Era', you know the plant is a cultivar, bred for human use.

Cultivars have decreased global biodiversity insofar as they have replaced landraces, traditional crops that have been bred over millennia. Humans first domesticated plants over ten thousand years ago, selected specific traits, and developed locally adapted varieties. Growing cultivars rather than landraces has led to genetic erosion. That Hass avocado? Its ubiquity comes at a cost. It is estimated that during the last one hundred years, approximately 75 percent of food plant varieties have disappeared due to the modernization of agriculture.[45]

Plant breeders create cultivars to match climates not just our tastes now. Drought, flooding, and climate change mean preemptive planning. It's worth asking: what do we want from flowers going forward? And what are we willing to give up?

There are few things that give me a greater thrill than seeing familiar garden plants "at home," growing in the wild . . . It is a little like a friend you think you know, and then visit in a family context; you see that person in a completely different light—sometimes exuberant and "larger" than you knew them, sometimes reduced in stature, even cowed.

—NOEL KINSGBURY

1 Catalog collage of cultivars I made during the pandemic.

Cultivated

What We Grow

America, all a-shimmer in its Gilded Age at the end of the nineteenth century, expanded. Puerto Rico, Guam, and the Philippines would fall into American hands at the end of the Spanish-American War, and while the Philippines gained independence in 1946, Guam and Puerto Rico are still territories of the United States. Of course, American expansionism predates these examples, given the country itself was cobbled together through alliances and wars with the Hawaiians, Spanish, Iroquois, Pequot, Shawnee, Cherokee, Lakota, Sioux, Apache, Seminole, Mexicans, and others, but for our purposes it's important to recognize how the American pursuit of territory and resources meant increased globalization of the world's flowers.

> **And what is the relationship between gardening and conquest?**
>
> —JAMAICA KINCAID

David Fairchild is considered by many to be the man who changed the face of American agriculture. In 1906, he noted that "no nation in the world has an agricultural territory with a greater range of climatic conditions than the US and its possessions."[46] He made it his life's work to find plants that fit not only the diverse landscapes of his expanding country but also the tastes of its people.

Working with the US Department of Agriculture and the newly created Office of Seed and Plant Introduction, Fairchild visited over fifty countries in what would be called the Golden Age of Travel, a time of steamer ships and slow rides. Traveling from Italy to Japan, Java to Africa, Greece to South America, and countless places in between, Fairchild was responsible for over one hundred thousand plant introductions to the United States, including fruits, grains, and ornamental plants. Many of the plants he collected would go on to supply the genetic material for American varieties of crops like cotton, pistachios, mangoes, and dates. He'd introduce kale a hundred years before it was appreciated and the ornamental cherry trees that now adorn the US capital in Washington, D.C. every spring.

I visited Fairchild's 1928 home on Biscayne Bay in Coconut Grove, Florida, now managed by the National Tropical Botanical Garden. As I wandered through the garden with the chair, Dr. Mike Rosenberg, we met a French botanist who placed a single scented bloom of *Magnolia champaca* (the Joy perfume flower) in my hand. Frenchman aside, it's a romantic place, the house trimmed in red, with giant figs, orchids, mangroves, and draping Spanish moss. As we talked, Fairchild became a part of the tapestry of my understanding of how plants moved and why, and how seeds, shoots, and whole plants have been shared, bought, stolen, and smuggled. Fairchild was more fair-dealer than swindler, but there's still a little pirate to his tales.

He saw himself as a fixer, a botanical problem-solver helping to feed the growing needs of his country. Do the housewives of America need citron for baking? Off he went to Corsica to smuggle some out. Was California in need of a drought-tolerant nut? Fairchild went to the Levant (Syria and Lebanon) and returned with pistachios. For "America's Egypt" along the Colorado River valley, Fairchild went to Nile to bring back cotton.

Zealous, indefatigable, patriotic, he wrote: "The Department of Agriculture is growing in this country some of the things that we now import and for which we pay annually many millions of dollars; it is forcing into public notice and encouraging the trial of foods that the people of other countries find excellent and of which we are ignorant; and it is bringing in from all parts of the world plants that are now wild, but that can be tamed by breeding with others now in cultivation, thus contributing to the creation of fruits and vegetables that the world has never seen before."

Today, most people wouldn't count the American diet as a particularly diverse one. As Michael Pollan notes, "There are some 45,000 items in the average American supermarket, and more than a quarter of them contain corn."[47] Why? Sixty percent of agricultural funding in the country today goes to grains and corn, not flowers, fruits or vegetables.[48] Gilded no more.

2

1 Vanda orchids bred at Motes Orchids in Homestead, Florida, captured by Robbie Honey.

2 David Fairchild.

Cuticle

Wilting and Waxes

Have you ever been in an environment so extreme you felt physically threatened, like you weren't adapted to live there? Now imagine you're a plant. A person takes you out of their house, pops you in the sun, you can almost hear the person thinking, plants like sun, right? And you're thinking, what happened the last time YOU went outside without sunscreen and baked for hours on the deck?

> If there is magic on this planet, it is contained in water.
>
> —LOREN EISELEY

How's a plant to adapt? In the case above, the plant can't. The change is too quick, the plant scorches, and if it's a just wee seedling, crisps up and dies. But given time to acclimate, plants adapt; they build up cuticles—waxy layers that form over their epidermis. The cuticle is an interface between the plant and the world that serves a number of functions.

Consider a leaf, where a plant converts UV-B radiation into heat, then vibrates it off while absorbing the red and blue photons needed for photosynthesis. How does it not scorch in the sun? The cuticles of plants miraculously generate their own form of sunscreen, both chemical and mineral.

In most flowering plants, the cuticle is thicker on the top of the leaf. The cuticle repels water (in plants like lotus and nasturtium the leaves are so hydrophobic they're self-cleaning) and offers a line of defense against fungi, bacteria, and insects. Want to find a pest on a plant? Look at its tender underside; lift the leaf.

Understanding cuticles can help inform our work with flowers. Plants breathe through their cuticles by opening and closing pores (technically stomata). The stomata regulate carbon dioxide absorption and the release of oxygen. But opening yourself up to the world can lead to water loss—approximately 90 percent of the water taken up by plants is lost through such transpiration. Yet transpiration is necessary to transport sugars and hormones and for cooling. It's a tricky balance to maintain.

Wilting is one strategy plants have—the plant collapses into itself in order to reduce surface area exposed to the elements, but that will work only temporarily. When cells collapse due to a lack of water, the situation can be reversed with a long drink, but not always, and repeated wilting can be fatal.

When cutting flowers, take these considerations in mind. Cut at a period of low transpiration, such as at dawn or dusk, or even in the dark of the night.

Hydration boxes have long served florists doing detailed work with flowers, providing a hydrating environment for corsages, headpieces, and other delicate materials. They can be as simple as a plastic tub with damp paper towel inside. The success of these boxes relies on a few things: the preservation of a dark environment (thus reducing transpiration), the maintenance of high humidity, and the regulation of temperature. Cut tropical flowers, which resent the cold, will still transpire when stored, but because many have thick cuticles, the flowers are slower to dehydrate.

A final quirky aside: In nature, as temperature increases, photosynthesis increases, but only to a point—about 85 degrees Fahrenheit or 29 Celsius, after which it's just too risky to continue growing. In deserts, where the risk of dehydration is so great, cacti photosynthesize at night. Wait? Doesn't photosynthesis require sunlight? Yes. The cacti suck in carbon dioxide once it's safe to open their stomata at night, then chemically store it for daylight. Photosynthesizing this way allows them to safely make fuel, silvery cuticles, spines, and all manner of beautiful things. After their work is done, they exhale the oxygen we breathe into the night.

2

1 Waxy cuticles of *Etlingera* and *Anthurium*.

2. I styled this in New York with the help of Abigail Sergent.

Demonstration

Designing with Style

Discussing art and technique on stage while using your hands is no small feat. Ask a celebrity chef. What do you talk about? In my last book, I included a section on "How to Speak About Your Work." In that lesson, I posed a number of questions to help designers figure out not only what to say but how they might say it. Here are some tips on actually presenting. (Note: I found it easier to write these bits in the second person because I think you do become different person on stage—you kind of have to—unless you're a true extrovert.)

> You don't want to give people what they want. Give them something that they didn't know that they wanted.
>
> —RUTH REICHL

Arrive earlier than early. You have learned that when you travel, things go wrong. Your baggage may be missing, the weather insane, the venue set up incorrectly, the volunteers clueless. Worse still, the flowers aren't great, so you need time to rummage through gardens or visit a wholesaler or a farm. So find a driver and new friend. The only thing you can control is your time: how much time do you have to fix the problem? Usually barely enough. Remember: a dress isn't worthy if it lacks pockets. Bring layers and wear nothing you can't secretly sweat in. Carry a first aid kit: Band-Aids, alcohol wipes, tweezers. You never know when a tick might attach to your neck after foraging or when you'll bleed on a tablecloth. True stories.

Articulate what you need and when. This can be as detailed as a sandwich or as simple as alone time. Schedule both.

Trust in technology, because despite your fears, you do know enough about it. Ask for the A/V person's contact information in advance. Worse comes to worst, you can have someone at home transfer your presentation slides. With a thumb drive and another device, you can almost always find a way forward (power outages not included).

Find a blank wall with decent natural light and a table to place your demonstration arrangement on. People will want to photograph it. It's wise to control how they do so before you're swarmed at the end.

Carry a self-care checklist in your mind in the minutes before your presentation: water, bathroom, and if you're really nervous, run warm water over your wrists until you feel calm. Blood flow is diverted to larger organs in times of stress, so warming yourself up can ease tension.

Okay, you've made it on the stage. Your demonstration will be timed like a cooking show but without the braised stew in the oven or the cake baked. You will wish every presentation stage had an overhead mirror because then you wouldn't have to spin the lazy Susan so much and explain so much, but you love words and people as much as flowers—that's why you are on stage as opposed to someone else, so keep up the banter even when you're bleeding from impaling yourself on a pin frog and blinded by the lights.

You have painfully learned that your floundering on stage isn't bad for the audience. Maybe they're thinking, what the heck is that?! Let them. In movies, a happy ending is always better if the lead has suffered first. So don't fret. Everyone is indecisive in front of beautiful flowers. Trust in the fact you will make something great under pressure. Added bonus: you get adept at uppity self-talk so that a hiccup mid-demonstration becomes, "Nicely done on building suspense!"

Chefs like to say they can only be as good as their ingredients, and this is true of plants and flowers too, but being snobby ("Normally I just pop out to my acres and pluck . . .") or proceeding from a place of lack isn't helpful to the audience. "You can't always get what you want, but if you try sometime . . ." You know the rest. Find common ground by remarking on the struggles of seasonality, the ephemeral nature of flowers, or how wholesalers think subbing a gold sunflower for a burgundy one is fair game.

You'll have a captive and captivated crowd of ten, sixty, or four hundred, so you can pepper your talk with miscellanea and push plant politics, all while distracting people with your hands. Don't ever, ever, ever miss a chance to feel like you're changing minds and the world. If your face is strained from smiling and talking, remember this tip from Robbie Honey: stick your tongue behind your front teeth and lift your cheeks.

No one knows how great you might have been. They only know how great you were.

1 Christi Douglas, owner of of the Botanical Gardens of Nevis.

Desiccated

Using Dried Plants

What's luck? For many, it's privilege. And for me it was in the story I'm going to tell you—sprinkled with a bit of flower magic.

One day I was hiking with a small group into the fynbos of South Africa. I'd been alone for a couple of days, the path was narrow, and I was grumpy because the group leader, an ecologist, was difficult to hear. Reluctantly, I gave up on learning plant names and started to chat with to two people on the trail. My luck: one would prove to be the second-largest dried flower exporter in the country.

His name is Johan Nel, and he's tall, blond, and rangy. That day he looked like a surfer, tanned and tousled. He was young, but I quickly learned he knew a lot, and he quickly learned I knew a lot, and so I pressed him on the environmental impact of dyed flowers.

"Food-grade dye," he said.

His wife, Este, had a face that suggested calm. We decided to chat later.

Time gives you distance, and distance gives you time to learn. "Lovely dead crap" was a subject I wrote about for my last book, advocating the use of dried flowers for sustainability reasons and to add a touch of nostalgia and whimsy to designs. I wrote about skeletonizing (see Glossary) and preserving, and the periods in Western history when dried flowers had been in vogue.

Bleached and dyed botanicals weren't as ubiquitous then as they are now. Today, as Johan said, "a grower can get ten products from one plant." For example, dip-dyed flowers, bleached flowers, sprayed flowers, flocked flowers, and glittered flowers are all traded in the dried flower market. And no, not all dyes used on plants are food-grade. Many textile dyes are used as well (see Dye).

Demand is high for colorful everlastings in part because faux flowers, those impossible plastic leaves and swags of wisteria, roses, and bougainvillea used for installation work on shop fronts and in restaurants, are (horrifically) trending.

Meeting Johan was a godsend for me. At Covent Garden Flower Market in London, I'd wander the aisles of dried plant parts and think: what is this? A gum nut? A chunk of something from a coconut? A collection of sepals? A cone from what exactly? And the fact I didn't know and the staff didn't know nerdily infuriated me. Just because something is dried or dyed, does it not deserve to be named? Have plants become simply decor?

When I next spoke to Johan I didn't lead with dye; I asked him about Kent Flowers, which his parents started in 1985. The farm trades in about 250 different species, with a strong emphasis on the protea family and other fynbos plants like hakea, brunia, leucadendron, aulax, and barbigera. Harvesting of wild species is managed by the governmental organization CapeNature, who issue permits for specific species and tally and inspect harvests (almost every South African I met praised CapeNature's oversight). Municipalities also offer permits for foraging, allowing the gathering of seeds, nuts, jacaranda pods, and foliage. Kent Flowers, a thirty-odd-acre farm, also grows artichokes, hydrangeas, and helichrysum to meet demand from European florists.

Plants are dried in simple sheds, open to the air. As flowers come into bloom year-round in South Africa, winter bloomers require extra fans and heat. Inputs remain low though; it wasn't until a drought in 2019 that a well had to be dug—a mountain spring had historically provided enough water for

2

1 Jessica Farrell at the Cambo Estate in Scotland, holding a bouquet by Louise Warner featuring the papery elliptical fruits of *Lunaria rediviva*.

2 Dried *Brunsvigia*, which grows from a bulb in the sandy soils of the Cape Province, South Africa.

3 Dyed *Protea repens* air-drying at Kent Flowers in South Africa.

4 A collection of Australian seeds and nuts.

5 Floral artist Rebecca Louise Law regularly uses dried flowers and copper wire in her installation work.

6 Workers at Kent Flowers in South Africa preparing dried *Leucadendron platyspermum* for shipment to Europe by sea.

3

4

5

the farm. Kent Flowers is surrounded by game reserves, conservation land, and apricot orchards. (Unlike orchards, Kent Flowers employs local workers year-round, in everything from horticulture to processing and packing.)

Ninety-nine percent of the flowers ship overseas, and quite literally too—on freighters. Twenty- or forty-foot shipping containers are loaded to the brim (given the relative low value of dried plants, they need to pack them in to make enough money to cover logistics) and driven two and half hours to Cape Town. From there they sail away, reaching Newark, New Jersey, in about four weeks and Hamburg, Germany in about three.

> If you think it is a garden, it is a garden.
>
> —JINNY BLOM

When asked about the issue of popular plants like pampas grass and eucalyptus, which can be invasive in subtropical regions, Johan said, "I believe it's crucial for florists to be mindful of the environmental impact of their materials. As for trading in these species, it's a complex issue. On one hand, they may be abundant and readily available, but on the other hand, supporting their trade could inadvertently contribute to their spread and ecological harm."

Considering what we know about the carbon footprint of flown flowers, the problems of repeated tilling, the electric drain of grow lights, the value of trees, shrubs, and perennials in sequestering carbon compared to annuals, the unsustainability of the cold chain, the irrigation of flower fields, the use of plastics, pesticides, and fungicides in greenhouses, the flawed ecologies and economics of bulb production, the heating of greenhouses, and how we need to protect biological diversity, in my assessment, buying dried wildflowers is a wise choice.

6

Dexterity

Hand Work

All that you touch, you change. All that you change, changes you.

—OCTAVIA BUTLER

Early in my floral career, I learned there were different types of floral folk. No great revelation that, but what struck me first was that some relished detail work and others loved a good saw. Some owned shops, some stands, some farms, some warehouses, some delivery vans, some estates, and some little at all. Yet all undoubtedly had hauled buckets of blooms and in one way or another, worked with their hands.

There's room for all in the trade—you could say floral design and gardening are professions that have tremendous range. But in my brief sojourn as a designer I quickly learned what I was not: dexterous. I'm a slugger and lugger, a gardener, and while the idea of knitting to audiobooks sounds like a very good and relaxing time, I'm just not sure I could get my fingers to literally do the work.

Many aspects of floristry require a high level of dexterity (and patience). Detail work such as wiring flowers and assembling wearables like leis, boutonnieres, corsages, and botanical jewelry require wrapping stems, bending fine wire, stripping small leaves, plucking flowers apart, tying knots, and using small tools. Needles need threading and seeds drilling, and the challenges of eyesight aside, many of these movements require sophisticated fine motor skills.

Thankfully dexterity can be learned. When my son was in a Montessori preschool I wondered about all the bead sewing and pegboarding he did—until his teacher put a pencil in his hand. He wrote early because he could physically; his fingers had been trained. Like children, adults can develop manual dexterity through training. Here are some tips for limbering up a couple of the best tools you have: your hands.

1 Range of motion is fundamental to health. Ball up your hands into a fist, then spread your fingers as wide as you can. Repeat!

2 Stretch your fingers. Lay them on a flat surface and manually lift each one up until you feel a slight stretch.

3 Add strength to your hands by squeezing a stress ball.

4 Each of our fingers has two knuckles, and some people can bend the top section independently. If you can't, try holding your lower knuckle straight and flexing the top bit of your finger. Like mini sit-ups, these exercises can strengthen your hands and provide you with more control.

Finger training involves neurological, muscular, and connective tissue adaptations, so be patient with yourself. Research has suggested that those who work with their hands have higher levels of inhibitory control, which means they are able to filter out extraneous noise in order to stay focused on the task (erm) at hand. Other reported health benefits of handiwork, including lessened anxiety and improved cognition, along with physiological enhancements, such as reduced arthritis in the hands and greater tactile sensitivity and coordination.[49] In many cultures, this work of the world, such as basketmaking, beading, winnowing, quilting, and so on, is accompanied by song, conviviality, and the weaving together of community.

2

3

4

5

6

7

1 Lei making supplies at Hawaii Flora + Fauna.

2 Flower vendor, Jaipur, India.

3 Plumeria weaving in Micronesia.

4 Torres Strait Islander Mariana Babia from Saibai Island with her Kulapiw Koewsa lei composed of a strand of kulap seed, timber beads, copper tube, nylon-coated trace wire, and crimps.

5 A vinok, or floral wreath traditionally worn by Ukrainian women and girls.

6 A display of decorative and functional household items in Aswan, Egypt, 2022. Nubians, including the local Kenuzi, traditionally use date palm leaves for weaving baskets and other items. The ornamental plates serve practical purposes but are also a testimony to the skilfulness of the girls and women in the household.

7 Born and raised on Maui, Lauren Shearer specializes in lei work in Haliimaile.

Diaspora

Culture and Horticulture

1

A composite of the Greek words for "scatter," "across," and "disperse," diaspora can be used to speak of language, plants, people, or culture. Among humans, diasporas are the result of complicated and often violent historical processes. For example, over a period of three hundred years, approximately 9.5 million people from Africa were enslaved and relocated to foreign countries around the world. Religious groups and ethnic groups, such as Serers, Jews, Roma, Sahrawis, Palestinians, Dogons, Syrians, Tibetans, and Ukrainians have been relocated or dispersed by force or killed. Today migration for work leads to the formation of labor diasporas, such as is the case with Mexicans, Filipinos, Indians, and other ethnic groups.

The word diaspora is significant to our understanding of plant use because it highlights how displaced people incorporate plants into cultural traditions and pharmacopoeias to maintain a sense of identity (and in some cases to simply survive). A diaspora may travel with seeds (as enslaved Africans did, hiding them in their hair) or find other means to grow plants native to their homelands. If the climate doesn't provide the right growing conditions, people are often forced to invent new cultural forms of expression with the plants and flowers of a new place.

Tulsi makes a good example. Related to pesto basil *(Ocimum basilicum)* and sometimes used in cut-flower bouquets for its perfume, tulsi is native to Asia, where the plant has been grown for centuries and has many regional forms. Used as a food, medicine, offering, and in cosmetics, tulsi is most often associated with India, where at least three different species of *Ocimum* are used. As the plant traveled west with its illustrious repertoire of uses, its name was Christianized to holy basil. In the UK, where a large Indian diaspora lives without all the diverse species of home, families still grow the herb—adapting to an African species of *Ocimum* that is more readily available. Among Hindus, the plant is considered a protector of the family.

The travels of *Hibiscus sabdariffa* tell a similar story. Traveling from Africa to the New World, many members of the Caribbean diaspora know this plant as sorrel. Brilliant red when steeped, the fresh calyces offer a tangy and fruity flavor to beverages throughout the islands and into Latin America. Given an analogous climate, the hibiscus benefited as its use spread through various ethnic groups, from place to place, while its name shifted again and again.

In a globalized world, diasporas might import familiar plants from home, particularly in major urban centers. One estimate from the Netherlands suggested that two thousand kilograms of plant material arrives into the country from Suriname every week.[50] In New York, Dominicans have access to familiar medicinal, decorative, and edible tropical plants, while in Cologne, Germany, Turkish immigrants can shop for familiar goods. Today the more than four million people of Chinese descent in America have access to traditional flowers—plum blossoms, orchids, bamboo, chrysanthemums, and other sacred and celebratory plants.

Diasporas have long altered floras and adapted to new botanical worlds. To paraphrase the great postcolonial thinker Édouard Glissant from Martinique, we live in a world of increasing diversities and confluences, which challenge the idea of universal truths. Diasporas challenge static worldviews.[51]

I change, and I exchange. This is an aesthetics of turbulence whose corresponding ethics is not provided in advance.

—ÉDOUARD GLISSANT

2

3

1 The wedding of Clive Gillmor and Manoj Malde in the Eastern Eye Garden of Unity at Chelsea Flower Show, England, 2023.

2 *Hibiscus sabdariffa* calyces for sale in the Caribbean.

3 Immigrants waiting to be processed at Ellis Island in New York, 1907.

Dye

Coloring Our World

> You may conclude that I consider ethics and aesthetics as one.
>
> —JOSEF ALBERS

Humans love color. We've mined minerals for blues, plucked the stamens off crocuses for orange, burned animal bones for white, scraped snails for purple, boiled barks for browns and plants for yellows, and harvested insects off cacti to create red.

The advent of synthetic dyes during the age of industrialization in the nineteenth century changed our relationship to color and nature. These dyes and colors altered how we saw the world, because color, once painstakingly difficult to produce, was suddenly everywhere—on packaging, advertisements, maps, and wallpapers, and in fabrics and paints. Inexpensive chemically produced paints were a boon to the Impressionists who, aware of the new science of color theory, relied on the optical mixing of color to create pleasing effects. Gardening changed in turn: Western gardeners designed immersive herbaceous borders so people might stroll through Impressionistic landscapes of shifting light and hue.

By 1910, two thousand colors were isolated. William Morris, the Arts and Crafts designer who championed artisanal production in England, said of the new strident synthetic colors of his time—puces, mustards, mauves, and blacks to name a few—"Every one of them is hideous." By 1939, 7,500 artificial hues had been created for industrial use.

When I tell this story of dyes and color, I don't tell the whole story, only mentioning in passing that I don't use dyed plants because "they're noncompostable." But a preference for hindsight can make you haughty; it can also skirt the subject of the future.

When it comes to dye used today, never before has the world used so much. Dried flowers get brighter and brighter in an attempt to compete with artificial flowers (also predominantly made of petroleum). Wholesalers present wilder plants by the minute—blue roses, Day-Glo baby's breath, brown tulips, yellow sweet peas, and painted branches in a rainbow of colors and lusters, from matte to glossy to metallic.

Today it's hard to find statistics on dyes because they've become so diverse: we have food dyes, acrylic dyes, solvent dyes, vat dyes, acid dyes, sulfur dyes, paint dyes, pigment dyes, and so on. In food we now call them colorants or color additives. What we do know about our obsession with color is that on the global pollution index, the dye industry today is among the top ten of the world's worst polluters, along with battery recycling, lead smelting, ore processing, and chemical manufacturing.[52]

The problem isn't at the user end—though this is an assertion of relative harm, not an exemption—it's on the production side. Take India: home to fifty large industrial dye plants and over one thousand small producers (on record), and all, according the watchdog Pure Earth, "disproportionately add to the problem of pollution."

Dyes made of arsenic, sulfuric acid, mercury, chromium, copper, and other metals require water to be produced. Dyeing also produces contaminated wastewater. People need water to live. And too many have too few choices of where they get it from, so in addition to ecosystemic impacts, dyeing adversely affects communities. Today, fabric dyeing and finishing are responsible for 20 percent of global water pollution. We need to ask ourselves who is bearing the brunt of our addiction to color.

2

1 Dyed Dutch tulips from the New York flower market.

2 Protea dyeing process at Kent Flowers, South Africa.

Ecological

Land and Livelihoods

1

Do you know what an umbrella species is? Think of pandas, jaguars, and spotted owls. The conservation "umbrella" around these animals protects other species in the same habitat. So what if a cut flower functioned similarly with the potential to help insects, animals, plants, and people?

This is the case with *Flor de Inírida* (flower of Inírida), which is the name of a town and a river in eastern Colombia, near the Venezuelan border, north of Brazil. This region is called Guainía, which means in the Yuri language "land of many waters." Some waters drain into the Orinoco basin, others toward the Amazon. The population density of Guainía is just over one person per square mile. More than three-quarters of residents are Indigenous (from numerous language groups). The town of Puerto de Inírida is the capital and has two roads leading out of it. The roads stop just past town. People mainly travel by boat.

The landscape of Guainía is a mosaic of tropical forest and floodplain savannas. Those with land produce food crops using *conucos*-style gardens, a type of traditional swidden agriculture where land is cleared of trees, crops are grown, and then the land is left to reforest. People hunt, fish, raise animals, and gather fruit. The floodplain savannas are sandy and nutrient-poor. It's here the Flor de Inírida grow.

Two species—from different genera—flower seasonally (one in winter, the other summer). If I could compare them to another flower, I'd do them a disservice as they're so unique—the genus name *Guacamaya* means "macaw" in Spanish, so that's a visual start. To me, they look like frosted, spiky gumdrops set atop long stalks.

Holding well in the tropical rain, drying to a warm brown, the flowers had traditionally been harvested from the wild for local markets. Community members wondered: what if the population of wild plants could be increased thus upping harvests? Could the flower work as a crop while also protecting land and biodiversity in Guainía? What about the local community?

The Indigenous people of the Amazon and Orinoco basins of Colombia have endured "five centuries of colonization, displacement, political imposition and cultural integration."[53] For one recent migrant to Inírida, now working with the flowers, picking through the local dump was once her only way to earn a small living.[54]

> There can be no sustainable development if people are hungry—hunger leads to more invasive and extractive practices.
>
> —FERNÁNDEZ LUCERO

Enter the bright Colombian conservation botanist Mateo Fernández Lucero, sagacious Indigenous farmers, sustainable development thinking, a local environmental group, trial and error, and today the flowers protect over ninety species of plants sharing the same floodplains by virtue of their value. A number of families work in processing the harvest.

This makes for a good story, doesn't it? Gardens America thinks so. They're the exporter now, branding the plant "Stella." After decades of flying out Colombian chrysanthemums from big-ag farms to Miami, they're finally on to a good thing. In this context, trading in sensitively cultivated wild plants benefits many instead of the few.

2

3

1 Flor de Inírida grows in sand savannas within biologically rich wetlands. Cultivation of the flowers has helped to protect other species and provide income to the local community.

2 Flor de Inírida (trade name Stella) has a vase life of over twenty-one days. A range of colors occurs in the species.

3 Cultivation of Flor de Inírida (*Guacamaya superba*), an indigenous species once collected from the wild along the Colombian-Venezuelan border.

Emergent

Flowers That Rise Above

Nelumbo: I love the shape of that word in the mouth. Nelumbo is the Sri Lankan word (and genus name) for lotus, which is an emergent. Technically an emergent is any plant that flowers above water or is taller than surrounding vegetation. Water lilies, papyrus, lotus, and bull rushes are all emergents. And all have rich histories of use.

> When nature is perceived as a web, its vulnerability also becomes obvious.
>
> —ANDREA WULF

Before we set off down the Nile, a short botanical mnemonic: sedges have edges, rushes are round, grasses have nodes from the top to the ground.

One more easy categorizer: water lily leaves float on the water; lotus leaves hover above the surface.

I didn't mention reeds yet. What's a reed? Reeds are aquatic grasses. Think of the dense thickets of *Phragmites*, a weedy reed growing everywhere from the tropics into the Arctic, its leaves emerging from nodes along the plant, its buff flower heads lifting twenty feet into the air spreading seed far and wide. Reeds are water filtration systems, bird habitats, the source of matting and flooring, and in the case of *Phragmites*, a global pest.

Papyrus the plant (not the paper product which shares its name) is triangular in shape (sedges have edges). At Lake Naivasha in Kenya (see Globalization), papyrus has almost seven inches between its edges. At lower elevations, such as historically the along the Nile, the plant reaches about fifteen feet high. Today papyrus has gradually shrunk through breeding to give us the horticultural varieties 'King Tut,' 'Prince Tut,' and 'Baby Tut.' The tokenism smarts. The plant was a cornerstone of a civilization, and yet today only about thirty acres are cultivated for papyrus production in Egypt while the plant is invasive in Florida, California, and Hawaii.[55]

There's almost too much to say about *Cyperus papyrus*. Egypt used a sustainable irrigation system for more than five thousand years, variously flooding land and leaving it fallow, and maintaining vast wetlands of papyrus for hunting, fishing, and material culture. Papyrus protects communities from floods, cleans water, and traps fertile sediment. The ancient Egyptians made boats from wild papyrus, farmed it for fiber, and used ropes of it to build the pyramids. The interior of the plant is built of cellulose and lignin, like wood. You can weave papyrus, burn papyrus, and eat papyrus. Hieroglyphs tell heroic stories of pharaohs hunting deep in papyrus, conquering that darkness, imposing order on chaos, and bringing the light.

I didn't see papyrus growing wild while sailing up the Nile, but I did see it etched on the walls of ancient tombs and temples. In heraldic terms, papyrus was more significant in the north of Egypt, and the lotus was more symbolic in the south. The sacred lotus was used in rites and rituals, and some scholars assert that the blue lotus (technically a water lily) treated erectile dysfunction. Ancient erotic images suggest the idea, and modern science has now proven the plant's ability to relax muscle tissue and "allow vasodilation within the corpora cavernosa, leading to penile erection."[56] It also works for the clitoris as well.

Water lilies, or the Nymphaeaceae, consist of five genera and about sixty species (and many cultivars). They're an ancient lineage of angiosperms, seed bearing, and yet wonderfully sophisticated when it comes to telling the time. The petals keep track of day and night, sensing when to be available to pollinators and when to close. The plant hormone group known as auxins controls this movement, triggering cells to shift from elongated at closure to stout during the day.

True lotus flowers are similarly amazing. The leaves repel water while the flowers use thermoregulation, much like mammals, maintaining a set temperature range even when day and night temperatures vary.[57]

We often forget how interconnected the ancient world was, but Indian traders brought both the true lotus and the Egyptian blue lotus to China before 200 CE. Sacred to both Hindus and Buddhists (to Buddhists the flower is a symbol of awakening and perfect fulfillment), the lotus is said to be the first flower ever to appear in poetry.

2

The plant has been in cultivation for more than seven thousand years.[58] Farmers plant root cuttings in the cool season into paddies. (Lotus, rice, and taro are some of the only crops that can be grown in flood conditions—something the world will likely face more of in the future.) Once the flowers are fertilized, a seedpod begins to form. All parts of the plant are edible. In China, varieties have been developed for root production, leaf and shoot production, and the flower trade. If the seeds are left on the plant to mature, eventually the seed pod, known as the lotus house, opens its doors and the seeds drop. This lotus house is the recognizable dried flower part for sale in floral markets the world over. These pods have a kind of holey look reminiscent of a lunar crumpet. In China, ornamental lotus flowers earn farmers about twenty times more than cropping the plant as a food.

1 *Nelumbo* 'Thousand Petal' in the garden of Billy Van Bakker.

2 *Nymphaea odorata* on the island of Martha's Vineyard, Massachusetts. The flowers can have both pink and white petals.

3 Jardines de Alfabia, Mallorca, Spain.

4 Collecting water lilies in Barishal, Bangladesh. Water lilies don't have strict requirements when it comes to photoperiod, but they do have internal circadian clocks, determining when they open and close, even once cut.

4

Endonyms

Naming Plants

1

A local name is an endonym. Places have local names, plants too. Let's start with a place: Montreal. In that fine city is a small mountain called Mont Royal. As far as we know, the French explorer Jacques Cartier climbed up the mountain in 1535 and called it that. *Mont* translates easily to "mount" in English, so some Montrealers call it that—Mount Royal. Quebec was colonized by France and is largely a French-speaking province today, so the city name is a kind of a hybrid: Mont-Royal (royal is a variant of the French *réal*) led to the name Montreal.

The First Nations inhabitants at the time of Cartier's arrival in 1535—who still live in and around Montreal today—included the Iroquois, who referred to Montreal as Tiohtià:ke, and the Algonquin, who used the term Moniang. These names reference beavers and rapids—Indigenous names often reveal a deep connection to the biogeography of a place.

The same is true the world over for plants. Rather than the names of explorers, we find associations, knowledge, ecology. In Micronesia, a plant can shift names depending on whether you're on the lagoon side of an atoll or not. Talk about place-based understanding! As such, endonyms aren't just words, but worlds.

> Once out of the Linnaean labyrinth, we have many choices.
>
> —BANU SUBRAMANIAM

In 1992, Antiguan American Jamaica Kincaid wrote an essay in the *New Yorker*, which I return to again and again. It's called "Flowers of Evil"—a provocative title for a provocative piece. In the essay, she struggles with naming and the way in which a history of conquest changed Indigenous plant names first to the language of the colonizer and later to Latin. It's a sticky piece because Kincaid presses the reader to think about what's lost when names change. As with many great essays, she struggles with her own associations and impasses; how she sat in gardens as a young woman looking at plants from around the world without questioning why those plants were actually there. She writes of this time, "This ignorance of the botany of the place I'm from (and am of) really only reflects the fact that when I lived there, I was of the conquered class and living in a conquered place; a principle of this condition is that nothing about you is of any interest unless the conqueror deems it so."[59]

I once had the great honor of commiserating with Kincaid at the New York Botanical Garden. In the previous forty-eight hours, COVID-19 had broken out in New York, and I was among a handful of plantswomen whose lives had been upturned in the space of a day. My friend Jennifer Jewell of *Cultivating Place* had invited me. She was interviewing Kincaid and asked her about naming. "Do we rename the dahlia back to what it was? Do we learn that name too?"

No doubt Jennifer had read "Flowers of Evil" in which Kincaid had written: "And so the dahlia: Who first saw it and longed for it so deeply that it was removed from the place where it had always been and transformed (hybridized) and renamed? Hernando Cortez would not have noticed it; to him the dahlia would have been one of the details, a small detail, of something large and grim: conquest."[60] (The dahlia began its cultivated life as a tuberous food crop for the Aztecs. Over centuries, it would captivate so many that forty-two species would be bred out into more than fifty-seven thousand cultivars—at last check.)

In conversation with Jennifer that rainy, bizarre day, when we all admired the bloom of a jade vine growing leagues away from its home in the Philippines, Kincaid said: "It's too bad that he named the cocoxochitl, which is the dahlia, after Andreas Dahl, which was one of Linnaeus' students. I wouldn't object to the renaming of the dahlia. They're renaming all kinds of things."[61]

In "Flowers of Evil," Kincaid had pressed the power button: "This naming of things is so crucial to possession—a spiritual padlock with the key thrown irretrievably away—that it is a murder, an erasing, and it is not surprising that when people have felt themselves prey to it (conquest), among their first acts of liberation is to change their names (Rhodesia to Zimbabwe, LeRoi Jones to Amiri Baraka)."[62]

Which brings me to another story, this time of having dinner with a book in Cape Town. The book was called *Birders of Africa*, and I'd picked it up in the lounge of my hotel. I'd been cramming botanical Latin on my flight over, dog-earing a wildflower book, narrowing down the genera I might see based on season and location. Birds seemed like a break. Then I read: "Linnaeus explicitly banned all names drawn from any languages other than Latin or Greek. He ruled that those nonclassical languages were 'barbarous' and 'should be considered as primitive ones because to the learned men, are their languages unknown.'"

Had I considered naming while studying my wildflower guide? South Africa is home to thirty-five languages, with no less than twelve of those official, and of course not

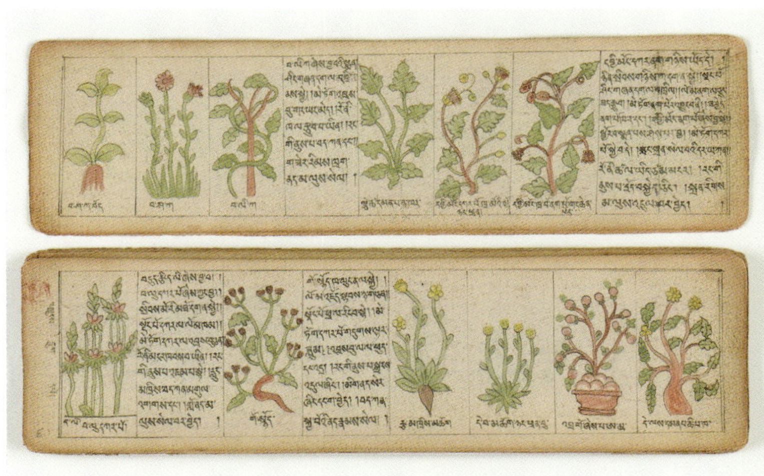

2

Plate 2
XIV
30
31
XV
32
33
XVIII
34
35
Crescentia cujete
Sesamum indicum
Bombax ceiba.
Theobroma cacao.
XX
36
XXI
37
38
37
39
40
41
42
43
44
XXII
45
46
XXIII
47
48
Zea mays
Cocos nucifera
Dioscorea sativa
Holcus sorghum
XXIII
50
51
52
53
54
55
56
Carica papaya.
Ants nest

one of them is Latin. So why was I memorizing this anachronistic language? I was trying to make sense of a flora, and given my background, training, and class, the Linnaean system was the most accessible one I had.

To borrow from the historian Dr. Lise Butler, the system of animal and plant classification that continues to structure our interpretation of the natural world today is rooted in Enlightenment doctrine—certain languages conveyed civilization and others did not.[63] Linnaean binomial taxonomy privileges not just certain people but also hierarchical forms of thought. Linnaeus himself was greatly influenced by Aristotle's development of a *scala naturae* or "great chain of being," which placed humans above other animals. But Linnaeus did not stop there; over numerous editions of his eighteenth-century *Systema Naturae*, he sought to categorize human variation—even developing subspecies. These ideas, which we would now consider racist in the extreme, would help shape the eugenics movements in Europe and the United States.

So how do we greet our botanical relations as we navigate our way through the world of flowers? Use local or regional names when possible. To borrow from the Red River Métis/Michif and settler scientist Max Liboiron, recognize that "the very idea of 'universalism' is a trick of Western imperialism."

4

1 *Magnolia grandiflora* aka Katlaha in Chotaw, Bull Bay, Southern magnolia, and Carolina Laurel. More than 150 cultivars have been developed.

2 Tibetan medicinal plant manuscript, date unknown.

3 *Sketches towards a Hortus botanicus americanus*, William Jowit Titford, 1811. The catalog identifies new and valuable plants arranged in the Linnaean system.

4 Darling Flower Show, South Africa.

Ephemeral

Living Lightly

> I've already lost touch with a couple people I used to be.
>
> —JOAN DIDION

I can't easily date the picture in my hands. Say, my early twenties. I don't recall my precise location, but I do know the latitudinal range and time of year: I'm about nine degrees north of the equator in August on an atoll in the Marshall Islands. Just looking at the picture reminds me of the prickly feeling of salt drying on my skin.

At the time, I was volunteering aboard a three-masted 156-foot schooner called the *Tole Mour*, which means "gift of life and health" in Marshallese. The ship was built by the Hawaii-based Marimed Foundation to support basic health care in the islands of the central Pacific. Our doctor and nurses were Marshallese, our dentist American.

The Marshall Islands is both a vast country and tiny one—spanning an area of 750,000 square miles, the total land area of the country is only seventy square miles. The population—only about forty thousand people—live on over a thousand different islands that rarely rise above six feet high. People live lightly on land.

The *Tole Mour* made medical rounds serving remote villages, some of which held just a handful of extended families (land passes matrilineally in the Marshalls and to simplify the social structure, such extended families form clans headed by a chief). The Marshallese have lived on their islands for approximately three thousand years, through cyclones capable of wiping whole atolls away.

Not long before the picture was taken, I dipped into the lagoon in my dress—nudity or exposure has been discouraged since missionary times, so I learned to wear a sticky sheath, a garment that could dry in minutes. One day, a manta ray came close to me in the water. Huge and black, skimming the turquoise shallows over white coral sand, its speed and size frightening, its elegance astounding. I'd been reading a book by David James Duncan at the time. "Wonder is like grace . . . it's not a condition we grasp; it grasps us," he wrote.

Walking back to the village, I found a huge green sea turtle (three hundred pounds?) lying on the beach, upside down, its eye slowly blinking, soon to be killed.

Portuguese explorer Ferdinand Magellan arrived in Micronesia first, then the Spanish, then much later the Germans and the Japanese. Imperialist exertions, missionaries, land grabs, sputtering colonization, attempts at resource extraction, and military operations, and then when the Americans occupied the Marshalls, things became worse. The already war-torn country became subject to thermonuclear bomb explosions—over and over and over again the mushroom clouds rose, each blast destroying lands, ecosystems, livelihoods, and people.

Twenty-eight explosions took place around Bikini Atoll—the Castle Bravo test bomb detonated in 1954 was over a thousand times more powerful than the one dropped on Hiroshima by the Americans in 1945. The fallout poisoned the Marshallese, sickened them for generations, and still does. Radioactive material traveled as far as Europe and drifted down to Australia. (Still, France would set off 193 nuclear tests between 1966 and 1996 in French Polynesia.)

At the time, I did not know all these details. I knew about Bikini of course, and how we were (apparently) safely about three hundred miles east of it, but I did not understand why my direct flight to Majuro suddenly dipped down over the vast Pacific to stop at an American military base a few hours out of Hawaii. Nor did I fully understand why diabetes has raged through the islands from the time of the American occupation, and why bundles of canned food, fishing nets, plastic toys, powdered milk, and rice were dropped by soldiers from planes in a training exercise called Operation Christmas Drop. I did not know that the reefs people relied on for food would one day be bleached or understand why, in the capital, rafts of plastic diapers, bottles, and bags collected in the lagoon.

But I was learning.

In the picture, I'm wearing a jasmine *mwaramwar*, a floral headpiece—a welcome gift made by women. On each island I received one; though I never saw anyone make one. The Marshallese always greeted us warmly. On some islands the young children cried, my blond hair so foreign I could have been a ghost.

And I was, in the grand scheme of things, a passing phantasm—even now I only have wisps of memory. I wish I could go back to that time and ask myself to pay closer attention. I didn't have much time on land, and what I remember wasn't the flowers so much as the food.

Taro, breadfruit, coconut, and pandanus traveled with the early settlers to the islands. These plants were farmed in agroforestry systems on what little land a coral atoll offered. Copra (dried coconut meat) was the only commodity I saw produced for trade—a few tarps drying in the sun by the lagoon, not anything that might be called an industry. People subsisted: they ate fish, turtles (eggs and flesh), shellfish, and the odd pig, farmed a bit, and bought rice, sugar, soy sauce, cigarettes, and clothes when they could.

On each island, once the doctor and dentist had served the community, we'd be hosted by the chief or head of the clan for a feast. The women wore bright bougainvillea flowers in their hair and sang songs of welcome and thanks as they carried in pandanus baskets brimming with food. We'd all sit on the floor of a crumbling concrete schoolhouse or on woven mats under the palms and eat fish, pit-cooked taro, breadfruit, and rice with our hands. Stories were told, though I couldn't understand them.

Recently I read: "Many Micronesian artistic endeavors are transitory; their emphasis is on the perfection of the performance rather than the creation of the lasting object."[64]

Our mwaramwars? We threw them into the ocean. We weren't too far from the time when everything single thing the Marshallese made (and used) came from, and returned to, the earth.

1 A work by Ren MacDonald-Balasia, the founder of the Los Angeles- and Honolulu-based floral design Studio Renko.

2 Oahu lychee, mangosteen fruits, miltonia orchids, and crepe myrtle by Ren MacDonald-Balasia.

3 Jaluit Atoll, Marshall Islands.

3

Exotic

Othering

1

I went into university hungry, ready to devour any idea that came my way. One of those ideas was Orientalism, as presented by a writer named Edward Saïd. An assigned reading first introduced me to his work, and I recall that it wasn't the words that appealed to me, but the writer's style of thinking; Saïd saw the patterns of economies, the biases of societies, the impact of culture on ideas and psychology, and somehow he synthesized that knowledge into a single word that spoke to the history of Western consciousness. I haven't recovered since.

One of Saïd's arguments is that Orientalism created a stereotyped image of the East (which historically referred variously to what was called the Near East, Middle East—both Eurocentric terms—North Africa, and Asia). This East was by turns, barbarous, feminine, sexualized, racialized, romanticized, and mythologized. By contrast, the West was presented as more rational and masculine. The East was "othered," as we might say now, and deemed "exotic."

Oh, how the West came to romanticize and fetishize the exotic. In the eighteenth century, when China began trading with Europe, motifs from East Asia (aka the Far East) trended in consumer goods. Fine porcelain with *nina-ki* (topiary trees) and tranquil pools spanned by intricate bridges would be one example, and fantastical landscapes of pagodas and flowers painted on cabinetry another. Western designers borrowed decorative styles often combining Indian, Japanese, and Chinese elements in design.[65] Was no one the wiser? It didn't matter particularly—the mystery and beauty of the East was what they sought to conjure. People wanted the exotic. The pagoda at Kew Gardens, built in 1761, was the first of its kind in Europe and still stands today as a testament to the fashion of chinoiserie.

I love rooms, not for the value of their furnishings, nor even because they may be of a certain taste, but because they mirror our lives

—MIGUEL FLORES-VIANNA

As the world's fairs began in the mid-nineteenth century, images circulated of the Orient, and early tourists returned with decorative objects such as sculptures, paintings, and carpets. When Napoleon Bonaparte invaded Egypt, the French not only looted the country of its obelisks (now in countless foreign parks, gardens, and squares), they incorporated Egyptian designs like hieroglyphs and sarcophagi into Empire-style furniture. Egyptomania ran rampant in fashion, leading to pyramid mausoleums, sphinx garden sculptures, and the design of the Washington monument.

Aristocrats and wealthy Europeans who had traveled on grand tours collected art and artifacts. I was once invited to teach at the Duke of Devonshire's home, Chatsworth, and was escorted through just such a gallery. It staggered the mind: museum-scale marble sculptures, tombs, busts, and towering tulipieres.

In the world of floral design, which is so often married to interior decoration, remnants of this acquisitive and collected design sensibility linger today. Collections of vases, kilims, chintz, patterned ottomans, silk embroidery, "tribal" textiles (in some cases attributed to no specific tribe), tiles, brass trays, and "Oriental" rugs now seem to fit with cluttered interiors and insouciant garden-gathered floral displays.

I must admit, it's an aesthetic I'm drawn to, and you can see the evidence in this book. Call it "haute bohemian," as Miguel Flores-Vianna did in his luscious book of a similar name. This term is not entirely apt: the original bohemians were outside society's conventions and had a contempt for money. Yes, they lived as aesthetes, but this historic antimaterialist element of nineteenth-century bohemian lifestyles, wherein people genuinely teetered on the edge of poverty or lived within it, seems to have disappeared under a surfeit of textiles. Today looking at interiors of decorative largesse, it's hard *not* to think about the money such a style requires (if the pieces are not reproductions and are truly collector worthy). Many true aesthetes collect out of a deep reverence for artistry and craftsmanship. Reproductions, appropriation, and merchandizing run rampant in the layered world of interiors today. The aesthetic endures, if not with integrity.

So what's all this got to do with the word "exotic?" Today we might describe a place or a floral arrangement as exotic without recognizing our own subjectivity. It's important to remember that exotic implies a kind of hegemonic othering, which, going back to Saïd, was an idea that helped missionaries and the colonial project, stripping millions of their land, language, culture, and power. So think carefully about using the word.

Thankfully botany makes things somewhat clearer—an exotic in contemporary botanical usage simply means a plant out of place.

3

1 Japanese flower seller, photographed by Kusakabe Kimbei, c. 1880. Kimbei often styled photographs for sales to Westerners.

2 Tebarek Allah, the Tangier home of Umberto Pasti and Stephan Janson.

3 Glass bell jars have long been used for horticultural and display purposes. Here a Himalayan blue poppy (*Meconopsis*), the seeds of which were smuggled out of Tibet in 1924 (and is now rare in the wild), fades.

Fair Trade

Consumption Philanthropy

Fair trade first arose as a way to promote equity in international trade. Seeking to support postcolonial communities in the global south, fair trade began in the 1950s and '60s in Europe, and earlier in the United States in 1946 when the Mennonite Edna Byler began selling Puerto Rican handicrafts out of her home in Pennsylvania. Today her project is named Ten Thousand Villages and is the largest fair trade retailer in North America, allowing artisans to set their products and keep 50 percent of profits. The company does over $42 million in North American sales.

> **Consumption philanthropy stabilizes, more than changes, the system . . . .**
>
> —ANGELA M. EIKENBERRY

The term is still used for businesses that emphasize people before profit, and despite the leftist connotations of the term, fair trade functions within a capitalist system and harbors a number of neoliberal principles. (There is so much to unpack here, and I have limited space, so if you want to learn more read *The Solidarity Economy: Nonprofits and the Making of Neoliberalism after Empire* by Tehila Sasson. I'll address what I can in the context of flowers).

According to the World Fair Trade Organization, fair trade fights poverty, gender inequality, and climate change by contributing to sustainable development. Today many of us know fair trade as Fairtrade International's certification system for agricultural products, yet economies of scale mean many flower farms in the global south still function on a plantation model. At a farm in Kenya producing Fairtrade-certified flowers, workers rioted after being fired for striking, having demanded fair wages and working conditions.[66] Yet still, businesses and farms that meet environmental, social, and economic standards are able to display a logo to consumers as a part of their marketing strategy. Skeptics argue that Fairtrade branding is a form of "cause marketing," designed to make us feel good.

Considerable research has gone into understanding how we shop, why we buy, and how many of us manage the tension of consuming foreign goods. Researchers use the theoretical lens of reflexivity, "which holds that individuals are tasked with the adaptive construction of their own identities in relation to a systemically uncertain social world."[67] Another way of saying this is that in modern life, many of us rely on our own judgment. We strategize and rationalize to make choices we can live with (often knowing that the systems we—and others—live within aren't always ethical or fair). We feel responsible to do the right thing: buy wisely or kindly, which in effect puts the burden for fixing the abuses of economies on individuals rather than the states.[68]

Transnational capitalism, individualism, systemic inequalities—these aren't things most Westerners contemplate while reaching for a pound of coffee at the grocery store or grabbing a bouquet at a corner shop. Marketers know this. Rather than deconstruct the notion of ethical capitalism or who truly benefits from continued global trade, they give us a comforting narrative, a story about how our purchases might help change lives in another corner of the world. To quote Bani Amor, "The mainstreaming of fair trade consumerism has offered well-meaning shoppers a bridge between charity and fashion."

One study noted that rather than change power relations on farms, fair trade campaigns actually sidelined meaningful discussions of labor standards. "Rather than bringing about a profound transformation of the production process," it argued, "these certifications obscure and even consolidate the existing socio-economic configuration of the industry. Certifications thus run the risk of having 'depoliticising' effects."[69]

We have limited agency as consumers, but for those of us who do have the choice of buying fair trade or not, it's important to recognize that real political engagement will do more to change the world than shopping ever will.

2

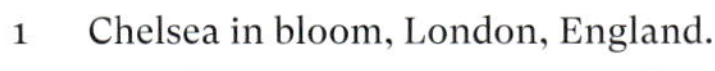

1 Chelsea in bloom, London, England.

2 A worker spraying pesticides at the Fairtrade-certified company Kiliflora in Tanzania, which grows roses for export.

Fernery

Farming Fronds

I am hungry for the touch of ferns

—ARIANNE TRUE

Between the 1840s and 1890s, a fern craze swept Victorian society. Enthusiasts scrambled to collect plants from the wild, pressed specimens, and hauled species home. Some ferns went into gardens, others into conservatories, and many into living rooms protected by an early version of a terrarium. Dr. Nathaniel Bagshaw Ward published *On the Growth of Plants in Closely Glazed Cases* in 1842, and his Wardian case allowed plants to survive salt spray on ship decks and tender plants to grow in the polluted air of the Victorian era's industrializing cities.

This pteridomania meant ferneries appeared—the word can mean a collection or a farm, and farm ferns people did—not only for nursery stock but the growing floral trade, and though the species have changed as fashions have shifted, ferns are still mainstays of bouquets today.

Join me in traveling to the self-proclaimed Fern Capital of the World, north of Orlando in central Florida, a region rich in lakes, but also hot, flat, and sandy. Florida traded hands many times in the colonial period, but let's start about sixty years after it became a territory of the United States, back when it was more of a floundering frontier than what we might imagine as the Sunshine State. The native pines and live oaks were cut and palmettos slashed from the underbrush. The settlers tried to grow things in the sandy soil.

Today an orange appears on the license plate of the state, but citrus wasn't easy in those early days. In 1900, when Florida had a population of about half a million, a hard freeze decimated citrus groves, only for another freeze to hit five years later.

What to do? Even today Florida weather is so wild—with hurricanes, tornadoes, freezes—it's difficult for nurseries to get business insurance. Survival required innovation, and along came Peter Pierson who had a brother in Connecticut with some trendy asparagus ferns people called plumosa. Said brother suggested to Peter that northeastern growers couldn't meet florists' demand; why didn't he try to grow it in Florida? With a new railway, Pierson knew he could get the ferns north to market.

Using seeds sourced from Italy, Peter Pierson went all in with ten thousand plants in 1904.[70] Savvy readers will have noticed the word seeds there and realized that asparagus fern (*A. plumosa*) isn't technically a fern, but an asparagus, a member of the lily family, reproducing not though spores as ferns do, but with seeds. In the twilight of pteridomania, it didn't matter much to consumers, so long as they could be sold as ferns.

In Florida, the "ferns" grew contentedly under the shade of native live oaks. (The plant originally comes from southern Africa, so heat and sandy soil was a good fit; today the plant is a widespread invasive in Australia). These oak hammocks, as they're called locally (a bastardization of the word hummock, I suspect), have closed canopies, punctuated with sabal palms, and are home to Florida panthers, bobcats, and rattlesnakes. Epiphytes abound in these hammocks: tillandsias, mosses, and real ferns hang from the trees.

Pierson built slat houses for his ferns to prevent scorching. They thrived without irrigation. Cuts were packed for shipping in the local Spanish moss and newspaper and the "ferns" successfully reached northern markets.[71] All went well for the asparagus fern until a true fern entered the picture—leatherleaf (*Rumohra adiantiformis*) from South America (or the Caribbean, no one quite knows). Glossy and easy to grow—you propagate it by splitting rhizomes.

Let's take a break from our historical narrative to fit in a bit of fern biology. Ferns first appeared in the fossil record about 325 million years ago, making them one of the earliest vascular plants (mosses and liverworts came first). They are ancient and elegant. Today there may be close to fifteen thousand species of ferns on the planet with more discovered every year. As mentioned, they reproduce sexually through spores, and some can tip a frond to the ground and sprout a plantlet from that point, while others colonize through spreading rhizomes. Leatherleaf offered growers two options—division and reproduction through spores, which I'll return to shortly.

2

3

While leatherleaf demanded irrigation, the Greek epithet of its Latin binomial suggests the reason for its ascendancy in the foliage trade today—*Adiantum* roughly means "does not get wet." The plant has both a waxy cuticle that sheds water and a slow transpiration rate, so by the 1970s the ferneries of Florida had moved on from plumosa (though there is still a town that bears that name.)

Panning around central Florida on Google Earth, it's easy to see the ferneries—acres and acres shrouded in black shade cloth. The cloth isn't just for sun—growers wet it when a freeze threatens, employing an igloo effect wherein ice insulates the plants below. (This works best if the plants are irrigated underneath.) In the 1980s, when more citrus groves froze, the ferneries survived, multiplied, and diversified.

Today, the Floral Greens Farmers of Florida in Pierson (yes, that Pierson of plumosa fame) is a cooperative of multigenerational farmers, some in their sixth generation. Many farms are still focused on leatherleaf and still tending plumosa patches under wild oaks, but others have diversified into aspidistra, umbrella palm (*Cyperus*), pittosporum, evergreen magnolia, elaeagnus, ligustrum, photinia, olive, foxtail fern, Leyland cypress, pine, and tree ferns. When flower production moved to South America, Florida growers moved into foliage. Alongside Costa Rica and Indonesia, Florida is one of the leading producers of cut foliage in the world today.

Mexican American laborers do much of the field work at Floridian ferneries, and most are paid by the stem, not by the hour. A recent study found that those working at a piece rate under shade cloth pushed themselves to cut without adequate breaks and hydration (drinking water when you're overheated can lead to vomiting, so many avoid it).[72] Sadly, many suffer increased rates of kidney disease.

Currently ornamental horticulture, not citrus, is the largest agricultural sector in the state. Dare we say Florida resolve its labor issues and put a fern on its license plate?

1 From Karl Blossfeldt's 1926 book *Urformen der Kunst* (*Art Forms in Nature*).

2 *Christmas is Coming*, Julian Ashton, *Illustrated Sydney News*, December 20, 1879. The tree ferns are likely *Dicksonia antarctica*.

3 Workers at Hagstrom fernery in Pierson, Florida, 1985.

4 Workers packing asparagus ferns for shipment, Casselberry, Florida, 1945.

4

Fix

A Sticky Subject

What's that trope about hominids? We use tools, so we're the cleverest creatures of all? Crows, otters, and octopuses use tools too, and just like them, we relish any new way of getting a job done without exerting too much physical energy. Take our kitchen appliances—I've got a range of modern conveniences run by energy I don't often think about. In the haze of a hungry morning, I push a button down and out pops toast. I don't consider that water nearby is dammed and flooded through a hydroelectric station to generate the electricity for me to have a bit of crunch on my bread.

I think of almost everything in terms of collage.

—AUSTIN KLEON

I continually bump up against this conundrum of the hidden costs of convenience in the world of flowers. Take glue. The floral powerhouse SmithersOasis claims that their adhesive "saves valuable time wiring and taping." It may, but what is it? I looked up the ingredients and can tell you hexane was pretty much the only word I recognized (it's a solvent used to extract oils from corn and soy). Hexane makes people giddy if they breathe it and causes neurological problems with regular exposure. It's volatile too: Oasis Floral Adhesive is so flammable it's potentially explosive. You shouldn't buy it, and if you have it, you shouldn't touch it. We know this because Smithers-Oasis tested the product on shaved rabbits (the Draize test for toxicity) and noted that it caused irritation to bunny skin and severe irritation to their eyes. No wonder you have to take it to a hazardous waste facility if you want to throw it out. Spray adhesives are no better.

So what do you do if you want to stick something to something else?

Zita Elze eschews floral adhesive for her work with flowers, opting instead for hot glue in her elaborate floral embroidery work. Leaves, however, are still applied to fabric with cold glue as the heat of the hot glue will otherwise burn them. Elze claims the hot glue seals off the flower stem and she is sure to use the rapid-melt style in her glue gun, not the slow-melt kind you'd find in craft stores, given it's too stringy.

You likely saw this coming, but any kind of a hot glue is a thermoplastic, which sadly renders floral artworks non-compostable.

Gelatin-based glues, on the other hand, are biodegradable and nontoxic. They're produced from the waste stream from slaughterhouses—namely animal bones, hooves, and hides, which are cooked down to extract collagen, precisely the kind a lot of people now eat as gummy supplements to thicken hair and fingernails. Gelatin is in everything from cosmetics to beverages, so a personal choice here is at play: you're either game for using by-products of the meat industry or you're not.

Yes, you could use tree sap to stick things and plug holes, as people long have. You could also use beeswax. You could use twine. You could weave. You could, like florists of old, learn how to wire flowers and reuse or recycle the metal. And you could, like many modern designers, say "stick it" to adhesives entirely.

1 Mexico City during Día de los Muertos, installation by Virro & Lola.

2 Postage stamp featuring *Plectranthus decurrens*, now in the genus Coleus, 1970.

2

Flora

Australian Flowers

Flannel flowers bloom after fire. A beloved group of pioneer species in Australia, *Actinotus* look like white fuzzy stars held aloft on silvery stems. Iconic, soft, with downy tomentose coverings designed to reflect light, the "petals" of flannel flowers are bracts; in some species, these bracts are so finely cut, so delicate they resemble feathers. There's something celestial about the flowers, particularly when they take advantage of the space and light created by bushfires and bloom in clouds of white in charred landscapes. One year, when bushfires had removed the forest overstory and heavy rains fell, a patch of flannel flowers reached 5.5 feet tall.

One observer of the super bloom noted that it's "typical of Australian plants and wildlife to have this boom-and-bust cycle . . . We have these really good rainfall events and then big droughts."[73] To many, the flower is a symbol of resilience.

> You go to places the whole world over No matter if it's near or far. But all their flowers will not entrance you Like the Wattle and Waratah.
>
> —NORMA HALL

A protected species in New South Wales, the harvest of flannel flowers from the wild has long raised a number of economic and ecological concerns. Can flannel flowers be harvested sustainably from the wild? If so, how many, how often? What are the environmental impacts of people venturing into the bush to pick them? In the words of Bettina Herron of WildFlowers Australia, the "wild harvest of flannel flowers (and certain other native flowers) for commercial sale is regulated by local (state) legislation through a system of permits; another layer of regulation is through export permits issues by the Federal government." With flowers being taken from both private and public lands, how can the government control harvesting? If people are poaching the flowers from parks, what resources do staff need to enforce laws?

Flannel flower seed is only about 70 percent viable, so the plant needs an abundance of flowers and seed to survive in the wild. Pink flannel flowers may stay dormant for over fifty years until conditions are right for bloom (and miraculously some will only germinate in the presence of smoke).

In New South Wales, the overharvesting of wild flannel flowers fueled conservation legislation, but wild harvesting is still a balancing act in the country today. There is insufficient enforcement of licensing requirements, and management plans need updating to ensure all species entering the cut-flower trade are protected if necessary.

The demand for native wildflowers in Australia has shifted over time. One reporter on the Sydney floral scene suggested that arrangements reflected the European cultures that shaped the country's identity and some "local designers were raised to regard native species as mundane and overly rustic."[74]

Things have changed. Today flannel flowers are cultivated on small farms to meet the overwhelming demand for them at home and abroad. Craig Scott is one such grower. A fourth-generation flower farmer, he grows on fifty acres of natural bushland, of which about twenty acres is farmed. He grows about two hundred types of flowers, almost all natives, and is licensed to collect seed from the wild.

Businesses like Scott's represent one of the possible futures of sustainable flower production. Native plants use less water than traditional florist flowers (think roses, lilies, tulips, ranunculus, etc.). Most can be grown outdoors, and many are woody, perennial, tough—adapted to Australia's climatic extremes.

The Australian cut-flower market was valued at AU$308 million in 2022–23. Of that, about 10 percent of the market are "wildflowers" with a strong impetus to produce more, making the country one of the world leaders in "wildflower" production for the cut-flower trade. I'm putting that word wildflower in quotes because according to Scott, "it was an umbrella term that was developed in the '80s and '90s by a number of producers of Australian and South African flora." Growers sought a term to delineate locally grown product from traditional florist flowers. "But there has been a lot of confusion in the industry on what's Australian and what's South African. And I think it's important in our marketing that we get that right."

So let's review: what flowers are uniquely Australian? Obviously there isn't room here to discuss the full flora of the country (estimates suggest there are about twenty-two thousand species of flowering plants in Australia and over 90 percent are endemic),[75] but here are some

3

4

5

flowers you may already know: kangaroo paw (*Anzigoanthus*), billy button (*Pycnosorus*, sun *Craspedia*), waxflower (*Chamelaucium*), wattle (*Acacia*), banksia, bottlebrush (*Callistemon*), tea tree (*Leptospermum*), waratah (*Telopea*), mulla mulla (*Ptilotus*), paper daisy (*Xerochrysum*), grevillea, pincushion tree (*Hakea*), and of course, the ubiquitous eucalyptus.

Despite increasing interest in wildflowers, wild harvesting is on the decline—in the 1980s, 50 percent of wildflower production in the country was from wild harvesting in Western Australia (a wildflower hotspot). Today that number is estimated to be under 10 percent, though foliage is still collected throughout the country.[76] Is that 10 percent even sustainable, people wonder? Conservation initiatives and environmental concerns have helped generate interest in native plant farming for cut-flower production and COVID-19 increased demand. Consumers learned that the vase life of natives far exceeded most traditional florist flowers. As grower Sus Bush said, "Wildflowers have a real advantage over traditional flowers; they just last so long."

So why can't they capture more of the market? Taste, culture, and capacity. According to Bettina Herron, "Some species take many years from seed to reach flowering—so cultivation isn't always a viable proposition."[77] But as people learn to think about where plants products are sourced from, how they are produced, and the high environmental cost of traditional florist flowers, the trade in wildflowers will grow.

Flower Industry Australia has recently found another angle: they are calling on the government to impose a levy on cut-flower imports.[78] Their argument? Biosecurity. Australia is an island continent that has routinely suffered from pests and diseases. The organization has noted a double-standard at work insofar as a foreign potted rose might spend six months in quarantine before heading out to the local nursery industry, but a cut rose can be cleared though a holding facility in the space of a day. (A brief historical note: Australian rose growers began importing cut stems to meet the local demand they could not supply. Today it's often cheaper to import roses than grow them in the country.) Flower Industry Australia argues that the sheer volume of imports means less than 20 percent of flowers are even checked for pests and diseases, a clever argument and one that supports local flowers.

One thread running throughout this story of Australian flora is the historical role the government has played in supporting research, developing legislation, and working with various interest groups in the flower trade. From limiting harvests to conducting scientific studies to inspecting plants to providing education and grants to growers, the government of Australia has engaged with the floral sector to bring benefits to the both the land and its people.

1 *Petals and Plumage*, by Pamela Pauline, celebrating Australia's biodiversity.

2 Craig Scott at his flower farm in New South Wales with kangaroo paw (*Anigozanthos*), which hails from Western Australia. Israel and the US also supply kangaroo paws to the trade.

3 *Crotalaria cunninghamii* grows in sandy, dry regions of Australia. The shrub can reach up to ten feet.

4 Cassia Heard with mulla mulla, *Ptilotus exaltatus* 'Joey'. Almost all *Ptilotus* are native to Australia.

5 *Actinotus helianthi*, aka flannel flowers, at East Coast Wildflowers in New South Wales, Australia.

6 Waxflower (*Chamelaucium uncinatum*) is native to southwestern Western Australia, where it can reach up to thirteen feet in height. Waxflowers are in the myrtle family and related to tea tree of essential oil fame.

6

Floriculture

A Hawaiian Story

1

In 2018, the Kilauea volcano on Hawaii sent lava fountains three hundred feet into the air. The lava moved down the slopes in wide flows, crossing roads, burning and burying as it went. The largest lake in the state evaporated as a result of the eruption, and the farmers who grew 70 percent of the state's orchids had mere hours to save what flowers they could.

Kilauea sits near the center of Hawaiian floriculture on the Big Island. After its eruption, more than thirteen hundred acres of arable land were buried. Eric Tanouye, then president of the Hawaii Floriculture and Nursery Association, estimated 70 percent of the orchids grown in the state had been decimated by lava.[79]

I had the great fortune of chatting with Eric at his farm, Green Point Nurseries, near Hilo, which supplies floral shops across the islands and ships about 30 percent of their tropical flowers and foliage to the West Coast of the United States. Green Point employs about fifty people, from growers and packers to office staff. We met outside an open-air processing building where flowers were washed, sorted, and packed.

Eric grows on about one hundred acres on land his father once farmed. "My dad grew up after the war, but the history in Hawaii wasn't easy. In the mid-1800s, plantations started here. It was more modern than slavery but a very difficult life. Other than sandalwood and supplies for ships in the early days, Hawaii did not have much to trade. So Hawaii picked export. But after the war, when the military was pulling out, the economy was so small . . . There was nothing but the big five." (Here, Eric is referring to the corporate sugar plantations, which benefitted from the US annexation of Hawaii through reduced tariffs on the trade.)

"When my father chose a career, he was thinking about agriculture, but he wanted to pick something that couldn't be salted, canned, bottled, or frozen because big business could do all that. Fresh flowers gave him an advantage."

Today the business specializes in the top tropicals in the trade, including anthuriums, orchids, heliconias, and gingers.

"In my dad's day he'd get maybe four to five years from one anthurium plant. Now, with good cultural practices, we get seven to eight. To be profitable, you don't replant. You keep your plants and soil well cared for." (His father used sugarcane bagasse leftover from processing to augment the soil, but Eric now uses the mineral-rich volcanic cinder from eruptions.) "I get about six blooms per year from each anthurium growing point."

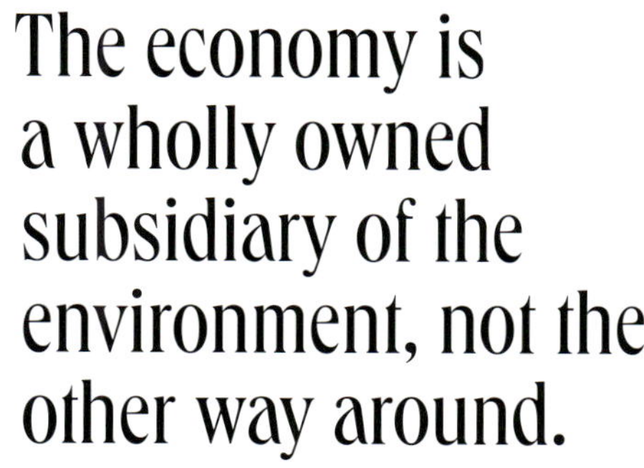

The economy is a wholly owned subsidiary of the environment, not the other way around.

—GAYLORD NELSON

It's a similar story for orchids—keep the plants happy and they'll bloom for years.

Hilo's first orchid society was founded in the 1930s after breeders, nursery folk, and orchid enthusiasts noted the east side of the island offered an ideal climate. A steady trade wind blows in moist air, perfect for the epiphytic varieties. Elevation provides a range of microclimates, so a diverse range of orchids can be grown: cymbidiums in the relative coolness of mountainsides, and arandas, mokaras, vandas, and dendrobiums on the sunnier and drier lowlands. The forty acres of orchid farms that disappeared in Kilauea's Puna flow grew cymbidiums, oncidiums, cattleyas, paphiopedilums, and dendrobiums.

Eric grows dendrobium for up to six or seven years and might cut twelve sprays of blooms per year as they only flower in summer and fall. Oncidiums produce year-round but only live for three to four years.

Business changed for the better for flower farmers like Green Point with the advent of the internet. "We don't supply much into the mass market. That model that demands you produce more each year and drop your price each year—it's a race to the bottom. In my father's time, we were stuck with one wholesaler in one city. Importers were the consolidators and the wholesalers were the gatekeepers. So to get out of that, my father sold to nonprofits, garden clubs, and direct to florists. "

I asked Eric how business was now. "Today FedEx takes about 15 percent, but you don't even have to own a truck. That's big. So nontraditional markets have become our traditional. But family farms are having a tough time. People are aging out, retiring. A lot of the farming in Hawaii isn't commercially viable; it's subsistence farming—growing a bit of food and some flowers. I don't think as a state we'll be able to meet future demand for flowers."

Later Eric showed me around the building where carpets of red and purple anthuriums sat in buckets ready to be graded, bunched, and shipped. A couple of desks overlooked the floor—the entire operation small enough you could wave across the room, share a smile, lend a hand. Garbage pails held five-foot-tall heliconias in water, their brilliant orange inflorescences hanging close to the floor. A few women in plastic aprons worked the baths, dipping gingers in soapy water to loosen bugs and spraying monstera leaves with water. A bulletin board of foliage plants suggested sizing, the plant names listed in Hawaiian, English, and Latin. In one corner, a woman prepared anthuriums to be shipped, slotting paper between the spathes, piles of shredded newsprint to her side.

Eric eschews plastic, has installed solar power, and tries to run Green Point as responsibly as possible. "A lot of energy goes into processing flowers. It's the processing side of agriculture which is demanding unless you have a lot of foresight—to build a building that can recapture water, that can capture sunlight, store energy . . . these types of ideas my father developed twenty or twenty-five years ago."

I asked where the greatest waste was in his industry. "If we didn't have to package flowers, we wouldn't. High material and labor costs."

Later when we walked the farm, Eric waxed philosophical. "The Hawaiian concept of *kuleana* means responsibility—for one's self and one's family, including the living things which support life. Flowers are Hawaii. The Hawaiian people have always used flowers and plants as a way to connect with their legends. They're expert storytellers." Three generations into a family business, Eric added, "they are our host culture."

2

1 Freshly cut anthuriums at Green Point Nurseries, on Hawaii.

2 Eric Tanouye of Green Point Nurseries, with *Heliconia vellerigera*.

Floristry

A New Age

1

> # If you think squash is a competitive activity, try flower arrangement.
>
> —ALAN BENNETT

The future of floristry lies in the hands of the educators and certification organizations who train designers. However, many are aligned with the flower industry, not the planet. Take the American Institute of Floral Designers (AIFD), considered the gold standard in certification in the United States, maintains partnerships with supply manufacturers, flower distributors, and grower conglomerates. Because designers must pass through levels of certification to have the esteemed AIFD after their name, these partnerships shape what students learn. For example, in 2022 the AIFD was proudly partnered with Smithers-Oasis, a floral foam and glue company; FTD and Teleflora, one-click corporations delivering arrangements of imported flowers in foam; Accent Decor, which distributes disposable vases and polyester ribbons; and Design Master, which sells spray paint and flower dyes.

AIFD receives a nominal partnership fee from each of these companies—$500 in 2022 (of which $50 is set aside for scholarships), however the industry partners receive more in return: product mentions in AIFD blog posts and reduced rates to feature their businesses at AIFD events. For an additional small fee, partners can also obtain the contact information for AIFD members, which allows them to send catalogs, marketing materials, and free samples directly to florists.

As the Japanese Canadian master florist, speaker, and educator Hitomi Gilliam once said, "The only way that sustainable floristry awareness can move forward is to disassociate from the marketing effort of the industry supply giants . . . So much of floral education over the years has focused on the supply line . . . by rethinking, reassessing different materials that can be deemed compostable, we can come up with new product lines that are more suitable for the new age of floristry."[80]

The Boerma Instituut in Aalsmeer, the Netherlands, has been teaching students since 1980. By the master florist level, students learn to design and support their own compositions. The intricacies of the designs amaze: you're likely to need a drill for wood as much as a pair of pruning shears.

Similarly, to become a certified floral designer through the Floral Design Institute, students learns how to make everything from wearables, like corsages and boutonnieres, to casket art. The course program includes a module on designing without floral foam, exposing students to techniques like building armatures, weaving foliage, and using a taped grid or chicken wire (aka floral netting). This is a step forward. If students learn the skills required to create art without waste, we all win. But it's a slow process.

A recent study suggested that a tension exists between the ethical decisions floral designers must make and the aesthetic choices of their customers. Sustainability for many designers is a moral obligation and foundational to their professional identity. Some have adopted the term environmental floristry to separate themselves from sustainability squabbles and highlight place-based aesthetics if not plants. Educating customers is one way these designers hold on to their professional integrity.

Still, many in the industry are aware of the wider problems in the world of floristry. For the educator and designer Susan McLeary, the future is about "technique, method, and sustainable solutions." Bashing on others about the ecological problems of floristry isn't a solution in her mind. "If you really care about change or progress and if you are not offering a solution or steps that people can take to be successful, you're not contributing to the solution."[81]

2

3

4

5

6

7

8

1 Azelle Chang modeling work by Francoise Weeks.

2 A shopkeeper in Jamaica Market, Mexico City.

3 Lei-making at Grace Flowers in Honokaa, Hawaii, owned by Alison Higgins (at left).

4 Mexican designer Leopoldo Gomez.

5 Pine, delphinium, and gloriosa adorning a pair of Meiji-era Japanese screens. A tea ceremony installation by This Humid House in Singapore.

6 Hitomi Gilliam with *Gloriosa* 'Southern Wind' at JA Kochi Misato Engel Kakibukai in Japan.

7 A young Kiribati woman in traditional dress.

8 From Japanese magazine *kimono-hime*.

Footprint

Accounting for Flowers

1

Carbon emissions have long been the focus of environmental campaigns, leading to exhortations to buy flowers that are "grown not flown," local, or regionally produced. Landedness has also come to define the sustainable floristry and garden-to-vase movements, but sadly many things contribute to the carbon footprint of flowers beyond travel, namely the level of mechanization involved in production, the type of flower being grown, vase life, soil mediums, and the materials used to package flowers and plants as they reach the consumer.

So what is a sustainable flower? Here are some questions you can ask yourself:

Is the flower dried? Painted, glittered, or dyed?

How long does the plant crop for? Meaning, does it offer up repeated blooms like an anthurium or is it a one-and-done flower like tulips, poppies, or flax?

Is the flower sterile? Has it been bred to have so many petals that it can't reproduce? If so, what might that mean for pollinators?

Is the flower corporately controlled or patented? Does it rely on tissue culture in a lab to be reproduced?

How long has the plant been in the earth? Think this way: trees are best, then shrubs, then perennials, then biennials, then annuals. Why? Carbon capture decreases down that list. Plus, more tilling means more carbon emissions from machinery and soil.

> Nothing is ugly as long as it is alive.
>
> —COCO CHANEL

How was the flower grown? On a farm? Was plastic used for weed suppression on the farm? Is the farm peat-free? Does the farmer practice no-till farming? Or apply chemical fertilizer? Pesticides?

Was it grown in or under plastic?

Does the flower come from a farm that practices regenerative agriculture? Has the flower been grown in a biodiverse agroforestry system?

Has the flower been irrigated?

Has the flower been hard grown outdoors or in a greenhouse? Was the greenhouse heated? (For example, Dutch roses imported to the UK have a higher carbon footprint than Kenyan roses simply because of heating.)

Where does the plant come from originally? Is it a high-latitude or high-elevation plant, or does it come from a lower latitude? Hardy or not? Plants from warmer climates and lower latitudes tend to bloom for longer periods meaning more bang for a grower's buck and often a more sustainable flower.

Did it grow from a seed or a corm or bulb? Is the bulb grown as a perennial or disposed of like commercial tulip and amaryllis bulbs after use?

Is it wild harvested? If yes, great. Let's see your permit. Harvesting indigenous wildflowers is unethical in many cases. However numerous flowers and foliage come from managed reserves. Non-timber forest products support ecosystem integrity and communities if managed properly. Often the only way to do that is through licenses and permitting.

Was it poached?

Was everyone along the supply chain—from gatherer or farmer to florist—earning a living wage?

Is the plant native to your region? Or a cultivar developed from a native plant? Does it serve local pollinators? Note that nonlocal species of a native may be cultivated near to wild populations. If these plants then cross-fertilize with wild populations, genetic diversity can be lost.

Was the seed open-pollinated? Genetically modified?

Was it grown under electric lights?

Does the flower have a robust cuticle?

Does it have a long vase life?

Does it "die" well? Can you reuse it dried?

Did your flower break the chain between producer and consumer?

Did you grow it yourself?

Is it an invasive species? Did you look it up? Did you check to see if it was harvested without encouraging its spread (dispersing seeds or pruning to stimulate growth)? If it is, can you now dispose of it properly?

Was it wrapped in plastic? Was it delivered to you in floral foam? Or a bioplastic that needs an industrial compost facility?

Was the flower flown? (Note how late this question comes up.) Or shipped by boat? How far did it travel to get to you?

Can you guess how long it might have spent in a cold chain or in refrigeration?

Do you feel okay about buying it or growing it? In other words: is it still sustainable enough for you after running through this list?

1 An aerial photograph of flower fields in the Netherlands.

Fynbos

Beauty and Biodiversity

This flora is adapted to burn; it needs to burn to live.

—DR. ADAM WEST

You can't plan a wildflower trip to South Africa. Not entirely. You can choose the season but not the weather. Unlike a guided safari, where you are almost guaranteed to see the "big five" animals in a national park, with flowers you can only put yourself in roughly the right place at about the right time and hope. You hope for the rain to fall and then not fall, for the temperature to hit 64 degrees Fahrenheit (18 degrees Celsius) so the flowers open, and you hope that the heat from the sun is not blown away by chilling winds. As you drive hundreds of miles through six types of weather, you hope you will make it before 3:00 p.m. when the flowers close, that the fog will drip and burn off, that you won't get a flat tire (I didn't) or lost (I did) or that the cell signal will hold (it doesn't) or the power won't go out for too long, and all the wondering and wandering will be worth it because you will lose your botanical mind.

Francis Masson, one of Kew's first plant hunters, wrote of South Africa in 1773 that "the whole country affords a fine field for botany, being enameled with the greatest numbers of flowers I ever saw, of exquisite beauty and fragrance."[82] He was correct: South Africa is home to approximately twenty thousand plant species (10 percent of all plants found on earth). The Cape Floristic Kingdom on the country's southwestern coast has about 9,600 species, 70 percent of which are endemic, meaning they grow naturally nowhere else on earth. It boasts ninety-four species per thousand square kilometers. (Compare that with other heathland ecosystems in California and Australia, which have twelve and fourteen species per thousand square kilometers respectively.) The Cape Peninsula, a smaller area known for its exceptional plant diversity and endemism has more than 2,600 plant species—more than in all of the UK—in an area smaller than London.

I went to South Africa to learn about the farming and wild harvesting of indigenous perennials and to see plants introduced to global horticulture in their native habitats. Many popular garden flowers and plants are South African. These include *Acidanthera*, *Agapanthus*, *Aloe*, *Amaryllis*, *Arctotis*, *Asparagus*, *Bulbine*, *Clivia*, *Crinum*, *Delosperma*, *Eucomis*, *Freesia*, *Gerbera*, *Gladiolus*, *Gloriosa*, *Ixia*, *Kniphofia*, *Leucadendron*, *Leucospermum*, *Mimetes*, *Nerine*, *Ornithogalum*, *Osteospermum*, *Pelargonium*, *Protea*, *Serruria*, *Strelitzia*, and *Zantedeschia*. These are among countless others whose origins trace to South Africa. Many of these South African plants have been hybridized by horticultural companies registered with plant breeder's rights with little money returning to the country (see Bioprospecting). One flimsy argument against sharing the wealth generated abroad from South African species is that their genetic material has been in the public domain for centuries. One estimate I read suggested that "the Netherlands earns more from South African flowers than South Africa earns from its gold."[83]

Fynbos is an Afrikaans name (loosely translating to "fine bush") for a type of biome characterized by proteas, restios, and ericas centered in the Cape Provinces. Much of the area has been converted to agriculture and urban sprawl, but fynbos, regenerated by fire, still covers the area's mountains, valleys, and coastal plains. Eighty percent of fynbos plants appear nowhere else on earth.

2

4

5

6

1 Fynbos flowers in Cape Town. There are more than 770 ericaceous plants in South Africa.

2 Fynbos landscape at Table Mountain National Park, South Africa.

3 *Phylica pubescens* at Kirstenbosch National Botanical Garden, Cape Town, South Africa.

4 Faldielah at the Trafalgar Place Flower Market in Cape Town, South Africa.

5 *Serruria florida*, aka blushing bride, is native to the Cape Province of South Africa.

6 Educational display at Kirstenbosch National Botanical Garden, Cape Town, South Africa.

Garland

Occasional Flowers

The word garland holds a world in itself, with so many iterations across cultures ranging from leis to flower crowns, laurels, wreaths, chaplets, necklaces, wedding, and memorial decorations that the possibilities are endless if you want to string or wire flowers. And people long have.

Aztecs strung tuberose garlands. Egyptians, lotus. Tamils, jasmine. Filipinos, ylang ylang. Romans, roses. Micronesians, plumeria. Mexicans, marigolds. Russians, roses. Maori, kōwhai (*Sophora* spp.) Hawaiians, maile (*Alyxia stellata*). Tahitians, gardenias. Fijians, tagimoucia (*Medinilla waterhousei*). The French, orange blossoms. And South Indians, tulsi.

In India (and throughout much of the garlanded world), flowers are "the food of the spirit, a sign of respect and love."[84] The anthropologist Jack Goody referred to India as a garland culture not a bouquet one, and historians can trace the use of garlands from India to the Pacific following the Chola dynasty, which influenced culture, religion, and architecture along a vast maritime network that developed before the common era and lasted into the thirteenth century. This Indosphere, as it is now known, lasted over 1,500 years and stretched from the Arabian Sea to beyond the Banda Sea in Indonesia. The religious teachings of Hinduism and Buddhism spread throughout this region along with a floriography both complex and holy. Today in India specific flowers are associated with individual gods: for Shiva, datura; for Kali, hibiscus; for Lakshmi, lotus; and for Ganesha, marigold. These floral offerings create a connection between the worshipper and the divine—by supplying the god with their aesthetic preference, the supplicant shows their devotion.[85]

People use their body adornment to become something else. You are capturing the audience. It is spiritual and social and creative.

—MARIANA BABIA

The meaning of specific flowers has shifted over time throughout the Indosphere. For example, in both Malaysia and India, frangipani (a New World plant) is associated with the afterlife and seen as a symbol of eternal life, but in Java, the tree is believed to bring bad luck. In Bali, frangipani is holy and planted near temples. In Laos, the plant is both sacred and the national flower.

In Thailand, intricately designed floral works and garlands are similarly used as offerings in temples and to bring good luck. The Thai word for garland is *malai*. Like in India and Malaysia, flowers are symbolic and intimately woven into religious life and social customs, appearing at special events like weddings, funerals, birthdays, housewarmings, and other auspicious occasions, while also being used in everyday life such as hanging from rearview mirrors in cars to honor the goddess of journeys, Mae Yanang. Traditional flowers include jasmine, gardenia, marigold, and champak (the beautifully scented *Magnolia champaca*).

In the Pacific, Polynesians spread the use of flower garlands throughout the islands as they traveled. Today about half of Hawaii's flora has been introduced, so foreign species have been adopted into traditional lei making and given Hawaiian names. This fits with the traditional process of *hānai*, whereby kinship is established through adoption. Today the native liana and maile (*Alyxia stellata*) may be used with tiny cuphea blooms, a plant native to the West Indies and Mexico. Scentless, the flowers are harvested from shrubs and strung together for Father's Day, anniversaries, weddings, and graduations. It's possible to find leis for men made of twisted ti leaves, orchids, kukui nuts, kukunaokala (the stiff flowers of a type of red mangrove, *Rhizophora mangle*), and he'e berries from the *Sida fallax*, an herbaceous sand-loving plant also known sometimes as the Christmas berry given its red color and use in holiday decorations.

What does decolonization mean for plants in Hawaiian ceremonies? Goodbye bark skirts at luaus (introduced by missionaries) and goodbye dendrobium tourist leis. According to Jen Murphy, "Now they will be made from locally grown flowers instead of orchids which are imported from Southeast Asia at high financial and environmental costs and have been used for decades only because White mainlanders found them pleasing."[86]

Things change, but our collective love of flowers remains.

1 A flower vendor outside the Mullick Ghat market in Kolkata, India. From the series Flower Men by Ken Hermann.

Globalization

A Kenyan Conundrum

The poet Gertrude Stein wrote "a rose is a rose is a rose" in 1913, and here we are well into a complicated twenty-first century and the rose has become a lens through which we might view the modern world.

In her wonderful book *Orwell's Roses*, Rebecca Solnit examined the many meanings and menaces of roses. I can't top her work, but I can try to expand on our modern relationship with roses in the context of globalization, because today the two are inextricably linked.

> Growth for the sake of growth is the ideology of the cancer cell.
>
> —EDWARD ABBEY

Let's start in the 1980s, when growing roses in the East African Rift Valley was considered a grand idea. Why? The equatorial sun shone twelve hours a day. At altitude, the climate was cool enough, labor was cheap, and the freshwater was free. An international market was a short continent away—nothing airfreight couldn't overcome with petroleum and policy.

A Kenyan rose did not spell love: it spelled money for the Kenyan economy to recover. Recover? From what? Recent decolonization. In 1963, Kenya declared its independence from Britain. In the postcolonial period, trade declined as it did for many developing nations. Many had borrowed as they sought to organize politically and modernize (in Kenya's case, they'd been an English colony for close to a hundred years). Then interest rates rose in the 1970s; the OPEC crisis hit, markets declined, and by the 1980s a series of debt crises wreaked havoc on the global south including Kenya, Ecuador, Mexico—many of the places we get flowers from today. The International Monetary Fund (IMF) stepped in to prevent a global financial crisis and together with the World Bank began negotiating loans to countries; these loans are known as Structural Adjustment Programs or SAPs.

What did these conditional SAP loans entail and what did the IMF demand in return? Privatization of state-run agencies, decreased public spending, decreased barriers to trade, and a devaluation of currency. In essence, these were neoliberal reforms, the kind of free-market thinking employed by leaders like Margaret Thatcher and Ronald Reagan and followed by "global-marketplace" advocates Bill Clinton and Tony Blair.

On script, massive investments in floriculture began. Countries like Ecuador and Kenya turned from food production (for local consumption) to corporate partnerships with foreign-owned companies to grow flowers for export. Food security decreased and infant mortality increased, and life expectancy and school enrollment decreased initially too. Money was made, yes, but as Manfred Steger explains, "When market dynamics dominate social and political outcomes, the opportunities and rewards of globalization are spread often unequally, concentrating power and wealth amongst a select group of people, regions, and corporations at the expense of the multitude."[87] Of the 123 companies in the Kenya Flower Council, a raft of them are foreign-owned, from Ball Horticulture (USA) to Flamingo (UK), plus a handful of Dutch-based businesses and companies based in the United Arab Emirates. Many argue that the SAP programs enforced a kind of imperialism through debt, a kind of contractual colonization. (Recently the World Social Forum, recognizing the worldwide disparities in wealth and well-being, has called for the blanket forgiveness of all these debts.)

Kenya now produces about 40 percent of Europe's flowers.[88] Much of the industry is focused around Lake Naivasha, which sits just above six thousand feet. This region produces 70 percent of Kenya's flower exports. The lake averages only about twenty feet in depth, spreading out to shallow beds of papyrus, which once filtered the water and kept it clean for people and their animals. "Historically there was public access . . . The flower farms now own much of the land around the lake."[89]

Today Lake Naivasha is struggling with silt, pesticide, and fertilizer runoff from the rose and flower farms lining its shores. Cattle herders have limited access. Some cattle have died from drinking water saturated with pesticides. Hippo numbers are a quarter of what they once were. Workers from the flower farms line up to get potable water from communal taps.

Recently, in a baffling testament to the globalizer's creed that technology might fix every problem, a Lake Naivasha sustainability project has been proposed to clean up the water. The plan? Floating *plastic* islands studded with papyrus.

1 *Garden Rose*, by Libby Ellis.

1

Gondwana

Ancient Lands

Why do so many tropical and semitropical plants show up again and again around the world? Before humans helped plants to move, plants moved themselves—through seed dispersal on the backs of animals or aloft on the wind. Some plants encased their seeds in tasty berries so they might fly in the stomach of a bird. That's the small stuff, historically speaking. Another explanation for plant migration is far, far bigger, supercontinental in scale.

Imagine Antarctica, Australia, Africa, India, and South America all adjoined. If you can, you have Gondwana, an ancient land that graced our planet for roughly four hundred million years. The climate was pleasant in the main, moist and mild, so plants grew lush. Cycads, tree ferns, mosses, and conifers would have looked much like they do today in a botanic garden's dinosaur display. Flowers, aka angiosperms, had yet to develop, so if you're still picturing an unbroken emerald forest, stay there a moment longer and take a deep green breath.

Gondwana covered about one-fifth of the earth's surface (Laurasia contained North America and Eurasia), and gradually broke apart during the Jurassic period, slowly though in geologic time. T. rexes came and went; plants too. Land masses drifted taking plants with them; their fossils and DNA tell us so.

Flowers developed about 130 million years ago, which isn't long in geologic time. *National Geographic* puts it this way: "If all Earth's history were compressed into an hour, flowering plants would exist for only the last ninety seconds."

Gondwana explains why monkey puzzle trees in Chile have relatives in New Zealand and how flowers we love from Australasia have sexier cousins in Brazil. Zealandia drifted away from Australia about eighty million years ago (before dinosaurs were extinct) and has more in common biologically with the Pacific Islands and South America than it does its neighbor.[90] Today New Zealand has only one terrestrial mammal, a bat, while having numerous flightless birds, the result of millions of years of no predators.

Much has changed, but Gondwana reminds us that studying the biogeography of plants can feel like looking through a kaleidoscope with beautiful patterns repeating again and again.

Where did the term Gondwana come from? We can thank a plant, *Glossopteris*, a now extinct flowering tree that a geologist noticed in the fossil record in India and South Africa, and later in Australia and South America.[91] He named the land after the Gonds, one of the largest Indigenous groups in India. Today Morocco, Oman, Turkey, the island of New Guinea, Thailand, and Laos have yielded fossils that share glossopterid affinity. Did they look like a ginkgo or a magnolia—other early flowering plants? No one quite knows.[92]

What *Glossopteris* tells us, and from what we know from human evolution, is that we are all connected, even if, to borrow from the archaeologist Andrew Sorenson, our family tree looks more like a braided stream originating somewhere in Africa than an oak.

In a time of so much human migration, it's worth considering how we are all connected. We may diverge, speciate, and adapt to new conditions, but history tells us life always relies on other life to succeed.

With your arms spread wide . . . to represent all time on earth, look at one hand with its line of life . . . in a single stroke with a medium-grained nail file you could eradicate human history.

—JOHN MCPHEE

1 On Australia's east coast, a series of UNESCO designated Gondwana rainforests run between Queensland and New South Wales. These forests are home to ancient lineages of plant and animal species.

Hegemony

Art, Plants, and Power

1

Dominance by force is one way of controlling people and taking power, but hegemony is often more subtle. In the context of culture, cultural hegemony refers to the way in which those in power use media, art, stories, or ideas to legitimize their dominance.

Given that there is an unequal distribution of power and privilege in our globalized world, it is important to recognize where cultural hegemony remains unquestioned. Art is not insulated from social forces, and neither are we in our judgment of it. We often don't question the ideas and values that shape our tastes.

Consider a floral foam company sponsoring a designer, workshop, or floristry school. The practice sounds like a simple marketing strategy to reach customers, but when the use of those products to create art is judged at an event or on television, well, to borrow from Marshall McLuhan, the medium (in material terms) really does become the message.

> Do we want to accept art is another ideology and its aesthetic just a part of it?
>
> —DANA ARNOLD

If I offer you a bouquet of roadside flowers in one hand and a bunch of fancy ranunculi in the other, you might instantly tally up the difference monetarily as much as assess the beauty of each bouquet. This idea—that the inner meaning of a work of art matters as much as the outer—is one developed by Jacques Derrida, who wrote of it in *The Truth in Painting*. Knowing you're standing in front of a floral painting by Vincent van Gogh would likely bring a set of thoughts and assumptions forward about the object's rarity, price, and status. Your knowledge of the artist may bear on your assessment in addition to the sense of wonder you might feel about its colors or the energy of the brushstrokes. You might experience awe simply because you know you are in the presence of what is known as a great work of art.

Now think about the building you might be standing in to view this painting, how it might function as a cathedral of sorts—hushed, grand, vaulted (likely in more ways than one). The museum acts as a sacred space. The architecture itself is linked with history, technology, and power.

These ideas aren't my own; they are those of Carol Duncan, a feminist art historian. She encourages us to think about how and where we view art, and explores the idea of the liminal ground, the "the kind of attention we call forth when we enter a sacred site, or when the lights dim in a theatre or concert hall or when we enter an art gallery."[93] In such a space, we're more susceptible to viewing works through a lens of connoisseurship. Now consider the florals at a couture fashion show—no matter what they look like, we assume they're on trend because they're surrounded by luxury. The installations bask in a rarefied glow.

If we give something aesthetic value we often imbue it with economic value too. As the sociologist Pierre Bourdieu suggested, aesthetically valued objects can be traded at higher prices, so it behooves Westerners to write about their historic language of flowers, to add meaning to the flowers they can access, and to promote the aesthetic they trade in. And it is not just the West that commingles aesthetics, art, power, and wealth of course.[94] As Jack Goody once extrapolated from the history of flowers in China, "The ruler or the ruling elite utilizes what is forbidden or unattainable to the rest, sometimes overtly with a religious or social rationale, more often covertly as the fruits of power."[95]

It can be difficult to understand how hegemony shapes popular culture, but it's important. Consider a flower magazine's use of an antique porcelain vase. The vase reinforces status.[96] We need to notice when (and how) the aesthetically valued art of the dominant class legitimizes its power. The sociologist Sam Friedman reminds us that value is ultimately arbitrary, and "it's only by revealing how arbitrary the ways in which we assign value *are* that we can tackle class and inequality."[97]

2

1 Learning about global floriculture inspired this collage I collaborated on with Ana Myerscough.

2 *Charles Townley in His Sculpture Gallery*, Johann Zoffany, 1782.

Hothouse

Growing Under Cover

> # Bricks to all greenhouses!
>
> —EDWARD ABBEY

In December 1934, a headline in the *New York Times* read, "Rare Park Plants Doomed to Die of Cold; City to End Hothouse Heat for Economy." Money was tight. After five years of the Great Depression, a third of New Yorkers were unemployed. The year before the headline, in 1933, New York, out of desperate necessity, built its first social housing. But housing plants? Ferns, palms, camellias, and magnolias were among the more than forty thousand plants in the Central Park Conservatory Garden slated to be auctioned off or left to die when the parks department decided to demolish their greenhouses. There were few buyers. The paper reports that "not even the large brilliantly colored goldfish, swimming placidly in their artificial brook in the tropical-plant building, drew a bid."[98] And so another symbol of America's Gilded Age came crashing down.

Long before the age of public greenhouses, people used cloth and paper to keep plants warm. In ancient Rome, *specularia* ("window panes") were built onto a type of wheeled raised bed and cold frame combo using oiled cloth or translucent stone like mica. In China, oiled cloth was used to trap steam from hot springs to keep plants warm. Throughout the history of horticulture, wherever there has been the will, we've almost always found a way to grow plants.

What's the difference between a hothouse and greenhouse? A hothouse is heated by artificial means, not solely the sun, as is the case with a greenhouse (though these terms are often blurred. A glasshouse might be passively heated through the sun or actively heated from a fuel source). Not all greenhouses are glasshouses of course—plastic and wood structures might be called a greenhouse too, though if it's curved it's often referred to as a hoop house or high tunnel.

Many of the large glasshouses seen in botanical gardens have been heated since the eighteenth century. When Kew Gardens moved from a royal institution to a publicly funded one in 1841, the shift necessitated a new form of curation for the public—they had to hide the messy business of growing plants. To borrow from Emmett FitzGerald, the garden's shift toward an imperial theme park meant barrows tucked behind walls and coal secreted underground to fuel the boilers. Today if you go into the Palm House on a winter's day, steam rises from the floor as if some unseen dragon lay below. As Mary Kuhn notes on this period, "Technology was not so much invading the garden as constituting it in the first place."[99]

2

Today greenhouse technology is still fully entwined with horticulture. Radiant heat (using water heated by liquid natural gas—LNG—or electricity instead of coal) is common. In the Netherlands, companies are experimenting with geothermal methods to reduce emissions. With nine thousand hectares covered with greenhouses in that country (imagine seventeen thousand football fields), finding more sustainable methods of growing plants is paramount.

Despite the Netherlands's long legacy of growing under glass, China, South Korea, Turkey, and Spain have the greatest density of greenhouses today, with China devoting a whopping 2.7 million hectares of land to agricultural production under either plastic or glass (with an area about the size of Maryland under plastic alone).[100] Many are passive solar structures—one-sided, traditionally using wattle and daub built of straw and clay bricks or more recently, thick concrete walls on the north side and plastic, which can be manually rolled up, on the south.

4

Japan and Singapore are innovating with vertical farming in old factories and car parks where plants are grown daylight-free, meaning under LED lights timed for maximum growth. The hothouse, the greenhouse, and the glasshouse may one day be relics of the past.

5

1 *Flower Composition with Figure, Logan Greenhouse*, Ludger Larose, 1899.

2 *Victoria cruziana* was a sensation in Victorian times. The leaves can hold a weight of up to seventy pounds. The plant hails from South America and will produce its own heat to attract pollinators. It also is transgendered. The plant first opens a scented white female flower to attract a scarab beetle, then closes, and next opens as a pink male flower, releasing the beetle to pollinate other flowers.

3 The Palm House, Royal Botanic Gardens, Kew, England.

4 Greenhouses used in the flower-export industry, Kenya.

5 Circa 1850s illustration by Thomas H. Shepherd of the Palm House at Kew Gardens.

Hybrid
Shaping Nature

A hybrid is technically any creature developed through a cross of species, varieties, or genera. The terms hybrid vigor or crossbred vigor are ones we use in reference to plants (as well as horses and dogs)—creatures bred for specific attributes, be it a shinier coat, shortened snout, or a longer pod. A crossbred dog, like a goldendoodle, is the offspring of two purebred dogs: a golden retriever and a poodle. Is the crossbreed dog healthier? Science tells us so. Purebreds, whether plants or mammals, have a limited gene pool, and when propagated continually can be subject to inbreeding depression.

> To make with flowers requires absolute love and patience.
>
> —KRISHAN RAJAPAKSHE

How does hybrid vigor matter to the floral industry? Let's say you spot a new color in a familiar flower one day. It's a freak, a mutant—or more accurately the expression of a genetic mutation.

Through hand pollination, you laboriously breed that one flower out until the seeds are stable (meaning it will reproduce reliably). You finally have enough seeds to sell and what happens? Because no one can patent a flower grown from seed, your competitors go out and buy your seeds, grow the plants, harvest the seeds, and sell it themselves.

Hybrids, on the other hand, do not reliably deliver offspring that resemble them. That's significant (though over time, hybrids can become more stable). The American Begonia Society puts it this way, "All hybrids are created from seeds but few can be propagated as such. Seeds grown from a hybrid, particularly those with complicated lineages, are unlikely to resemble the original hybrid even when self-fertilized."

Let's go back to Gregor Mendel and his peas. Say we've got two great parent flowers with noted pedigrees developed through selection and breeding to have useful or pretty attributes, such as velvety petals or reflexed leaves. If a farmer or seedsperson who understands the parents' pedigrees (and the science of heredity) sexually crosses those two plants, the resulting hybrid (denoted as the F1 generation) will have the dominant features of the parents, but also the benefits of that wider gene pool, which may convey traits like greater resistance to disease, more robust stature, or better overall health.

The parents were inbred after all, so you could say the vigor is relative, but that would be missing my point that I'm desperately trying to get to: F1 hybrids have forever changed life on earth.

Today, from food systems to floriculture, seeds are big business. Case in point: hybrid begonia seeds by weight are more valuable than gold. Begonia seeds are minuscule, so a grower might get over a million plants per ounce. Is it worth it? In the bedding plant industry, it is. While begonias can be propagated in other ways, vegetatively or through meristem culture, our need for seeds remains.

In food systems, F1 hybrid seeds have historically had a darker side. In the 1950s and 60s, the trifecta of hybrid seeds, petrochemicals, and mechanization allowed crops to move into climates where their ancestral relatives may never have grown (think maize in Africa). These uniform high-yielding hybrid plants required advanced machinery and high inputs of water, and fertilizers and pesticides. In developing countries and postcolonial economies, like that of India, hybrid seeds were the cornerstone of the now controversial Green Revolution, which allowed productivity to increase dramatically, but also saw indigenous seed varieties sidelined in favor of corporately controlled hybrid seeds (which meant a loss of biodiversity and demanded machinery and petrochemicals few farmers could afford). Because hybrids don't reproduce to type, new seeds needed to be purchased year in, year out from foreign corporations, creating cycles of dependency. Many activists have noted that poor farmers can be forced into a kind of seed slavery. In 2022, it is estimated more than eleven thousand Indian farmers took their own lives.[101]

In agribusiness today, vertical integration means plant breeders work for seed suppliers and seed suppliers sell pesticides matched to the crop. Farmers produce so much food today that some estimates suggest we could feed an extra three billion people (40 percent of food is lost or wasted).[102] As physicist, food activist, and ecofeminist Vandana Shiva recently noted, "76 percent of all commercial seeds are in the hands of ten companies. Most of the genetically modified seed is in the hands of one company. And sadly while we could be eating 8,500 species of plants, our cropping systems have been reduced to four . . . ."[103] These are sugarcane, maize, rice, and wheat—the food equivalents of roses, carnations, gerberas, and chrysanthemums.

Hybrids are such a big topic, but I can't help reflect on another form hybridization—that of thought. When I was in my twenties, I studied with Shiva. She was teaching at Schumacher College in England, an institution that grew out of non-Western thought insofar as E. F. Schumacher—English economist and author of the 1973 book *Small Is Beautiful*—was heavily influenced by his time in Buddhist Burma in 1955. One of his realizations, which feels almost anachronistic now but certainly wasn't mainstream at the time, was that "production from local resources for local needs is the most rational way of economic life."[104]

As a student at Schumacher College, you worked with your hands and heart, not just your head, and so one night after a day of lectures and discussion, I found myself alongside my heroine preparing eggplant for dinner. She asked me, very directly, as is her wonderful open way, "What do you really want to learn?"

I remember saying something about plants and then slightly regretting it, given it was too simple a noun, that complexity could have better tied to me her. The program she was teaching was nothing less than quantum physics, systems theory, and ecological thought. I was fully up for it, but I had no idea how my sensual connection to plants would serve me intellectually.

"Botany?"

I shook my head, recounting a story from my first year at university when I couldn't properly weigh salt, cheated in a lab, and promptly dropped the class in favor of Chemistry and Society.

She had a doctorate in physics but laughed. And though I can't recall after all this time what she said in reply, I'm reminded of that old adage that it's not what someone says that you remember, it's how they made you feel. I bloomed.

2

1 *Shapeshifter no. 1*, by Jennifer Latour, 2023.

2 Soy cultivation in the Brazilian Amazon.

Indigenous

Knowledge and Respect

> # Every empire sings itself a lullaby.
>
> —LENA KHALAF TUFFAHA

Globally, Indigenous people comprise fewer than 5 percent of the world's population but help protect 80 percent of the world's biodiversity.[105]

What does indigenous mean? Is the word capitalized or not?

Indigenous is applied equally to plants and people today. So let's start with a basic definition: indigenous means naturally occurring in a particular place, not introduced. In terms of plants, indigenous vegetation usually references a smaller area than the word native. Indigenous often overlaps with endemic, which means to be born of specific locale.

Easy enough. But when we get to the term Indigenous (often capitalized when applied to people), it's important to know the history of the word. As Wade Davis recently wrote: "There are words that, through overuse, lose their power and authority, causing the eyes to glaze over. Sustainability is surely one. Indigenous may be another."[106]

The word Indigenous gained acceptance in the early 1970s, when anthropologists began to question the language of their discipline. Namely, as Davis writes, by "referring to living peoples and cultures as 'primitive' and 'savage'—words that appeared without shame in the early ethnographic literature."

The United Nations Declaration on the Rights of Indigenous Peoples codified the word in 2007, defining Indigenous peoples as those "having historical continuity with pre-colonial societies that developed on their territories" and, Davis reminds, consider themselves distinct from the "societies now prevailing on these territories."

So who is this Davis? He's not Indigenous, but he was one of the leading thinkers in ethnobotany when I was an undergraduate in British Columbia. He wrote beautifully, and went everywhere a man of his talent, vision, and privilege could go: deep into the north, the Amazon, and eventually wherever his *National Geographic* explorer status took him.

After a double major in anthropology and environmental studies, I was perfectly poised for a career in ethnobotany, and I did, through field studies, check it out. But at the time, the power dynamic of flying into a place to chronicle plant use bothered me. And yet, in some ways, the work of ethnobotanists like Davis created conversations between cultures, elders, and governments and have led to some reconciliation. Significantly, the documentation of traditional land use has helped with land repatriation.

Thinkers now recognize the term Indigenous does not recognize the multiplicity of lifeways, languages, and cultures still extant on this earth, nor does it do the harder work of naming groups of peoples individually. Davis argues that the word simply highlights "the myriad cultures that have a shared history of subjugation and subservience, and whose traditional homelands are encompassed by the web of boundaries that mark the arbitrary limits of nation-states forged for the most part from the wreckage of nineteenth-century colonialism."

In Brazil, there are more than three hundred ethnic groups within the Indigenous population: in Thailand the Hmong, Karen, Lisu, Iu Mien, Akha, and Lua (to name a few groups); and in Australia, the Pitjantjatjara, the Warlpiri, and the Arrernte are among many more. Indigenous human cultures are diverse. We must be more specific.

So what do we do with this word indigenous today as plant people? If we're discussing a plant's used by a nation, tribe, or cultural group, we are as specific as we can be.

2

1 Wild blue *Heliophilia* with *Ursina.*

2 Biedouw Valley tapestry, South Africa.

Installation

Creating Space

1

What makes a critical mass? In politics, it has been said that for women to make real change, they need to assume at least 30 percent of elected offices. In nuclear physics, where the term originated, it means the point at which a reaction will become self-sustaining. I like that definition in terms of flowers—as our eyes take in a room or a display, at what point do we feel sated, like what we see is just enough?

Research in landscape design has shown people respond favorably to about 26 percent floral coverage at any given time. A person's taste influences that percentage of course. There are minimalists and maximalists, those who like the sway of green grasses, say, and those who love to swim through flowers.

Does the percentage hold indoors? Or in the context of installation work? Not usually. Recently, the style of massing industrially grown flowers (and using very little foliage) has been on trend. Walls of roses, hummocks of hydrangeas, giant puffs of carnations—every year when the Chelsea Flower Show runs in London, the business community creates shop-front displays and pavement "gardens." Giant cherries, bumblebees, crowns, elephants, popsicles, butterflies, and other creatures and shapes might be made from flowers, while billowing clouds of dried, artificial, and dyed plants spill off buildings. Floral percentage? I'd say 75 percent (Chelsea is a flower show after all), but concerns about sustainability have led to the appearance of native plants, dried grasses, and the odd reconstructed mini-meadow on sidewalks.

Many floral designers think of installations as gallerists do, not as photo backdrops but as designs in conversation with a space. They might aim to create intimacy, a sense of surprise or wonder, to design something site-specific (whether indoors or outside) to conceal elements of architecture or lighting, or to highlight the very same. Experience matters—often the goal is to conjure emotion or encourage thought.

Chloe Rose Quinn developed Make A Scene in Bali with Gus Ari after Ari designed a wedding using only woven local coconut leaves, pioneering what is known as the "re.green" movement in decoration. Quinn has a theater background and said this of their work: "It's all about the shared intention of elevating craft. We transform spaces with Art. We don't want to take anything away from the space, instead we want to engage with it. When we create new designs we want to bring a sense of theatre to a place. When you are around our 'woven scenes' you are inescapably in Bali—It's a celebration of nature, skill and culture."[107]

> I have a strong sense of imagining how things will be and making them be. It is art and it is design. What is intangible becomes tangible.
>
> —AYAWAL MANIN MARIA BABIA

I recently learned of the work of Canadian artist Kapwani Kiwanga. In her Flowers for Africa series, she looked back to archival photos of heraldic moments when flowers helped to mark occasions such as the "signing of an accord . . . a negotiation between two hostile parties [or] a celebration of a country that becomes independent from its protectorate or colonial overseer."[108]

Kiwanga created reproductions of these floral designs in stark white exhibition spaces. Vases of flowers sat on plinths and hung from the walls. The flowers were not watered and thus spoke to time—how dreams might fade, how struggle and suffering are still a part of life in postcolonial Africa. As she says, "Pan-African dreams have been eclipsed by the everyday difficulties of the average African citizens."[109]

I mention her work here because it embodies Saul Bass's idea that "design is thinking made visual." Technically, the word install means to put something inside of something else.[110] Installation art often aims to put ideas or emotions into us as viewers. As the Tate Gallery puts it, "What makes installation art so different from sculpture or other traditional art forms is that it is a complete unified experience . . . ."[111] Even at a wedding or event, designers think sensually—of scent, touch, and perhaps even sound. As the floral designer Emily Thompson (who regularly does installations for large-scale events) once said, it's "storytelling through design and art."[112]

1 Work by Make a Scene, a leaf-creation studio in Bali that highlights traditional leaf weaving techniques. Using *busung* (the young yellowish tender leaves), *slepang* (the older darker leaves) of the coconut tree, and *lontar* from the fan palm *Borassus flabellifer*, the design company builds biodegradable sculptures, installations, and artworks.

2 A Lunar New Year installation by This Humid House in Singapore featuring the roots of princess vine, aka curtain vine (*Cissus verticillata*). The aerial roots of the vine provide one strategy for the plant to spread, its berries another. Considered highly invasive in many parts of the world, the plant is native to the Neotropics.

2

Invasive

A Thorny Issue

The first time I stepped on a fire ant nest I was taking a shortcut on Nevis. I was staying with my in-laws, shortcutting to—you might have guessed it—a bar. Dead set on a rum punch and silence, I ducked under some shrubs on sandy soil and within seconds got swarmed. The bites burned and blistered, and that rum punch came with a bag of ice for my sorry foot and little sympathy at dinner. At the time, I didn't know much about the ants, but if I had known they can kill through allergic reaction, that they have eaten sea turtles and occasionally deer,[113] I might have milked my suffering, but given I'd sheered off from the group for a tipple, comeuppance it was.

> The restoration of degraded ecosystems is like the restoration of personal health. In restoring the health of a loved one, no one, I presume, expects that the sick person returns permanently to their youthful selves. Rather, that person is, at best, returned to the path they were on before they fell ill.
>
> —LIAM HENEGHAN

The great entomologist E. O. Wilson (who we can thank for the lovely term biophilia) was thirteen years old when he discovered Brazilian fire ants. The ants were a recent introduction to the United States in the 1930s, and he tracked their spread from a port in Alabama to Texas to Missouri and beyond. The government learned of the threat, sprayed organochlorines and pesticides in an eerie, early *Silent Spring* parallel, and killed not just birds but cows, and yet, almost a hundred years later, fire ants still claim ground.

Wilson researched fire ant plagues in the Caribbean. One species he tracked to the early colonial period in the 1500s and the other to an African fire ant, which he guessed traveled on an early slave ship. The ants, loving disturbed ground, ran rampant with plantation development in the 1700s. My Nevisian fire ants' ancestors may have traveled by boat from an adjacent island or arrived in American sod used on the island's only golf course in the '80s, but no matter the mode of transport, fire ants are still on the move.

By the 2000s, when the ants hit Australia, the insect was so red-listed it even had a scary-sounding acronym: RIFA—Red Imported Fire Ant. The Australians knew the threat: RIFA are considered one of the most noxious invasive species in the world along with cats, rats, kudzu vine, and cane toads. Repeatedly, Australian authorities have beat back incursions, with over a billion dollars committed to their destruction in Queensland alone.

Invasive species usually follow a significant other: humans. As we invade, expand, excavate, deforest, trade, farm, or garden, we unwittingly spread pestilence, disease, and species that undermine native ecologies. This ultimately threatens us of course, but in the age of the Anthropocene, when our actions shape the very climate, what can we do?

As plant lovers, a lot.

There has been much discussion in floristry circles about the use of invasive species. Some view their use as positive, a kind of beautification-through-eradication approach that I advocated in my last book. Rather than import flowers, let's use those carbon-neutral nasties in the neighborhood! Just be sure to dispose of them responsibly, I implored. But sadly, the research doesn't stack up to be a forage florist. Here's why:

Invasive species often thrive on disturbance; that's why they're so successful at colonizing roadsides, stressed ecosystems, and places where humans have interfered with natural landscapes. As such, they might take your presence (and use of it) as a good sign to grow more. Remember that plant in Harry Potter called Devil's Snare? Hermione and Harry have to remain calm to defeat it. Hack at it they could not. Devil's Snare isn't far from the truth of some invasive shrubs; as gardeners know, a good pruning often stimulates growth.

Disposal isn't easy. Ever tried a ritual burn of plant material after a wedding? Chances are it was not successful. Used plant material, even when composted, may not always reach high enough temperatures to destroy seeds.

Flowers often contain unseen seeds that fly off in transit. Let's use coral vine (*Antigonon leptopus*) as an example. Used in floral design for its beautiful racemes of delicate hot-pink

2

3

flowers, the plant runs rampant on roadsides in the tropics, and in the midst of all that abundance you think, will my actions really make a difference?

Well, you decide: coral vine was introduced to Florida as an ornamental. The plant, likely from Mexico, has Spanish, Palauan, Chamorro, Tongan, English, French, and other names because it has spread almost everywhere, from Queensland to the Galapagos and from St. Kitts to Hawaii to Singapore. Why? It grows to up to twenty-five feet, smothers other species, tolerates a variety of lean and limey soil types, can defoliate in drought and come back stronger after a rain, is a prolific producer of winged seeds (which can float), resprouts if cut back, and can, like morning glory, root from any bit of buried of stem that has a node if someone tries to excavate it.

Like fire ants, coral vine is aggressive and invasive through both remarkable adaptations and aplomb. Does that mean florists should not use it? With a rap sheet like that, I'd give serious pause.

Spreading invasives can lead to extreme eradication measures by municipalities and governments who may have no recourse save spraying herbicides, which threaten human and animal health.

The writer Hussein Omar noted that in Egypt, the bougainvillea's name is the infernal one, derived from the Quranic word for hell.[114] Sounds about right.

Cutting feels like helping, I know, and eschewing imported flowers in favor of local ones is a climate-friendly choice. Plus, the use of foraged plants appears democratic insofar as anyone can afford to harvest them (given the time and resources to acquire them), but showcasing invasive species forces a lot of tough questions your way: how do you destroy it? How do you ensure it doesn't spread? Did seeds drop in transit? Is it okay to promote a known invader without acknowledging it's invasive somewhere, even if it's not in your area?

I think not.

We use so many words to describe plants: endemic, endangered, rare, pioneer, naturalized, common, threatened, alien, etc., that if you're confused, it's no wonder. It wasn't until 1999 that the United States established an Invasive Species Council noting that "invasive species" means an alien species whose introduction does or is likely to cause economic or environmental harm or harm to human health."

We tread at our peril.

1 My husband wearing coral vine, or corallita (*Antigonon leptopus*), which was introduced to Caribbean gardens in the 1940s. Researchers on Sint Eustatius estimate 33 percent of the island is now covered or partially covered in the vine. This wasn't very responsible of me, making this headdress, as seeds were likely spread during collection and construction, but I did bag the vine after the picture was taken.

2 Volunteers burning *Rhododendron ponticum* in Wales. In 2020, the National Trust of Scotland started Project Wipeout to remove invasive species. It's estimated that half of Scotland's rainforests are choked with these rhododendrons.

3 South African ice plants (*Carpobrotus edulis*) on the California coast. About 60 percent of California dunes are covered with ice plants, which were introduced in the 1900s to prevent the dunes from migrating into pastures. Given the moist climate, these plants can spread up to three feet in a year.

4 The papery bracts and flowers of bougainvillea.

4

Jungle
Imagined Forests

1

In one of Henri Rousseau's most famous works, a naked white woman lies supine on a couch in a fantastical tropical forest, giant blue and pink lotus flowers, lions, palms, and citrus in the mix. In another of his jungle paintings, tigers stare from between aloes and yuccas—creatures that naturally appear continents apart. Like that of the Dutch masters who assembled still life bouquets from sketches of individual plants and flowers, Rousseau's work is filled with odd juxtapositions. In *Tropical Landscape: American Indian Struggling with a Gorilla*, the title alone takes us beyond fact.

As a plant person, when I first saw *The Dream* at the Museum of Modern Art in New York, I wondered not so much over the grand sense of scale in the work but over the mash-up of species. How did a man who never left nineteenth-century France know these tropical flowers, these animals, these plants? And why did he pull them together as he so wonderfully did? Certainly books and magazines chronicled species new to the Western imagination, but I felt there was something more experiential in his paintings, more tactile and real.

Rousseau painted about twenty-five surrealist *jungles luxuriantes*. In his time, the word jungle covered wide swaths of the tropics, leaped from continent to continent, conjuring a lush green world. The true origins of the word come from the Sanskrit *jaṅgala*, and various iterations have appeared throughout India and beyond, referencing tangled vegetation and dense growth. The English word jungle developed in the eighteenth century, decades before Rousseau painted, and referred to humid tropical forests, which is an interesting shift from the word's origins—jaṅgala originally referred to disturbed landscapes, places where native vegetation had been removed and aggressive colonizing species moved in.

Rousseau did not visit jungles; he visited gardens. "When I go into the glass houses and I see the strange plants of exotic lands, it seems to me that I enter into a dream," he once said. Rousseau worked for the customs service in France, picking up a paintbrush in middle age, determined to be an artist. He was a Fauvist by circumstance—the word *fauve* roughly means "wild beast" in French and refers to a group of French artists (many of whom worked with a knowledge of color theory). Self-taught, he is called a naïve, a painter who just did what he did, stretching brilliantly from his own time toward the future (and some say, paving the way for the surrealism of Pablo Picasso).

> One of the commitments that I've found with biodiversity and betadiversity conservation is that it's not aesthetic conservation. It's not: "This place is beautiful I'm going to conserve it." It's: This place is necessary.
>
> —HALEY MELLIN

We know Rousseau visited the Jardin des Plantes in Paris and marveled at the Exposition Universelle in 1889. The Exposition was a world's fair spread out under the new Eiffel Tower. Queen Victoria and Prince Albert (who created the V&A Museum in London) had unveiled the first world's fair in 1851 at the height of Empire, displaying technological exhibits and curiosities from twenty-five countries. The French went further—a Mexican palace was reconstructed on-site, and the world's Indigenous peoples were presented in displays alongside animals to gawking crowds.

To borrow from the writer Michael Brooks, the lifestyles of colonial subjects, the foods they ate, the clothes they wore, the animals they hunted, were displayed in idyllic and picturesque manner, devoid of any notion of resistance, conflict, or violence.[115] Why? Not everyone supported the idea or expense of imperialism. The expositions were a form of PR.

Today it's still a jungle out there. The writer Upton Sinclair titled his socialist takedown of immigrant wage slavery in early twentieth-century Chicago *The Jungle*. Later, Jamaican reggae star Bob Marley spoke of urbanity as a concrete jungle. In modern English, the word often refers to a place of overwhelming complexity. But darker allusions linger—that of *The Jungle Book* and Tarzan, swinging out from a rapacious and racist past when, in the words of Hamid Dabashi, tropical forests had yet to be "conquered, assayed, exploited, colonized, and destroyed."

2

1 *The Dream*, Henri Rousseau, 1910.

2 Henri Rousseau in his studio, 1910.

Killers

Gloves On

1

The beauty of petals is both a blessing to a farmer and a curse. Pests can hide in the folds of flowers. The sticky nectar of tropical flowers is a food source too—for pollinators of course but also for pests such as aphids and the ants that farm them for their own sustenance.

Plants grown in artificial environments, such as greenhouses or plastic tunnels, and those grown in monocultures are more susceptible to disease. Growers need to combat disease to make money, so a breakout of ants, mealy bugs, mites, aphids, thrips, or scale will mean hard losses, particularly if the crop only flowers for a short time. One of the quickest fixes is to apply chemical pesticides. You may think these wash off by the time the flower gets to you, but many pesticides are designed *not* to be water-soluble for obvious reasons, so consider washing both your flowers and hands in sudsy water if dealing with commercial product. Better yet, wear gloves.

> If control is the problem, then, by the logic of the Anthropocene, still more control must be the solution.
>
> — ELIZABETH KOLBERT

As Amy Stewart noted in her book *Flower Confidential*, an exposé of the floral industry, flowers are among the most toxic industrial crops in the world. One Greenpeace study of bouquets in the Netherlands found forty-three different pesticides present on the flowers being sold, flowers that we know people often stick their noses into to immerse themselves in pleasure.[116]

In addition to pesticides, insecticides, herbicides, and chemical fertilizers being used on cut flowers, antifungal treatments for root rot and mold are particularly common. For example, flowers may be dipped in benomyl, an inexpensive DuPont chemical fungicide that has been around since the 1960s and is toxic to earthworms. The other treatment for mold is not much better: thiabendazole, which is used both as an antifungal and antiparasitic, is carcinogenic in high doses or with extended exposure.

But what's a grower to do? Hawaiian-grown ginger is often treated post-harvest with insecticidal soap, not in itself a bad thing if naturally derived, but pyrethroids are often used as well. Botrytis is everywhere; it thrives in damp, cool settings, feeding on decaying plant material and affecting orchid greenhouses, houseplant production, storage facilities, and endless spaces in the cold chain.

A recent study suggests three reasons ornamental horticulture and floriculture are one of the most toxic types of farming.[117] First, the plants have been genetically altered or bred to a degree that they can no longer defend themselves against pests. Second, consumer demand for perfect flowers leads to more spraying. Third, there simply isn't an international body governing residue limits. While the EU has banned countless toxic compounds, they import and sell flowers without screening. The effects are felt by florists. One study out of Belgium identified dangerous pesticides in the urine of florists who worked without gloves.[118]

So do be careful with imported mass-produced houseplants and flowers. Protect yourself, those who grow flowers, and the earth as best you can.

2

1 Nicotine has been used as a pesticide since the seventeenth century. Today synthetic neonicotinoids adversely affect pollinator populations, water quality, and human reproduction.

2 A soapy bath at Green Point Nurseries in Hawaii. Light washing with a gentle soap and a spray with fresh water is sufficient to remove insects from tropical flowers.

Liana

Our Love of Rattan

What do Victorian wicker loungers, basket chairs, shipwrecks, and boho bedsteads have in common? A palm called rattan. If you're getting confused already—wicker isn't a material but a style of weaving, and rattan (*Calamus* sp.) is a group of more than sixty spiny palm species from a number of genera, many of which act like vines or lianas, and some of which are capable of growing up to five hundred feet in their pursuit for light in tropical forests.[119] It is estimated that more than seven hundred million people worldwide trade in or use rattan.[120]

> A vine becomes whatever it needs to be and does whatever it must to make real its fabulous pretensions.
>
> —HOPE JAHREN

For millennia, rattan has been used for basketry, food, matting, thatch, dye, medicine, fishing poles, furniture, handicrafts, and webbing. To get a sense of how long Westerners have been coveting rattan, consider the story of the *Orange*, a trading ship engaged by one Elihu Yale of the British East India Company, who in 1692 emptied the ship's hold of Sumatran rattan in Madras, India, where (we can assume) it was woven into furniture. (Historically rattan is often simply called cane.) Mr. Yale, "a prominent diamond dealer, slave trader, and alleged poisoner of troublesome opponents," then reloaded the vessel with valuables from China, seeking to make a bundle.[121] He did: some of those proceeds later were donated to the Collegiate School of Connecticut in 1718, which later became, you guessed it, Yale University.

But back to rattan. Is it a vine or a liana? It's woody, so the latter. Lianas can't support themselves—they clamber up other plants. The scientist Hope Jahren writes eloquently of how vines and lianas move through forests. They "resolve to fight their way up to the light by any means necessary. They do not play by the rules of the forest: they place their roots in one optimal spot and grow their leaves elsewhere, a different optimum, usually several trees over. They are the only plant on land that grows farther sideways than it does up. Vines steal. They steal patches of light left unattended and rivulets of rain. Vines do not enter into apologetic symbiosis, but instead grown bigger at every opportunity. A dead scaffold being just as good as a living one.

"A vine's only weakness is its weakness; it desperately wants to grow as tall as a tree but it doesn't haven't the stiffness necessary to do it politely. A vine finds its way to the sun using not wood but pure grit and undiluted gall."

So back to that five-hundred-foot-long liana we call rattan. The harvest of rattan is labor intensive, given the most flexible material comes from the shoot tips often high up in the forest. Spiky bark sheaths the pith. Harvesting is done by hand and on foot with simple tools. In Borneo, a man can harvest about seventy kilos a day after commuting by boat to the forest. It can't be harvested wet—a tall order in tropical peatland forests.

Rattan is soaked for three days before being dried for transport to a peeling and splitting facility. Thin rattan is put under tarps and smoked with sulfur, while thicker rattan is boiled in oil; then the rattan is dried. In 2022, according to *Business Insider*, a rattan harvester in Borneo earned about 14 cents for each kilo of raw rattan; meaning all the work of paddling, hiking, pulling, cutting, stripping, hauling, and transporting might earn a harvester less than $10 a day.

Rattan is lightweight and durable, and costs about three times that of bamboo. While rattan is a sustainable forest product in theory, unmanaged wild harvests and deforestation have created the need for rattan enrichment programs in Southeast Asia. Seedlings are now distributed to rural communities to bump up local harvests (it takes about six to ten years for a rattan palm to reach harvestable length).

Given rattan's popularity and potential (socially and environmentally), the World Wildlife Fund has made the plant one of its focus areas. Rattan gardens, such as those

2

nurtured in Indonesian agroforestry systems, create biodiverse habitats protecting a wide range of associated species. The sustainable harvesting of rattan, they say, is helping to keep the forests of Borneo (home to critically endangered orangutans) standing in Indonesia and supplying the local population with income where resource extraction (logging, oil palm plantations, and coal mining) have irreversibly scarred the islands.

While Indonesia is home to about 80 percent of the world's rattan trade, immense pressure is on wild rattan in places like Vietnam, Cambodia, Laos, India, Thailand, Malaysia, and the Philippines—so much so, that many areas are turning to rattan plantations. (A vine needs to grow on *something*, so support trees are required.) What's wonderful about rattan is that it can be grown in degraded landscapes and improve, through shading, the quality of land beneath it.

So what's all this got to do with flowers?

Rattan is the source of *midollino*, an Italian term for the dried strips from the inner core of the rattan palm, which is used in in a range of applications in floral design. Once soaked, midollino is pliable and strong.

Currently, the world trade in rattan is close to a half a billion US dollars annually, and recently demand has increased with the fast furniture industry mainstreaming caning in its search for ecological options (produced inexpensively abroad). Check the provenance on rattan if you're in the market.

3

1 Redouan showing me his work in the straw market of Tangier, Morocco.

2 Harvesting rattan, central Kalimantan, Indonesia.

3 Children weaving in a village outside Cebu, the Philippines, 2002.

Line

Vitality and Vision

At the Halekulani Hotel in Honolulu, monstera leaves, ti leaves, and fan palms "grow" up from the burnished base of an old tree in the lobby. The hotel has long followed the Sogetsu school of flower arrangement from Japan, renowned for modernizing the art of ikebana and shifting design from classical forms to more creative practice. The founder of the school, born in 1900, Sofu Teshigahara, once said: "Sogetsu ikebana can be created anytime, anywhere, by anyone, and with any kind of material."

There are no lines in nature, only areas of color, one against another.

—EDOUARD MANET

You don't need flowers.

Sogetsu ikebana emphasizes the space between materials and gives a strong emphasis to the design principle of line. But what is line? And why is it so important? You likely recall from grade school that a line is the distance between two points, but some lines in design don't technically exist at all.

Let's say you've got a bunch of red and yellow flowers. You trim their stems to a variety of lengths. You arrange them, stand back, and notice you've created a yellow C. The yellow flowers aren't connected, but your mind has connected them—this is called an implied line. Color can create line as can the replication of form.

Flowers themselves are forms of course, so what to make of them as we think about line? Sogetsu practitioner Marzena Joseph explains, "In ikebana, the line is often represented by the stem, the mass by the flower head, and the colour by the petals. But these are just literal interpretations." She goes on, "The beauty of ikebana, and indeed any form of art, lies in the endless variations and expressions of these elements."[122]

There are so many types of lines: spiral lines, helical lines, hanging lines, weighted lines, static lines, curvilinear lines, radiating lines, and broken lines. I like the American Institute of Floral Designers' definition of a line as "a visual path that directs eye movement through a composition."[123] In a way, a line can be both what see and what we feel.

In Chinese floral art, line is related to vitality. A line's attitude or inclination also might suggest an idea or an emotion. In a composition, the major line or lines "convey the dominant idea of the entire work, while subordinate lines add further ideas and give balance and unity to the whole composition."[124] This relates to the Confucian ideal of equilibrium and also to the importance of subordination of parts to a whole. In Chinese floral art, symmetry is often related to dualism.

In other words, a line isn't always just a line. It can point to a deeper understanding.

We can use linear plants to punctuate, demarcate, abbreviate, and endlessly create. The Japanese artist, filmmaker, and designer Hiroshi Teshigahara (the first son of Sofu Teshigahara and who became the third *Iemoto* or grand master of the art) worked extensively with one of the most linear of plants—bamboo—making vast installations, splitting and bending the plants into forms, lines, and spaces. He transformed museums, rooms, and stairways. He said, "My goal of 'playing with space' is moving away from stand-alone ikebana that we only look at, and toward the creation of an environment that embraces people . . . However, the time in which this composition can be maintained is the same as a flower's life, and when time passes it disappears without a trace and remains only in people's memories."

Hiroshi Teshigahara has been described as a "modern traditionalist or a traditionalist modernist" who linked his work with plants to art and society.[125] In 1994, he wrote, "In the pursuit of affluence, semi-permanent cold spaces made of steel, glass and concrete were created all over Japan. And inside them, things are packed tightly, people are stuck in a state of immobility. Isn't now the time to question whether such a constricted state of immobility is genuinely affluent or not?"[126]

English is loaded with idioms about lines. We cross them, draw them in the sand, and fall into them; we have fine lines, hot lines, lines of duty, and lines of fire; we lay it on the line, toe the line, and hold the line. Lines hold meaning across cultures and between them.

1 *Frozen Flowers*, Azuma Makoto, 2019, created in Hokkaido. Japan.

2 *Maitake (Dancing Bamboo)*, Hiroshi Teshigahara, 1997, Hiroshima City Museum of Contemporary Art, Hiroshima.

Memorial

Farewell Flowers

Not many of us want to plan for our deaths. Yet those who do make it easier for the rest of us.

I considered this recently as a friend picked me up with a basket casket hanging out of the back of her pickup truck. Our mutual friend had died, and we were delivering the casket to the funeral company then performing ritual washing, oiling, and dressing of the body before burial.

I state this matter-of-factly now, but it was hard and healing and beautiful at the time. A green burial it would be, which brings me back to the casket. It was handwoven willow with an opening lid hung with cedar bark cordage. On the day our friend was buried in the earth, her linen-shrouded body was surrounded by flowers.

> Lots of people have terrible taste and make a damn good living off of it.
>
> —DIANA VREELAND

We have long adorned the dead. Pollen from fifty thousand years ago tells us Neanderthals placed flowers with their loved ones at burial. Among the Asante people of West Africa, plants were used as symbols of mourning—the *Cardiospermum* we call love in a puff or heartseed for its little heart-shaped seeds were in the Asante language "tears."

Visit a cemetery today and plastic flowers, flowers in plastic, and wilting flowers in plastic foam abound. Farewell flowers and sympathy flowers are big business. The florist Lori Poliski recently estimated that if "just one funeral flower arrangement using floral foam was present at half of the 2.4 million funerals held in the US . . . that would be 1.2 million pieces (of foam) entering the landfill in just one year. Many funerals have more than one floral tribute, so the number could actually range from 1.2 million to 3.6 million."[127]

It's high time we rethink our exit strategies.

A Cornell study showed that in the United States, twenty million board feet of hardwoods are used for coffins while 1.6 million tons of concrete and sixty-four-thousand tons of steel are used for housing the dead. Embalming with formaldehyde (a known carcinogen) is on the decline, yet the country still uses about four million gallons annually. Cremation is still hot (forgive the pun, but bodies are burned at 1900 degrees Fahrenheit, meaning a single cremation releases about as much carbon dioxide as driving a car six hundred miles).

What are we do to with ourselves?

In densely populated Europe, discussion about recycling grave sites and crypts is a necessary fact of life (and death).[128] Human composting is now approved in a number of US states (each of us makes about one cubic yard of soil), and green burials are feeding woodlands all around the world. Research has found inoculating caskets or baskets with mycelium can speed up the decomposition process and help forests.

One clear way we can green funerals is by removing floral foam, building naturally compostable (instead of industrially compostable) botanical tributes, lobbying the death industry to ban plastic, and collectively dialing down our expectations and cultural associations of what funerals ought to look like.

I'm one to talk; when my friend died I sent her mother flowers. A bouquet of sweet peas cut on the vine, locally grown, wrapped in paper, but delivered a few miles nonetheless. Did I need to do that? Not entirely. Arriving at her house a couple of days later, bouquets of flowers sat languishing by the front door, an abundance of sentiment she couldn't manage.

When Queen Elizabeth II died, heavy machinery had to remove dunes of plastic-wrapped flowers. The spectacle made me think of the old adage: presence not presents. Legacy and tribute should not cost us the earth.

2

1 Garden flowers supported by chicken wire and a pin frog.

2 Victorian cabinet photograph of funeral flowers, 1884.

Meristem

On Orchids

1

People have coveted orchids for millennia. These beautiful, dramatic, and mysterious flowers prompted Charles Darwin to publish a book on the role insects played in orchid pollination in 1862, heightening fascination with the plant, but gardeners continually struggled to get orchid seeds to germinate. If an orchid is epiphytic and lives on a tree, it's not as if you can sow the seed in earth. People wondered: what does it grown in? Moss?

In 1889, a French botanist discovered mycorrhizal filaments on orchid roots. What was the fungus offering? Scientists didn't yet know, but a food source, it turned out. Orchid seeds lack an endosperm and a large embryo, so we could say they require external (or ecosystemic) support to grow. In 1921, an American biologist developed a gel technique to provide orchid seeds with the sugars, salts, minerals, and moisture sufficient for orchid seeds to successfully germinate. This nonsymbiotic method heralded in a new era of hybridization and cultivation.

Between 1925 and 1949, the director of the Singapore Botanic Gardens, Dr. Richard Eric Holttum, developed a lab for germinating seeds from crosses made in the garden. Holttum's success led to Singapore registering over two thousand varieties of orchids.

Breeding was one thing, however mass production another. Orchids were still slow to produce. A cattleya, once called the queen of orchids, takes five years to bloom from seed. Cultivation remained the purview of the scientific, the affluent, and the enraptured.

Let's roll the clock back for an example: cattleya orchids arrived in England as packing material for a shipment of plants hailing from the mountains around Rio de Janeiro in 1818. A Mr. William Cattley nursed them to bloom, and the flower appeared at a flower show in 1829, sparking an orchidmania. Commercial collectors from nurseries around the globe went in search of new species, felling trees to reach the epiphytic plants. To give you a sense of the scale of bioprospecting, one company in England, Veitch Nurseries, employed more than twenty plant hunters in the second half of the nineteenth century. One collector in search of odontoglossum in the Andes provided Indigenous workers with axes. They "cut down some four thousand trees" to secure "about ten thousand plants."[129]

Given the climate requirements of orchid cultivation in the UK, orchids remained specialty plants since few could afford a glasshouse, let alone amass a collection. Enter William Cavendish, the sixth Duke of Devonshire, who was excruciatingly rich and an avid horticulturalist. He not only hired Joseph Paxton (who would later design the Crystal Palace) to build him a glasshouse for his collections, he funded orchid-hunting expeditions (by the 1830s he had over three hundred species).[130] The duke once paid the equivalent of £10,000 for a single butterfly orchid. Suffice it to say in the nineteenth century, orchids required vast amounts of wealth. As Judith Taylor notes: "Growing orchids was rather like playing polo or keeping a yacht. If you had to enquire how much it cost, it was clear you could not afford it, to paraphrase the wonderful maxim of J.P. Morgan."[131]

All this changed with the discovery of gel propagation and later the development of meristem culture in the 1950s and '60s. A meristem is a portion of plant with a high rate of cell division. All plants have them—on roots or shoots, or wherever a high rate of growth needs to occur. A meristem can be the size of a period—tiny, yes, but bigger than many orchids' seeds.

With meristem culture, a young shoot could be sliced off, sterilized, placed in a test tube with some nutrients and moisture, and grow under artificial lights. As the *New York Times* reported in 1964: "For the commercial cut flower producers, the method means a sure crop of quality flowers when needed for holidays and weddings."[132] Thousands of dendrobium, oncidium, odontoglossum, and paphiopedilum plants could be produced in laboratories and grown in greenhouses to meet demand.

Today you can buy a phalaenopsis, or moth orchid, for under $10. Groups such as the Taiwan Sugar Comporation produce five million plants a year at four nurseries in Taiwan for shipment overseas. Various countries specialize in different areas of the supply chain. As Noel Kingsbury notes, "Phalenopsis orchids have become one of the most traded of all plants, which in a series of complex exchanges, varieties may be bred in the United States, tissue-cultured in Japan,

> I need to remember the botanists and botanical guides who were erased from the herbarium archives.
>
> —PRUDENCE GIBSON

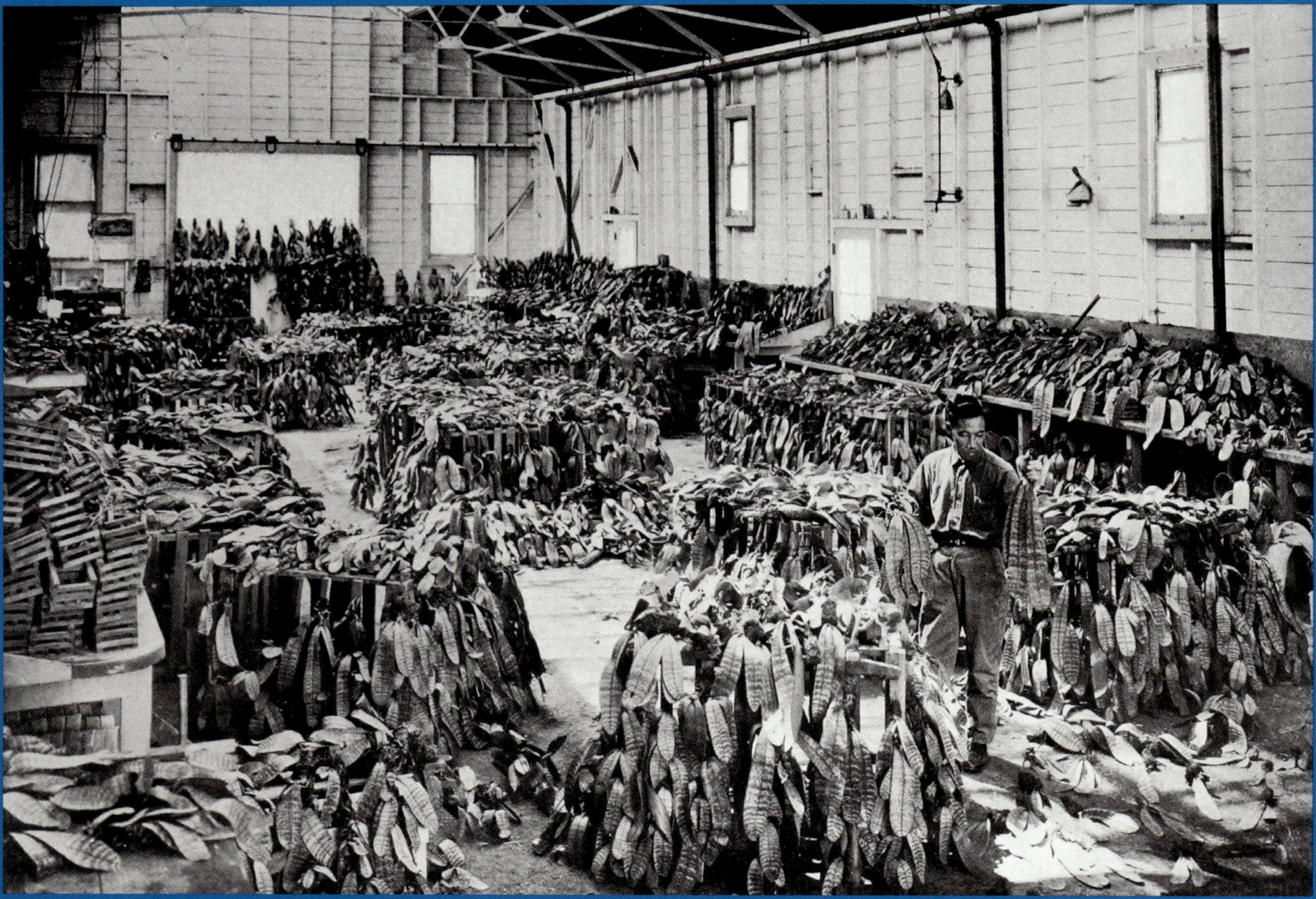

3

ORCHIDEES
6. L'Odontoglossum
PRODUITS LIEBIG: AMELIORENT LA CUISINE.
Reproduction interdite
Explication au verso.

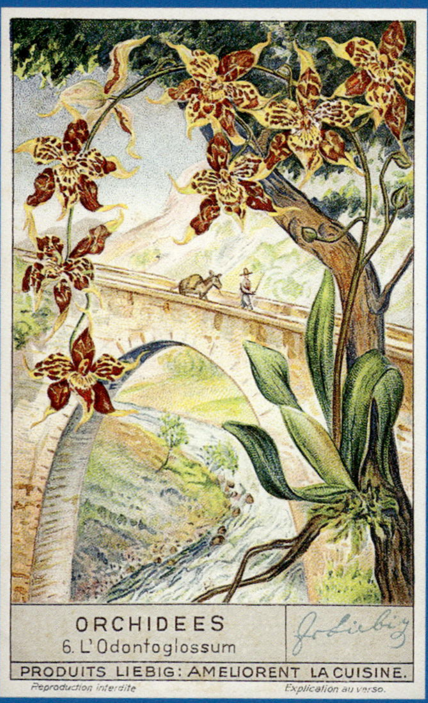

4

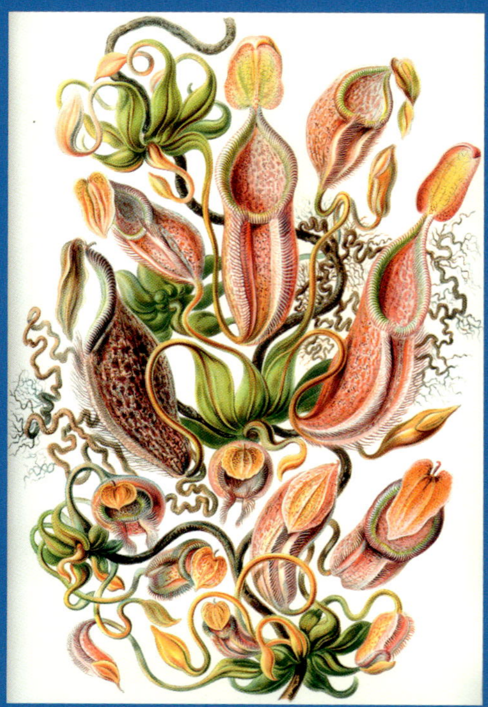

5

grown on in China or Taiwan, and then grown to retail size in the Netherlands."[133]

When I see videos of cultured orchid plants stuffed in peat being robotically wrapped in plastic under LED lights on conveyor belts in glasshouses, I have difficulty seeing the beauty in the flowers. But dare I say, not all orchids are created equal.

Susan Orlean wrote of the incredible diversity of orchids still collected today in her book *The Orchid Thief*: "There were orchids for sale . . . a madhouse of orchids in every color, in every shape, with wide leaves and skinny leaves and no leaves at all, with fat jutting lips and lips cupped like thimbles, and with blackish-red hoods and freckles, with ruffles, with pleats, with corkscrew curls, big as fists, small as fingernails, smelling of honey, grass, citrus, cinnamon, or of nothing, not a smell at all but just the heavy warm quality that air has after it has been sitting in a flower."

6

Given their diversity and glamour, orchids are still loved, but our rapaciousness means that roughly half of the extant species of orchids left on this earth are threatened with extinction. All trade in orchids is governed by the Convention on International Trade in Endangered Species of Wild Fauna and Flora (CITES), which lists 27,922 species of concern on their site. Nepal has more than four hundred species of orchids, one hundred of which are traded illegally. Mexico has close to a thousand epiphytic orchids and some researchers found over 333 taxa available for sale in markets.

It's worth asking, what drives humans to collect rare species? It's not solely the beauty of the plants or the money gained in trading in them, surely, but also the emotional experience of rarity. And here we come to a psychosocial phenomenon known as loss aversion, whereby the emotion of a loss is felt more intensely than an equivalent gain. I'll explain: this phenomenon is at work in last-chance tourism where "people are twice as likely to book a trip to a see a destination that is in danger of vanishing than they would be to go to another equal destination that offers nothing but ongoing positives. Scarcity increases perceived value."[134] Plus, the get-it-before-it-goes idea captures a sense of urgency for collectors in a fragile world (botanists among them).

Thankfully meristem culture has been a boon to endangered species, allowing rare plants like nepenthes and orchids to be propagated (thus reducing pressure on what wild populations there are left).

1 A collection of *Bulbophyllum oxypterum* by Robbie Honey. The orchid is found in woodland and riverine forests in South Africa.

2 *Ansellia africana* (syn. *Ansellia gigantea*) stamp, c. 1952.

3 A shipment of more than ten thousand varieties of wild-harvested *Phalaenopsis* from the Philippines received in San Francisco on April 11, 1914, by the MacRorie-McLaren Company. At the time, *The Orchid World* reported that this was "the biggest shipment ever made to America and represented many years of collecting."

4 Trade card, 1937.

5 *Nepenthes*, Ernst Haeckel, from *Kunstformen der Natur*, 1904. Haeckel was an ardent plant eugenicist.

6 Propagation of the endangered Canelo Hills Ladies' Tresses orchid (*Spiranthes delitescens*) at the Desert Botanical Garden in Arizona.

7 Mass production of lab- and greenhouse-grown *Phalaenopsis* in the Netherlands.

7

Microplastics

Ecosystems over Aesthetics

Cleaning the ocean of plastic is like sweeping in the desert.

—CRISTINA ROMERA-CASTILLO

Plastic is everywhere, and it's one of those subjects that's so big I just want to shrivel up and hide. So if you're thinking, yeah, I know, while giving a defeatist shrug, I share your apathy and sense of being overwhelmed. Packaging, plant pots, gloves, tags, buckets, tools, crates, wire, tape, ribbon: everything is plastic or plasticized today. It's inescapable and easy to feel trapped in a world you don't agree with, yet continually, begrudgingly, participate in.

Was I responsible for a handful of the five hundred billion PET water bottles produced in the last year?[135] Yes. Did I ever turn down a coveted plant because it was in a plastic pot? No. So let's draw a comparison here: I don't want to write about plastic, and you likely don't hear about getting rid of it entirely, because *you already know*, but plastics are relatively new; that means we *can* get rid of them.

Plastics are made of petroleum. First invented at the dawning of the twentieth century, plastics didn't begin to replace metal, paper, and glass until the postwar period.

What can we do? Focus on substitution. Polyester gloves? Use leather or cloth. Plastic grow crate? Use compressed manure pots or earth. Plastic bucket? Metal. Tarp? Waxed cloth. Tape? Use wire. Floral foam? Change your expectations (or use chicken wire or twigs). Fifty-eight percent of all the microplastics in rivers, streams, and oceans are from paint.[136] But paint doesn't have to be plastic—it's just cheaper to produce.

Recently, I heard Rita Feldmann of the Sustainable Floristry Network discuss the issue: "Ten or fifteen years ago we thought we needed to make biodegradable plastics. So out come all these industries creating all these biodegradable plastics, but this concept of biodegradability is very loose. It might take ten thousand years to biodegrade. It doesn't say how long or under what set of conditions . . . . Biodegradable plastics just fragment and make their way into the environment more easily."[137]

And from the environment into us: microplastics are traveling across placentas now and are lodged in our brains. As the oceanographer Cristina Romera-Castillo said, "Now we can only wait for those little pieces to end up sedimenting and end up buried in the seabed, forming a layer that in the future will be a witness of this era of 'plasticene.'"[138]

The attention on fast fashion and on synthetic fabrics, dyes, and cheap clothes (produced by underpaid people) can teach us a lot as flower lovers. The fashion industry is responsible for 10 percent of global carbon emissions. Why has no one tallied the impact of the floricultural and horticultural sectors? We're likely hidden in agriculture and not capturing the full story.

Recently, the *Financial Times* reported that in the EU approximately fifteen thousand metric tons of floral foam—equivalent to 2.5 billion plastic bags—is sent to the landfill every year by people who purportedly love flowers.

An aesthetic shift needs to happen, but instead the industry is turning to bioplastics. But there's a hitch: waste systems are not yet set up to capture some new bioplastic products. There just aren't enough industrial composting facilities that reach high enough temperatures to digest the bioplastic. As Rita Feldmann notes, "I get concerned that people hear key phrases like sustainable or bioplastic and they don't truly grasp what's going on. For example, there are sleeves or buckets that are supposedly recyclable but the problem is there's only five places in the country that recycle it. So it doesn't get recycled because it can't easily be."[139]

If we can't shake our addiction to cheap conveniences, to poured and shaped forms, and governments aren't banning plastics or building industrial bioplastic composting facilities to deal with these new technologies, what do we do? We can try to consider these words: "Ecosystems over aesthetics." We can try to prioritize environmental justice over the whim of the creative.[140] Muse, look out.

1 *Lotus Garden*, Mandy Barker, Hong Kong Soup: 1826 Series, 2014. This collection of discarded artificial flowers was gathered over three years on Hong Kong beaches.

Modernism

Avant-Garde Gardening

1

The animated movie *Inside Out* is largely set in a child's brain. At one point in the film, three characters, Joy, Sadness, and Bing Bong, are on a quest to get to the Train of Thought. Bing Bong suggests a shortcut that Sadness knows is dangerous—a tunnel called abstract thought.

Once inside, the characters visually morph. Bing Bong's pink face reassembles into something like a Picasso painting, then his lips pop off, while Joy's yellow arms become floating triangles, and Sadness has to grab her blue head from the void, yelling "We gotta get outta here before we're nothing but shape and color!" Finally, three flat nonfigurative forms slide out under the door.

I saw *Inside Out* while thinking about modernism, wondering how I might write about the word without relying too heavily on the history of painting. Abstraction, deconstruction, the emphasis on shape and color—*Inside Out* nailed it, but how could I discuss modernism in the context of plants? And why did I feel I needed to?

> A garden should be cohesive and self-contained, if it cannot include the landscape it had better reflect the environment in which it is born.
>
> —ROBERTO BURLE MARX

Then I remembered the gardens of Roberto Burle Marx.

Marx was a Brazilian landscape architect, environmentalist, painter, printmaker, and polymath who worked from the 1930s through the 1990s. After founding his studio in the 1950s, he designed more than two thousand gardens (many with his associate Haruyoshi Ono). He created the iconic two and half mile black-and-white mosaic of the Copacabana promenade in Rio de Janeiro, Miami's groovy Biscayne Bay boulevard, and countless international urban parks, private gardens, and public spaces. Marx has variously been called "a painter working in landscape,"[141] and "the father of modernist landscape architecture"[142] in addition to a visionary. He recognized the value of the Brazil's native flora and condemned the destruction of the Amazon, and today more than fifty species bear his name.

In Brazilian gardens, Marx created vast checkerboards of alternating varieties of buffalo grass (aka St. Augustine, *Stenotaphrum secundatum*) and sweeping forms of maroon *Alternathera* in lawns. He painted as he planned and planned with plants and planes in mind. He said he used "natural topography as a surface for composition, taking mineral and plant elements found in nature as materials for aesthetic organization, just as other artists use canvas, paints and brushes for their compositions."[143] His work has been described as anti-memetic, which roughly means life imitating art.

Generally speaking, one of the hallmarks of modernist design is minimalism, embodied though a rejection of decoration, sentimentality, and illustration.[144] The Cubist Garden in Hyères, France, developed in 1925 by Gabriel Guévrékian, contains geometric forms such as boxes and triangles—some planted, some not. Looking at it today—you can visit—the garden looks busy with the repetition of geometric forms.

The garden historian Lorraine Harrison suggests that concrete "freed designers" to make curved walls, sculptural shapes, flat planes, and shallow reflecting pools.[145] Marx experimented with these shapes, including some reminiscent of seashells—Archimedean spirals and nautilus-like curves. He set Cubist sculptures in plazas and slim horizontal fountains into walls and designed blocky pergolas that separated light and shadow into wide stripes reminding me of that glorious poem "Clear Night" by Charles Wright, which begins:

Clear night, thumb-top of a moon, a back-lit sky.
Moon-fingers lay down their same routine
On the side deck and the threshold, the white keys
and the black keys . . .[146]

Looking at the rhythm and repetition of light and dark in Marx's work, be they the tile keys of a promenade or the towering spires of cacti casting long shadows through a garden, it's affirming to read his words: "One may even think of a plant as a note. Played in one chord, it will sound in a particular way; in another chord its value will be altered."[147]

2

Of his influences, he said: "I explain my developments in relation to my reality of my generation, when painters were faced with Cubism and abstractionism. Juxtaposing of the aesthetic attributes of these art movements with elements from nature was what drew me toward new experimentation."

The writer Rebecca Solnit captures some of this spirit of twentieth-century modernism when she writes about seeing one of Diego Rivera's murals commissioned by Henry Ford's son in Detroit. She writes, it was "one of his grand murals celebrating industrial labour and production . . . and I wondered why an avowed communist was working for one the world's most successful capitalists . . . Gazing upon the walls, filled with images of auto assembly lines and workers dwarfed by machinery, I realized that capitalists and communists of the era shared a devotion to mechanization and to industrialization as phenomena that would allow human beings to transcend the limits of nature."

Avant-garde artists in what we call the modernist period looked forward to a shining future, and it's easy to see this energy in Marx's work, while his deep relationship with plants reflects a postmodern environmental ethic. He gardened, and as his knowledge of plants grew, his work was changed through his knowledge. He wrote: "From Nature we can accept with humility its laws and suggestions, always acknowledging it to be the greatest artist of all, with more to teach than one can learn."[148]

3

4

1 *Pot of Flowers*, George Valmier, 1922.

2 Roberto Burle Marx holding *Heliconia hirsuta burle marxii*, one of the many plants that bears his name.

3 Garden design by Roberto Burle Marx for the Ministry of Education and Health in Rio de Janeiro, 1936–1938. The garden sits on the roof of the second floor with offices rising sixteen stories above, so Marx kept these viewers in mind. Some say this was one of his first experiments with organic forms.

4 Copacabana mosaic and boardwalk designed by Roberto Burle Marx in Rio de Janeiro, Brazil.

Motif

Elements of Design

1

I love the title of the book *The Grammar of Ornament*. There's friction between the nouns, a spark of conceptual contrast. Grammar is foundational, almost elemental, and yet there stands an filigreed word next to it. As people might say today, ornament feels totally extra.

All sorts of things in this world behave like mirrors.

—JACQUES LACAN

But is it?

The author of the book, Owen Jones, didn't think so. An architect, designer, and polymath, Jones published his first book almost 170 years ago, in 1856, and it has been in continuous production since then. Composed of over one hundred stunningly beautiful color plates of global decorative styles, the book also provocatively sets forth thirty-seven "propositions" concerning "the arrangement of form and color."

These range from the pragmatic, "In surface decoration all lines should flow out of a parent stem. Every ornament, however distant, should be traced to its branch and root,"[149] to the esoteric, "True beauty results from that repose which the mind feels when the eye, the intellect, and the affections, are satisfied from the absence of any want."[150]

I was introduced to the work of Jones through the architectural historian Olivia Horsfall Turner of the Victoria and Albert Museum. We met at the Art Workers' Guild in London, a quirky club of sorts founded in 1884 by members of the Arts and Crafts movement who sought to "create a meeting place for the fine arts and the applied arts on an equal footing." In keeping with its history, today members include architects, landscape designers, weavers, furniture makers, hatters, and craftspeople of all kind (though no floral designers as yet). I once hosted a lecture at the Guild, and I could imagine no better a place to attend a talk on ornament.

The word motif had been niggling me prior. Was it simply a repeating pattern? In film and literature, a motif is a recurring element that supports or emphasizes a theme. A musical motif is similar and can be as simple as a few notes or as complex as a repeated rhythm. I thought of weddings and how as a part of my own, I'd used the image of the island we now live on part of the year—on the invitations, place cards, thank-you notes, etc. Others do this with flowers, developing motifs to build the theme of an event.

Jones believed ornament should carry symbolism, that meaning is a part of ornamental charm.[151]

The subjects of motif, ornament, and pattern became hot topics toward the end of the industrial revolution, when mechanization and factory production impacted the decorative arts. By the 1840s, wallpapers were mass-produced, rugs woven by machines, and all manner of domestic goods created for a growing consumer market. The societal changes wrought by mechanization were of great concern to Arts and Crafts thinkers, like William Morris (a past master of the Guild) and John Ruskin, who believed that goods created by machines and laborers subject to producing them in mindless repetition "drained . . . products of meaning and wholeness."[152] Veneered furniture was seen as a sham and decorative illusion almost morally corrupt.[153]

As Turner noted in her talk, "In mid-nineteenth-century Britain, discussions about wallpaper were a microcosm of design reform debates. Far from being superficial, wallpaper encapsulated the core questions that obsessed theorists, inspired practitioners, and vexed manufacturers."

One fundamental issue centered on representations of nature. Ruskin advocated "for artists to reform their work by producing the most accurate representations possible of the natural world." As Turner noted, this was "an exhortation that had been zealously taken up by the members of the Pre-Raphaelite Brotherhood, founded in 1848."

Jones wanted greater abstraction. He argued that the country seemed trapped in repeating cycles of decorative revivals—Gothic, Greek, Egyptian—conjuring up pastiches instead of creatively striving to form a unique pattern languages of its own.[154]

One side of imperialism we aren't trained to consider is how the exploits of empire can reveal the deficiencies of the colonizer. For Jones and his cohort of design reformists, the Great Exhibition of 1851 held in the Crystal Palace brought England's failings into stark relief. As Turner noted of the international displays at the Exhibition, these "wares were manifestly more accomplished in design and execution, thereby destabilizing Britain's ideas of racial hierarchy and progress."[155]

2

How could England improve? Education was needed, the reformers concluded, so an exhibit was held in London to showcase "False Principles in Design" a year later. The exhibition was intended as an educational event for students, designers, manufacturers, and the public. The show garnered attention: newspapers of the time referred to the hall where an array of English chintz and wallpaper samples were displayed as "The Chamber of Horrors."[156] Arguments were made that flat patterns should cover flat surfaces, so naturalistic roses, lilacs, or horses shouldn't be woven into rugs or used on walls. Direct imitation of nature was discouraged. Jones put it this way: "True art consists in idealizing and not copying the forms of nature."

Like the False Principles show, *The Grammar of Ornament* was intended to inspire and guide. In the last section of the book, plates of leaves appear in outline, and a collection of flowers drawn by Christopher Dresser, a protégé of Jones's (who would go on to become a professor of botany and has been called the first industrial designer), are presented to remind the viewer of the primacy of nature in the development of ornament.[157] Jones writes, "We believe that if a student in the arts, earnest in his search after knowledge, will only lay aside all temptation to indolence, will examine all the works of the past, compare them with the works of nature, bend his mind . . . he cannot fail to be himself a creator, and to individualize new forms."[158]

William Morris would be one English designer to carry Owen's vision forward. He designed his first wallpaper in 1862, six years after Owen's book was published, and today looking at his willow boughs, acanthus leaves, violet motifs, stylized irises, or the beautiful symmetry and movement embodied in the *Strawberry Thief*, nature, ideated and idealized, endures.

1 City Palace, Jaipur, India.

2 One of over a hundred plates in *The Grammar of Ornament* by Owen Jones.

3 For Owen Jones and his cohort of design reformists, the Great Exhibition of 1851 brought England's failings into stark relief. The skill of decorative arts in the colonies far surpassed those of England. In 1852, an exhibit of "False Principles in Design" was held in London to showcase flaws in English decoration.

3

Naturalize

Homing Instincts

In a globalized world, themes of indigeneity, invasion, and naturalization recur when speaking of people and plants. Given the dual meanings of words like alien and naturalization, it's easy to make the leap between culture and nature. Human immigrants become naturalized when they obtain citizenship in a country other than the one of their birth. In plant ecology, a naturalized plant is a foreign plant (like people, they can be deemed an alien) that reproduces consistently without direct intervention by humans (or in spite of them). Naturalized plants do not necessarily become invasive.

Some gardeners have asked: is naturalizing with foreign species okay or should the maintenance and restoration of indigenous biodiversity be the holy grail? Can we live with foreign species companionably? The arguments seem to vary by region (and the ecological pressures faced).

The English gardener Gareth Richards recently opined, "Botanical incomers enrich the fabric of our nations, and their roles will become ever more valuable in a future dominated by changing climates and shifting pathogens. Our collective failure to appreciate this points to wider societal issues. Sadly xenophobia is alive and well even in the 'caring' world of nature conservation, where sneers about 'invasive non-natives' often take on a human tone."[159] Richards is referring to what some would argue are the nativist politics of purity that can be at work in conservation biology (and in human societies as well).

How and why and where we classify plants as undesirable is part of the story of our ceaseless attempts to draw boundaries between nature and culture, wildness and domestication.

—RICHARD MABEY

In some gardening circles today, naturalization can be considered a hallmark of success in an established garden—it means you've succeeded in matching plants to a place. Gradually the flowers reproduce, but their success in naturalizing initially (and often) relies upon human interaction. In this context the verb naturalize can refer to both foreign species and indigenous ones.

One of the most inspiring gardens I've visited is set on a hillside overlooking the Atlantic Ocean in Morocco. The project of Italian novelist Umberto Pasti, the Garden of Rohuna features meadows of rescued indigenous plants such as crocus, scilla, iris, narcissus, and gladioli. While Rohuna is unique in that many plants were relocated to the site and encouraged to naturalize, it is not solely a native plant garden nor an ecological restoration project, though one could argue, those are among its most inspirational features.

Most botanists tend to think of introduced species on a continuum, from alien (introduced), casual (reproducing occasionally), naturalized (reproducing regularly), to invasive (reproducing and spreading over substantial distances from sites of introduction).[160] Today naturalizing often happens accidentally through ornamental horticulture, when escapees find a foreign climate compatible—as is the case with the more than five hundred species of plants from South Africa that have naturalized in Australia.

In the Caribbean, a comingling of European settlers with Amerindian and African people is known as creolization. Culturally, this cross-fertilization led to new cultural forms and languages, but it's hard to argue that in the natural world, a creolized landscape is an ideal one. "When it is life forms rather than cultural forms that are at stake, the interaction between organisms from widely disparate places of origin often entails environmentally perverse rather than progressive effects," one critic has said.[161]

Before European contact, plants traveled around the Caribbean with the Taino and Kalinago people. These people farmed but lived lightly on the land (meaning disturbance—a plant's opportunity to claim space—was kept to a minimum). The plants they introduced eventually naturalized in small regional communities over centuries. Then came slave ships carrying human cargoes, foreign plants and animals, and the wholesale destruction of indigenous vegetation for plantations. The landscape was inexorably changed—in as little as a hundred years, twenty times the number of plants were introduced than in the two thousand years prior to European contact.[162] In the Caribbean today, more than 220 tree species have been introduced, and 179 of those are now considered invasive. This pace of change is a hallmark of the modern age, and from an environmental perspective, one we're all struggling with now.

2

3

4

We've long known that when it comes to plant introductions, we are playing with fire, but the idea of biosecurity is a relatively recent one. In the United States, it wasn't until the late nineteenth century that the country began to grapple with biological pathogens (precisely when the nursery trade and the Department of Agriculture were importing plants with wild abandon and industrialized agriculture was taking hold). Blights and agricultural epidemics led to the 1912 Plant Quarantine Act to safeguard the country. As the landscape scholar Anna Li notes, like many countries' foreign policy at the time, "US foreign policy oscillated between cosmopolitanism and nativism, molded by the forces of a globalizing market economy."[163]

Culture and nature are often intertwined in the popular consciousness, and today we're still grappling with the meanings and associations of naturalization. With plants, we have the benefit of hindsight and research, and can ask: Will the plant serve local insects and wildlife? Will it spread too far? Those questions are always site-specific and plant-specific. But thankfully the information is there for all who care about what they put in their garden or their vase.

1 Umberto Pasti with *Gladiolus byzantinus* on his property in Rohuna, Morocco.

2 Salvaged *Iris tingitana* naturalizing in Rohuna, Morocco.

3 Many *Echiums* hail from Macaronesia, the islands off North Africa. I photographed this in the garden of Lily and Gene Walsh in La Jolla, California. Many plants, like *Echiums*, have found climate analogs. Today Vermont farmers are experimenting with growing rice from Hokkaido, Japan, in an effort to increase food security in a changing world.

4 *Cecropia*, native to the neotropics, with *Agapanthus* (from South Africa), on Maui.

5 Pomegranate, *Punica granatum*, is native to southern Europe and northern India but has naturalized in various regions of the world.

5

1

Occupy

Decolonizing

During the era of transoceanic exploration, a framework of laws known as the Doctrine of Discovery gave European powers the right to claim "uninhabited" land and all that was on it. Uninhabited was deemed terra nullius (vacant or no man's land) and defined as land not inhabited by Christians. At this time, most European vessels were searching for trade routes and precious goods like spices and gold, not pursuing the accumulation of territory. Nevertheless, over centuries two kinds of colonization took place.

The first form involved claiming sovereignty over land, establishing a presence in the form of administrators and occupying troops, then using various means to control trade, the territory and its people. Examples would be Indonesia ruled by the Dutch and India under the British.

The other form of colonization involved similar mechanisms, but with the added pressure of European resettlement. Think of the United States, Canada, or Australia, where settlers moved in, and Indigenous peoples were displaced and enslaved as well as decimated through disease.

A third form, what I consider a later development, is exemplified by the actions of the United States, who created what some have referred to as a hidden empire by acquiring overseas territories after the settlement of the western states. To borrow from Alex Von Tunzelmann, the United States waged a "secret war in the Caribbean that destroyed any hope of freedom in democracy in Cuba, Haiti and the Dominican Republic. It toppled democracies, it supported dictators, it licensed the worst excesses of those dictators, it financed terrorism, it set up death squads, it turned Cuba communist and kept it communist for half a century. It did massive and permanent damage to the international reputation of the United States, and it nearly triggered a nuclear holocaust."[164] Many say that empires require occupation, but consider that by 1920, American companies owned two-thirds of Cuban land.

The term decolonization is often used metaphorically today—politically, psychologically, and sociologically—but historically, decolonization meant throwing off the yoke of a colonizing power. For Frantz Fanon, a Caribbean-born theorist and activist who wrote the influential book *The Wretched of the Earth* in 1961, decolonization was firmly tied to racism, power, and violence. "Decolonization never takes place unnoticed,"[165] he wrote.

Yet today, a teacher may seek to "decolonize their curriculum," or a botanical garden an exhibit. Nuala Caomhánach, in discussing the decolonization of botanical gardens, suggested that "decolonization is both a movement and an ideology, to acknowledge, examine, challenge and eliminate the disproportionate legacy of white European thought." For her, decolonizing is "about decentring white supremacy over the world, and in particular the natural world."[166]

While Fanon suggested decolonization was a process at once psychological, epistemic, and political, contemporary usage speaks more to critical theory and organizational change than its original intent. Some contemporary thinkers, notably Eve Tuck and Wayne E. Yang, have asserted that this "metaphorization of decolonization makes possible a set of evasions, or 'settler moves to innocence,' that problematically attempt to reconcile settler guilt and complicity."[167] They argue that decolonization should not involve equivocation. Decolonization should center on the repatriation of land.

> For a colonized people the most essential value, because the most concrete, is first and foremost the land: the land which will bring them bread and, above all, dignity.
>
> —FRANTZ FANON

Consider Hawaii, annexed in 1898 by the US. Hawaiians have yet to achieve self-determination through nationhood, but we might hear that Hawaiians have sought to "decolonize" by challenging imperialist American beliefs and histories. This is decolonization as metaphor and empowerment, not sovereignty over land. Today, some estimates suggest Hawaii only produces a small percentage of its own food, and relies on the mainland to feed its population.

Four-fifths of the land on earth was colonized or semicolonized[168] by European powers[169] by 1914. Today, fewer than two million people live in the remaining seventeen non-self-governing territories of former imperial powers. Many are small islands in the South Pacific and Caribbean, with France, England, New Zealand, and the United States functioning as administrative powers.

As Fanon predicted over sixty years ago, decolonizing is complicated and not everyone can manage it given the social and psychological legacies of the colonial period and the fraught ecologies and economies left in its wake. Systems that perpetuate injustice (such as neocolonial education systems, foreign ownership and management of resources, and economic models I mentioned in the section on globalization) make emancipatory futures more challenging to effect.

2

1 *Monument au Conteur (Alin Légarès)*, Adeline Rapon, 2022. The artist provided this caption: "This is a portrait that symbolizes the heritage that should be celebrated in Martinique, which means the 'Culture des Mornes,' associated with poor and dark-skinned people from the country. Alin is a very well-known teller, specialized in death ceremonies, which is very specific in Martinique but also is a job that's dying with the dominance of religion—especially evangelism, doing the work of colonization again. The pedestal he's sitting on once held the statue of Joséphine de Beauharnais, a wife of Napoleon's from a slave owner's family. Her statue was moved by Césaire when he was mayor of Fort-de-France and later decapitated in the '90s. In 2020, RVN activists, led by women as part of the movement to decolonize cities completely, broke the statue, along with others in the city. Replacing a White slave-owner by a "Vié nèg" (old negro in creole) is a statement and a reappropriation of what's supposed to be celebrated."

2 A collection of bromeliad flowers on Hawaii.

3 Aechmea in an old sugar mill building, Nevis.

4 *Cassia alata*, currently renamed *Senna alata*, is valued for medicinal and ornamental use but is now considered invasive in Austronesia.

5 From the front page of the *Philadelphia Press*, August 14, 1898.

3

4

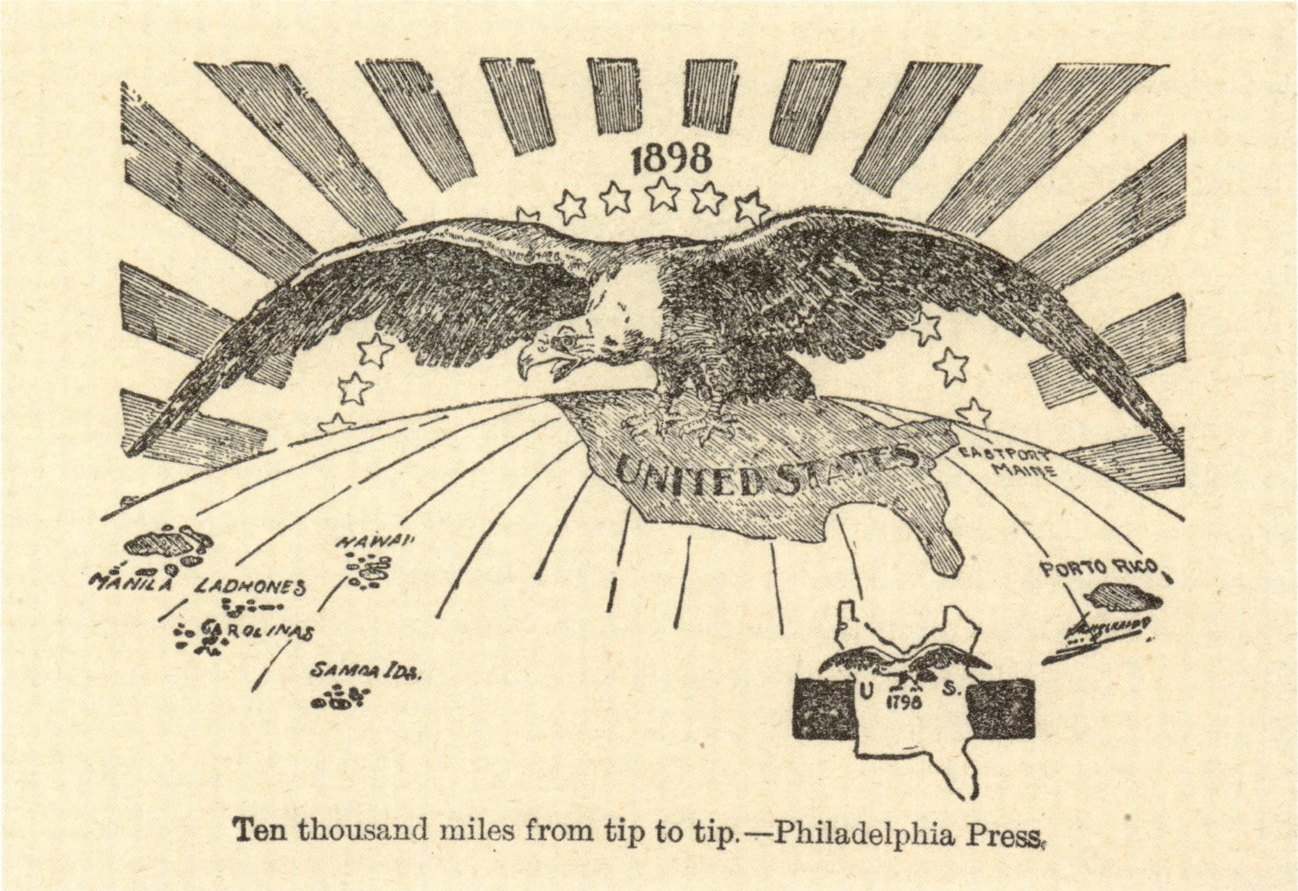

1898

UNITED STATES

EASTPORT MAINE

HAWAII

MANILA

LADRONES

CAROLINAS

SAMOA IDS.

PORTO RICO

U. S.

1798

Ten thousand miles from tip to tip.—Philadelphia Press.

5

Pantropical

Phytosynthesis

There should be a term for botanical déjà vu, that kind of have-I-been-here-before moment where you look at the plants around you and can't place yourself. Let's call it phytosynthesis.

It recently struck me in Antigua at Nelson's Dockyard, a UNESCO World Heritage Site in English Harbour. The legacies of the colonial era surrounded me, and the wider landscape told a story of deforestation, initially for shipbuilding and fuel, then cotton, tobacco, and sugar. I was staying in a small inn that had served as an old pitch and tar store for the servicing of vessels. I'd arrived in the late afternoon, learned I would be alone in the hotel, and was sent a pail of ice and jar of rum punch by boat. I took myself for a walk, admiring the building (built in 1788) and the plantings of palms, ferns, orchids, and hibiscus. Perhaps it was the rum, but a green wave of phytosynthesis washed over me—I couldn't locate myself through my knowledge of plants. Surrounded by ixoras from India, pride of Barbados (*Caesalpinia*) from Madagascar, crotons from Southeast Asia, cordylines mainly from the western Pacific, snake plants (*Dracaena*) from West Africa, I had no botanical sense of place, save sea-level tropical.

> Tourism is like a fire. You can either cook your food with it or burn your house down.
>
> —BRANDON WITHROW

Research has shown that the composition of alien flora in a region varies depending on the colonizing power.[170] One of the oldest tropical botanic gardens in the western hemisphere lies south of Antigua on the island of St. Vincent. Founded in 1765 to facilitate plant introductions and exchanges within the British Empire, the garden's initial focus was on medicinal and edible plants. A map of the garden from 1773 shows plots of turmeric, nutmeg, and mango, none of which are indigenous to the Caribbean. Useful plants preceded ornamental ones, and while the Dutch had their plants and the English, Spanish, and French theirs, the legacy looks similar: according to the Convention on Biological Diversity, today only 11.3 percent of the Caribbean is biologically intact.

Any species distributed throughout the tropics is referred to as pantropical. The word didn't enter our lexicon until 1913, when a catchall was need to reflect the redistribution of plants of around the globe.

Today pantropical plants speak to the homogenization and corporatization of horticulture as much as they do the legacies of colonialism. The botanic expression of a colorful tropical aesthetic is sold to tourists, almost as if Tahiti or Dominica should resemble Disney-World in Florida (and standing in a hotel courtyard, they often do).

In Antigua, I hiked above English Harbour through scrubby forest up onto the rocky headlands, the soil so thin in places it barely could support life. It was the end of the dry season, and some broad-leaved trees had defoliated to survive. Invasive snake plants scrabbled along the forest floor. Epiphytic tillandsias caught moisture from the wind, lizards scurried, and native cacti poked out between rocks. Doesn't sound very tropical, does it? Nary a hibiscus to tuck behind an ear. The words of Antigua native Jamaica Kincaid settled in: "and since you are on your holiday, since you are a tourist, the thought of what it might be like for someone who had to live day in and day out in a place that suffers constantly from drought . . . must never cross your mind."[171]

Atop Shirley Heights, the site of an old English naval base, at the edge of what felt like a hardscrabble savanna, I found the country's national flower in bloom—the towering succulent *Agave karatto*, rising from a cliff edge, its ten-foot bloom, elegant and proud, standing like a testament to the need for reparations and an Antiguan ecology restored.

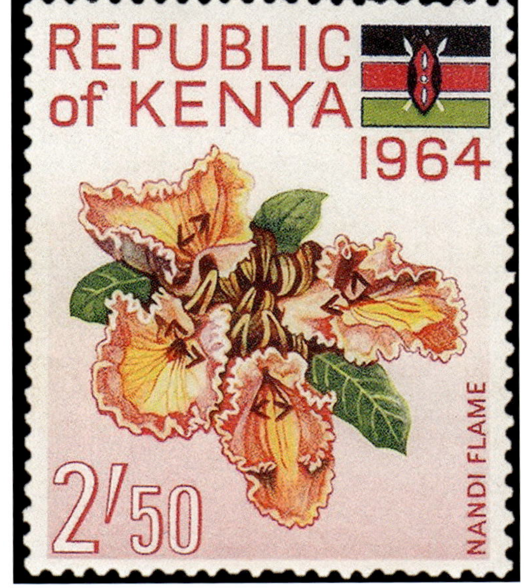

2

1 A bloom from the Hong Kong orchid tree, *Bauhinia × blakeana* at the Hermitage, Nevis.

2 *Spathodea campanulata*, known as the African tulip tree, is native to Kenya and surrounding countries. It has common names in countless languages, indicating its spread throughout the world as an ornamental (and invasive) species.

Pastiche

Making Art

Once every few months, a painter tags me on Instagram to thank me for inspiring them with one of my floral arrangements. Sometimes the work is a detailed copy of my photograph rendered in paint; sometimes it's a loose approximation. Sometimes I post the artist's work in my stories, and sometimes the work is too awkward (or do I say emergent) for me to promote.

Many painters ask me for my consent prior to using my work, and others ask me if it bothers me to have my work copied (with or without consent). I do a teensy bit, but not enough to stop putting my work out in the world free for all to use.

> To be original is not the most important thing, is it?
>
> —I.M. PEI

I see such painters' work as a form of pastiche. It's simulacrum, an attempt to create from a creation. The painters don't have the flowers in front of them; they have an image, a photographic artwork where some of the problems of light, color, and proportion have been solved. I rarely envy the struggle of working in paint, but I do honor it. When I was lured by the light and energy of Dutch still-life paintings into working with flowers, I recall once pointing at an image and asking a photographer, "How do I do *this*?" Homage is helpful. Teachers have us copy to learn, to gain skills, before we face the challenge of charting our own creative path.

The word pastiche can be used in reference to many art forms—dance, architecture, music, and literary work. We can say, "The interiors of the hotel were decorated in a pastiche of Egyptian motifs," or "Her speech was a rambling pastiche of therapy-speak, and I left more baffled than inspired." These examples reveal the origin of the word: pasticcio—a kind of Italian pasta pie (the Greek version is similar) in which a range of ingredients are brought together before being baked. A pastiche or a pasticcio is a mixture, an assemblage, and in some cases, a mess.

I once heard that one floral queen shunned another for "stealing her idea of spray painting vases," and the other never forgave her. Designer egos are often more delicate than vases at times, but we all borrow styles. If we borrow them to mock a style, that's parody (and postmodern). In this example, sadly that wasn't the case.

It's important to recognize the difference between pastiche and misappropriation. Pastiches may mix genres or styles, use borrowed elements, and repurpose or recontextualize them, and thus provoke questions around art and originality. Appropriation art such as Andy Warhol's Pop art soup cans created in 1962, use repetition to underscore the dominance of advertising and consumerism in contemporary culture.

Misappropriation involves misuse, particularly when a work of art has been entrusted to you and you manipulate to meet your own ends. Misappropriation also occurs when settler artists appropriate styles or motifs gleaned from Indigenous artists. As Cherokee scholar Dr. Adrienne Keene explains, "There continue to be instances where artists use what they (mis)understand to be merely a 'technique' or 'style' of Indigenous art to create their work, without realizing that Indigenous hereditary rights often govern the usage of such designs and technique."[172]

Appropriation art is not without its challenges and legal battles. One famous case involved the photographer Patricia Caulfield, who published a series of flower images in a magazine in the 1960s. Andy Warhol used these images, without consent, as a basis for a series of silkscreen prints that made him a fortune. Caulfield successfully sued for misappropriation.[173]

1 American artist Andy Warhol in 1973, with one of his renditions of a photograph by Patrica Caulfield.

1

Peat

Old Plants, New Ways

In my twenties, I interned at the Royal Botanic Gardens at Kew and encountered what was called coir for the first time. It came in big plastic bags and looked like shaggy coffee grounds, nut brown and light to the touch. Scentless, absorbent, and at the cutting edge of horticultural practice at that time, this coco peat comes from the husk of coconuts. Coconut husk fibers have been used throughout history—for matting, and as fine decorative line, thick ropes, and a supplement to horsehair in upholstery. By the time I got to Kew, it had found a new use as a substitute for peat in soil mixes.

I'm Canadian, so let me say right out of the gate, Canada is the world's largest exporter of peat. Look at a map of northern Canada or Russia and you might wonder what's there—vast expanses of boreal forest punctuated by water and long-legged moose. In Canada, that's peat country, a vast area roughly twelve times the size of Portugal. (The peat is covered by a layer of sphagnum moss, which is also exported.) Canada's peat reserves are estimated to be about a trillion cubic meters; the country is home to about 25 percent of the world's peatlands. We often think of rainforests as carbon-rich, but square meter for square meter, Canadian peatland stores five times more carbon than an equivalent area of forest.[174]

Peatlands are increasingly rare—globally they cover only 3 to 4 percent of the planet's land surface while containing close to one-third of the world's soil carbon. According to the UN, "this is twice the amount of carbon as found in the entirety of Earth's forest biomass."[175]

How so? Peatlands store plant matter. They're literally old growth. In cold environments, peat accumulates at the near glacial pace of one millimeter per year, meaning it takes about one thousand years to reach a depth of one meter.[176]

Remember the Tollund Man? His skin stained brown, held tight to his face after 2,300 years in a bog? His remains were found more or less intact due to a lack of bacteria. Leaves, plants, flesh—in anaerobic environments things don't fully decompose. Anaerobic bacteria don't discriminate latitudinally, north to south, so even though the word peat might conjure a smoldering fire in a damp pub somewhere in Ireland (or a pernicious Canadian forest fire that burns underground), 33 percent of the world's peatlands are in the tropics.

Consider Indonesia, where peat swamp forests cover roughly twenty-two million hectares of the islands that make up the country. Globally significant, these carbon sinks are being logged and drained to create oil palm and rubber tree plantations. Jobs are created, yes, but the money soon leaves the country and an ecocide is left in the wake. Environmental organizations in Indonesia are working hard to keep the peat forests and the diverse livelihoods that rely upon them.

I'm writing this near Easter, when attractive plastic pots of tulips line shelves at garden centers and "sustainable" flower farmers force tulips in heated greenhouses from crates filled with peat-based soil mix. I know most of us want to grow, but with UK gardeners going through five hundred million new plastic plant pots every year, I have to wonder if the Edenic myth we sell around gardening is just a marketing ploy.[177] For me, the mental health benefits of gardening are increasingly eroded by the cognitive dissonance surrounding the surfeit of modern gardening products. It makes one want to return to the basics. As Jo McKerr recently wrote of the trouble with plant starts: "To garden with seeds is to shun the 'instant garden': the garden as a product."[178]

Thankfully, the Royal Horticultural Society's gardens in the UK are now 98 percent peat-free, and the organization aims to hit the target of 100 percent by the end of 2025. Sally Nex, of the UK's Peat-free Partnership, would like to see legislation to "outlaw its use altogether."[179] She writes, "there's no need to use it: these days there are some really high quality peat-free potting mixes available, made

> You can't teach an old dogma new tricks.
>
> —DOROTHY PARKER

from renewable, often reclaimed or recycled ingredients, so you can grow very nearly everything just as well but without the environmental damage."

As the American gardener Margaret Roach said, "No product is without an environmental footprint—whether from its production, transport to market, or both. Coconut coir, sourced predominantly in South Asia, requires large amounts of fresh water to wash and prepare. Perlite, mostly sourced from Greece, and vermiculite, from South Africa, require furnaces to process. Even local, easily renewable materials like wood, fiber, and bark, require energy to process."[180]

As such, many gardeners are aiming to avoid such products entirely and trying to close the loop, preferring to reuse, recycle, and reclaim, and build their own composts and soils. Making media: a workshop coming soon to a garden near you.

2

3

1 New York houseplant shop on 28th Street.

2 Bolivian worker drying peat near Ushuaia, Tierra del Fuego, Argentina.

3 Peat removal in Quebec, Canada.

4 Biodiversity and Betadiversity Series, Haley Mellin, 2024.

Perennial

Future Farming

The oldest task in human history is to live on a piece of land without spoiling it.

—ALDO LEOPOLD

Picture an English border in full rolling bloom—say in June: frothy alchemilla, cornflowers, tall delphiniums, roses, biennials like foxgloves, honesty, perhaps some puffs of peonies, punctuated by spires of sweet peas. Sounds like a dream? It is, but like real ones, spectacular and brief.

To paraphrase the inimitable Sarah Raven, you must measure the productive profile of your cutting garden, evaluating each plant not solely on the basis of beauty, but also the volume of blooms delivered per week. If you care about flowers, ask of your plants: how long will you bloom?

In a talk given at a Gardens Illustrated festival, Raven outlined her research into the productivity of various cut flowers and highlighted the value of semi-tropical plants. Plants like dahlias (native to Mexico) bloom for weeks on end, delivering more blooms over a season than any traditional cut flower—a rose, say, or a peony.

One of the terms used for such plant is "cut and come again." Raven advises: "If you think about a half-hardy annual, let's say, cosmos, and you compare it to a hardy annual like a cornflower . . . most hardy annuals flower for about ten weeks. Half-hardy annuals flower for about twenty weeks . . . they hail from places with longer growing seasons." She added, "It's exactly the same with perennials. If you think about comparing a hardy herbaceous perennial like a peony with a tender perennial like a salvia, you've got a bloom period that's three to four times that of the peony."

Unlike many traditional florist flowers—sunflowers, tulips, or ranunculus—many tropical flowers live year in, year out, in place. They're perennials, not annuals, which means farmers don't regularly release the carbon from their soil in order to grow them. What do I mean by release? Well, without getting too technical, let's say a farmer plows in the spring. There's some plant growth likely incorporated in the soil at that point, hopefully (but not always) a cover crop that is churned up and returned to the soil to feed it while carbon-rich organic matter from the soil is exposed to the air, meaning oxidization takes place and the carbon stored in the soil turns into carbon dioxide. Add the tractor emissions used to plow and you get more carbon dioxide.

Simply stated, using perennials in floral design means fewer greenhouse gas emissions. For example, a Hawaiian grower may get seven years of production from an anthurium or dendrobium. By contrast, California growers may turn over a field for stock, then rotate the same land to sunflowers, tilling at least twice a year.

All that disturbance to the soil doesn't just mean an increase of carbon emissions, it also means disturbing the living roots in the earth, which in turn means less water retention and fewer coexistent fungal relationships that benefit plants (see Regenerative). The topsoil is drained of life, so chemical fertilizers and often pesticides are needed. Then there's erosion.

Given that conventional agriculture produces 24 percent of global greenhouse gas emissions, many farmers are shifting their growing practices.[181] No-till methods are catching on as people recognize the dynamics of soil and how no-till methods conserve the micro- and macroorganisms vital to plant health. Regenerative agriculture similarly focuses on soil health, increasing biodiversity, conserving natural vegetation, practicing water and waste management, and lowering the inputs of everything from labor to chemicals.

Many of these methods have been practiced by Indigenous peoples and non-Western cultures for millennia, using livestock to graze as part of crop rotation and growing a wide variety of crops as opposed to monocultures. These growing practices nurture soil health and plant health.

Regenerative agriculture is both our past and our future. As the plantsman Kelly Norris notes, "resiliency means more to me than sustainability because lots of things are sustainable with the right number of resources. The limitation on resources is what we must get serious about."

Designing with perennials is a big step in the right direction.

1 Christmas palm fruits *(Adonidia)*, beach spider lilies *(Hymenocallis littoralis)*, hibiscus, and *Dracaena*.

Photoperiodism

Timing Is Everything

Because the time is ripe, the age is ready

—CHARLOTTE PERKINS GILMAN

A flower opens when it senses it is the right time. I'm not being coy—plants have receptors that track darkness, light, and solar intensity. An organism's response to this miraculous measurement is called photoperiodism. A flower simply knows when it is time to bloom just as a bird knows when it is time to sing.

Petals move, as we do, in space. Together we travel along an orbital plane on a spinning sphere, completing a full rotation every twenty-four hours. The solar day sets a plant's circadian rhythm much like our own.

But consider that we travel around the sun too. We spin along a slightly elliptical orbit every year. At times we're closer to the sun or further from it, but those distances alone don't make a season. How not? The elliptical orbit we might have drawn as a child is actually more circular than oval. Seasons change largely because of our angle of approach.

The earth tilts significantly—spinning on an axis set around 23.5 degrees. So depending whether you're in the northern hemisphere or the southern one, you're either receiving the sun's rays directly (in summer) when you're closer to the sun or obliquely (in winter) when further away.

How does this matter to living things? It doesn't much at the equator, where day length is about twelve hours no matter the time of year. (The equator actually receives the greatest amount of solar radiation at the two equinoxes; plants there respond to the qualities of light as much as the subtle measures of it.) But the situation changes drastically in higher latitudes, whether going north or south, with photoperiod controlling bloom time for many plants.

Understanding photoperiodism is critical for producers, so temperate and semitropical plants are generally sorted into three general categories: short-day plants, long-day plants, and day-neutral plants.

Short-day plants like chrysanthemums and poinsettias need a long night to bloom. They are, chicken or egg, perfectly timed for Thanksgiving and Christmas. (Poinsettias are the world's most economically significant potted plant.)[182] Long-day plants require exactly that: a midsummer's long day. Day-neutral plants are indifferent, responding more to temperature and other factors independent of light.

Today many greenhouse-grown flowers are manipulated into flowering by electric lights. Another reason roses are so ubiquitous in the floral trade? They're day-neutral.

Obviously rainfall or drought can trigger flowering, and changes in soil temperature do too, but if we remove those seasonal climatic variables, say in a place like a tropical rainforest, slight variations in photoperiod come back into play. So one last wonder before I leave you musing about this beautiful planet we're traveling on: synchronous flowering.

Scientists discovered this phenomenon in tropical rainforests where individual trees of the same species might be as much as a hectare apart. These rainforests are dark and crowded with species (about five hundred different species in one hectare), so it's hard to find a mate (forgive me, but when it comes to dating, it's a jungle out there). What will increase a lonely tree's chance of reproductive success? Blooming at the same time as a favored mate. So after measuring the sun's rise and set and the subtle variations in wavelengths of light, flowers open on separate trees in the forest, far apart—sometimes for only a few days. Synchronicity gives the plants the best chance of success.

1 'Platinum Blonde' dahlias with zinnias, sunflowers, and the citrine-colored pea *Lathyrus chloranthus*. Dahlias bloom with twelve-to-fourteen-hour day lengths, sunflowers vary, but longer day lengths lead to longer stems, and zinnias prefer shorter day lengths in warm climates.

2 *To Stand Outside of Yourself*, Kara Taylor, 2009.

Protea

A South African Story

When Freddie Kirsten handed me a worn and plastic-covered copy of *Protea Cultivation: From Concept to Carton* by Gerhard Malan, I realized my questioning had gone a little too far.

"Call Gerhard. Go over," Freddie suggested. "He lives nearby."

I'd been peppering Freddie with questions about the productivity of his proteas. How long do they live? How many flowers did he get per plant?

"A twenty-five-year-old king protea? Three to ten stems, depending on the pruning regime."

"That's it?"

"That's it."

"What about . . ." and off he went to fetch the book.

> What would they see, those who come seeking vast, empty plains, yearning for the untamed wild?
>
> —DANIEL NAAWENKANGUA ABUKURI

Freddie is a fourth-generation farmer in South Africa. He grows table grapes and cultivars of native leucadendrons, leucospermums (pincushions), and proteas on about 150 acres near Paarl in South Africa, in what he describes as "three different microclimates and soil types."

We met in his office behind his Cape Dutch farmhouse surrounded by vines. I'd hoped to see his proteas, but he didn't recommend going up the roads in the weather. Low winter clouds hung on the mountains.

"Too wet," he said.

When a plant lives twenty to thirty years, time apparently isn't of the essence. Freddie told me that some smaller proteas can live for forty or fifty years, depending on the variety.

I flipped through the book: leucadendrons live for ten to fourteen years. Pincushions for ten years and, depending on the variety, can yield thirty-five to sixty stems per year.

"Incredible." What if floristry could be more sustainable by moving to shrubs? I thought. What if the Proteaceae, in a warming climate, could . . .

Proteas are a botanical family (the Proteaceae) that contains a number of popular cut flowers including leucadendron (usually grown for foliage and fruiting heads), leucospermum, blushing bride (*Serruria*)—all of which are South African—and grevillea, banksia, and waratah from Australia, to name a few.

Proteas are ancient plants, not quite as old as cycads, but still related to the proteas of old that lived on the continent of Gondwana. That's why the greatest diversity of proteas are in Australia and South Africa. Many are adapted to fire through the development of something called a lignotuber, which sounds as tough as it is—the tuber holds buds ready to emerge after rain even if the plant has been burned to the ground. (Other proteas have seeds that sprout after being exposed to smoke.) In South Africa, where the king protea (*P. cynaroides*) is the national flower, there are about 330 species of protea in the Cape Floristic Kingdom alone. Worldwide there are more than 1,400 cultivated varieties.[183]

"Where do you get your cultivars?" I asked, knowing Hawaii was a big breeding center.

"Future Fynbos, a South African breeder. We plant cultivars under license, and we pay an annual royalty."

I asked Freddie about water, not an issue in winter, but the lack of it meant summer stress on plants. "Proteas can be drought tolerant," he said, "but if you're growing commercially you need stem length. And for that you need irrigation."

"What's the stem length the market requires then?"

"Sixty to eighty centimeters for export. Fifty is fine locally."

Interesting: consumer demand demanded more water.

"Where are you selling to?"

"In twenty-four to forty-eight hours we can get flowers to Europe, Dubai, Saudi Arabia, and Singapore. These are on passenger flights mainly. There's space. The holds on those planes might be 10 percent luggage and 90 percent flowers."

I knew proteas were cold tolerant, and thus could be shipped easily through the cold chain. But Saudi Arabia?

2

I asked him why are proteas popular there—other than being beautiful, of course.

"They're big. Plus, value for money. They've got a two or three week vase life."

Later we drove in Freddie's truck out to a field of *Leucospermum* 'Tango.' The soft greens and peaches blended into the pale distant mountains. I asked Freddie what sustainability meant to him.

"It's about using water well, conserving what we can, and growing plants that are native to the region. We don't grow in greenhouses, and even though there are lots of fynbos flowers grown in the Cape, you can't say the flowers are mass-produced. Beyond that, we match the plants to elevation, soils. We don't spray unless we need to. Not preventatively, only if we absolutely need to. And we keep natural buffers around the fields too. It keeps everything healthy."

On my way back to Cape Town, the fields became vineyards, the buffers became hillsides, the hillsides became mountainsides, and the fynbos rolled on.

3

1 King protea cultivars with Ericaceous fynbos plants.

2 *Leucospermum* 'Tango' growing at a FreshCap property near Paarl, South Africa.

3 *Protea barbigera* at Kent Flowers in South Africa.

Queer
Plants and People

Are plants queer? Very. Most plants are hermaphrodites—they contain both male (masc) parts and female (femme) parts. A female flower can, depending on environmental factors, develop a male reproductive organ to self-pollinate. Avocado flowers can shift gender expressions in the space of a day, opening in female form then closing to reveal male sexual parts later. You could say plants can be hermaphrodite, bisexual, asexual, and polyamorous.

Some queer folk refer to themselves as perfect flowers. The term is botanical in origin and refers to flowers that are both male and female.

There's no question that most queer, intersex, and gender-nonconforming people, if not plants, have been made to feel unnatural (and been persecuted for it). Yet science tells us that nature is wildly diverse in its presentations. Understanding how plants and animals live in a multiplicity of ways and how transformation is natural resonates with the fluency of identity many queer and gender-nonconforming people's experience.

> Inside of me is expanding, like a beautiful time lapse of an opening orchid, and I don't want you to worry.
>
> —LORETTA RIACH

To address this impasse between fact and fiction, queer ecology has become a burgeoning field that explores the intersections of environmentalism and queer culture. Queer ecologists and gardeners argue that queering biology might "free other species from the script of the history in which they've been written about," particularly, "in a white, European, straight, male context." In scientific terms, a queer ecological perspective might "help illuminate areas of research that may be obscured when viewing human and nonhuman biology through a lens of heteronormativity.[184]

In many ways, queer ecology reaffirms Indigenous ways of knowing. Alex Wilson from the Opaskwayak Cree Nation explains: "The Swampy Cree dialect of our community has no word for homosexual and no gender specific pronouns. Rather than dividing the world into female and male, or making linguistic distinctions based on sexual characteristics or anatomy, we distinguish between what is animate and what is inanimate." Wilson suggests that in her culture, lesbian, gay, bi, and trans people may choose to describe themselves as two-spirit, which "may encompass all aspects of who we are, including our culture, sexuality, gender, spirituality, community, and relationship to the land."[185]

Queer gardeners today also consider the act of gardening itself to be a kind of querying or queering, an interrogative process of being in dialogue with the self, the earth, and plants. Some frame their work with plants as a form of protest—growing one's own food may be anticapitalist and creating community gardens subversive. In a culture that devalues queer identities and nature, there's commonality. Cooperation and found families in queer ecology communities emphasize connection with others and mutual empowerment. The Institute of Queer Ecology suggests that "on a rapidly changing planet, Queer mutability and mutualism can guide us toward adaptation and survival."

2

1 *Helleboriosus exquisitus* created by Brandy Kraft.

2 Quebec designer Marc Sardi.

Regenerative

Welcome to the Rhizosphere

1

The first time I heard the flower farmer Jenny Love use the word rhizosphere I thought she'd made it up. Love is a bit of an alchemist, concocting life-giving potions for her flowers, practicing no-till farming, and supporting wildlife to manage pests. I was once a passionate mushroom hunter and knew about the mycorrhizal associations between fungi and plants, but a rhizosphere? What was that?

A German scientist coined the term in 1904 to refer to the layer of soil with the most life—the place where roots engage in biogeochemical processes.[186] Like our intestines, roots absorb and secrete. A microbiome is integral to the functioning of both systems. One teaspoon of healthy soil contains more microorganisms than there are people on earth, so the exchanges made in the rhizosphere are incredibly diverse, important to plant growth, and at the forefront of regenerative farming.

Regenerative agriculture has been practiced throughout the world. The polycultural system known as milpa in Mesoamerica involves intercropping maize with climbing bean vines that fix nitrogen and squash or melons along the ground, which control weeds. The system is more complex than that of course—fruiting trees, jicama and chilis, and other food and medicinal plants might be grown as well. In West Africa, multistory farmers might grow oil palms, ground crops, and root crops such as yams or cassava underground. In Bali, a salak agroforestry system might include (from high to low) mangoes, coconuts, jackfruit, durian, cloves, cacao, bananas, citrus, forage plants for livestock, sweet potatoes, peanuts, taro, gingers, lemongrass, and turmeric.

Regenerative agriculture weaves together a complex set of ecological (and sometimes spiritual) ideas that put soil first. Some of the key tenets include keeping living roots in the soil, growing diverse species, minimizing soil disturbance, and keeping the soil covered.

A healthy forest might lose only seven inches of topsoil in five hundred thousand years. Contrast that with conventional agriculture, where that same amount of topsoil will be lost in eighteen years. Regenerative practices reduce moisture loss, lessening the need for irrigation, and reduce erosion. (And it's not just the loss of topsoil that's a concern—it's where it goes too. Silting of rivers and marine systems harms habitats. In the southern hemisphere, sediment transport increased 36 percent between 1984 and 2020, largely due to land use changes.)

Mariam Mayet of the African Centre for Biodiversity once said, "We only have a future with agroecology," referencing Africa's food security and seed security, which like India's, relies upon growers saving seeds and caring for soil.

Rheanna Chen, who worked as a regenerative flower farmer in Trinidad, noted the struggles of restoring productivity on mismanaged agricultural land after volunteering at the Allerton Garden, a part of the National Tropical Botanical Garden on Kauai. "Thirty-eight years ago, due to the colonial past, a lot of the land at Allerton was plantation—they were doing coffee, they were doing cacao, they were doing citrus. There were lots of chemicals used on the land, so the soil was depleted." She went on, "Similarly in Trinidad, the soil has been so damaged by sugarcane, we have been stewarding the land to increase productivity. It's a slow process toward restoration."

If you are concerned about the health of your soil, take comfort in the fact that you can nurture soil over time. The rhizosphere will help you silently and miraculously underground.

We know more about the movement of celestial bodies than about the soil underfoot.

—LEONARDO DA VINCI

2

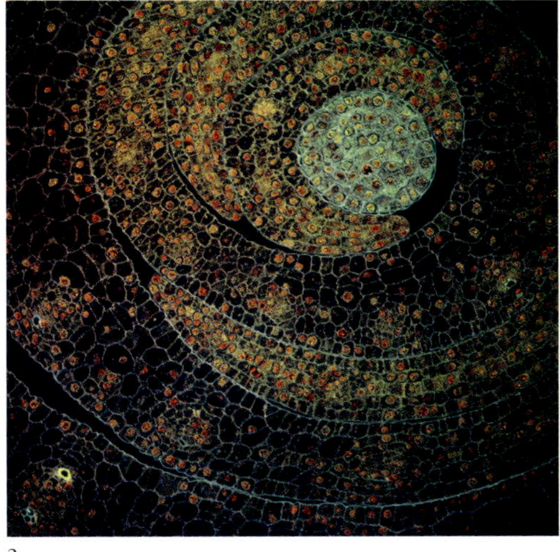

3

1 Stowel Lake Farm flowers on Salt Spring Island in British Columbia. Designed by Star Maracle.

2 *La Cosecha del Cacao, (The Cocoa Harvest)* Diego Rivera, Palacio Nacional, Mexico City, 1929–35. The image shows *chinampas*, artificial islands made by Aztec farmers to support floating gardens. This form of regenerative agriculture is still practiced in some regions today.

3 Cross-section through maize leaves.

Ripe

Hormonal Fluctuations

Oh, how I thought this would be an easy section to write! I thought I might talk about the forced ripening of fruits, but no, ethylene is more than a gas—it's a hormone too. Who knew? Once I learned that fact, I couldn't help draw a comparison between plants and certain animals, most notably myself. Ethylene's role in a plant's cells acts a bit like the estrogen that used to be in mine. So it goes (or rather went), but I recall not long ago when a woman remarked on my writing and peripatetic lifestyle and suggested that obviously, I wasn't menopausal.

I laughed it off at the time, but for most of my life estrogen coursed through me, first regulating growth and then maintaining my reproductive system. I released an egg every month and was lucky enough to not think a whit about hormones. That has markedly changed, but it got me thinking how ethylene plays a similar role in plants: it signals ripening. Ethylene also engages in cross talk with other hormones, messaging when it's time for root development or to grow "hair," or later in a plant's life, when it's time for a plant to senesce. Intimately involved in maturation and both naturally occurring and human-made, ethylene exposure can change everything when it comes to fruits and flowers.

But only *some* flowers and fruits, not others. Need to ripen a peach, mango, or banana? Put it in a bag with an apple, or just leave it to ripen on its own. Need to ripen an orange, strawberry, pomegranate, or cherry? You can't.

Are fruits and flowers treated (gassed) with ethylene today? Yes. Fruits such as pears, plums, grapes, mangoes, bananas, tomatoes, apples, apricots, and peaches are often ripened after transport at their destination market. You know, when the time is ripe.

With flowers, things are more complicated. The control and management of flowering time is critical to floriculture. Ethylene can cause plants to abort flowers and buds. In general, the industry avoids ethylene, which is seen as a pollutant. Transportation exhaust and greenhouse heating units emit ethylene, so growers try to manage exposure.

In addition to ethylene pollution, transportation is stressful for both cut flowers and live plants. Plants emit ethylene naturally, but when jostled in travel they emit more. Rough handling and injuries increase ethylene and shorten vase life considerably. Given cut flowers are often packed tightly in transit to lower costs, together they, erm, egg each other on to ripening faster. What's a grower to do? Spray compounds like EthylBloc or silver thiosulfate on flowers and plants to help them through the cold chain.[187]

It's worth knowing which flowering plants are sensitive to ethylene. These include petunias, salvias, begonias, dianthus, impatiens, tomatoes, marigolds, bugle lilies (*Watsonia*), bouvardia, gardenia, gloriosa lily, ixia, kalanchoe, kniphofia, Vanda and Odontoglossum orchids, Philippine ground orchid (*Spathoglottis*), penstemon, philodendron, and harlequin flowers (among others). If sold in live plant form, these flowers might be sprayed with ethylene to stimulate branching, before being sprayed again with an ethylene inhibitor for travel to retail locations.

Some flowers are immune to ethylene: heliconias, lachenalia, Christmas bells (*Sandersonia*), blushing bride, strelitzia, pagoda flower (*Mimetes*), and the foliage plants monstera, yucca, bear grass, bottlebrushes, date palms, and pittosporums to name a few.

Why all this variability between species? I don't yet know. Plants have the ability to cease and resume growth. Animals do not. That alone gives pause for serious thought.

Life shrinks or expands in proportion to one's courage.

—ANAÏS NIN

70122
Partardia
H. E. Van Deman
Miami,
Fla.
Mary D. Arnold
2-16-14
3-1-14

3

4

1 Sri Lankan bounty styled by Thanushi Eagalle.

2 *Citrus paradisi: Patardia*, Mary D. Arnold, USDA Pomological Watercolor Collection.

3 *Without Airs (Paradise is Paradising)*, Lilian Martinez, 2023

4 Detail from a watercolor by Mariko Ikeda, *Pandanus boninensis*, 2016. The plant is endemic to Japan's Ogasawara Islands.

Scent

Luring and Alluring

1

For a flower, a scent is a lure, a signal, a means of enticing a pollinator to visit. For a human, a scented flower is alluring too, a nose-in-petals moment of regret or rapture, a layering of experience and memory. In India, "to kiss" means smell—for isn't that what we do? We lean into a moment of intimacy.

For people and plants, there's power in scent. Our olfactory system is directly linked to the limbic system of the brain, which processes emotions and encodes memory. While the science of scent is not a mystery today, our experience of scent often beguiles, in part because it can be difficult to name what we smell. Perfumers don't always smell more than the rest of us but rather train themselves to decode, distinguish, and describe. For a word lover like myself the lexicon of scent, like that of wine, feels extraordinarily extravagant: sweet, spicy, woody, fatty, phenolic, warm, waxy, mint, tobacco, honey, herbal, linden, clove, carnation, cinnamon, hawthorn, cheese, butter, fruit, pine, terpene, citrus, fresh. A gardenia? More green, moist siren scent than sweet tropical.

> Millions of flowers, branches, pieces of bark and drops of resin are tipped into stills, all of them bearing the particular mark of their natural environment.
>
> —DOMINIQUE ROQUES

For millennia people have captured the ephemeral scent of flowers. Enfleurage is one traditional method, using oil or fat. The process is labor intensive and can be done "cold" by simply placing and replacing flowers on or in the fat, or the flowers can be macerated and stirred into melted fat. The flowers diffuse scent into the fat, are strained out, and replaced until the desired level of saturation is reached.

The resulting solid perfume (which melts on skin contact) is a called an enfleurage pomade. Washing or soaking the pomade in ethyl alcohol was the traditional means of getting scent molecules into alcohol. Once finished, you would have an absolute.

The volume of flowers required for natural perfumes staggers. To make a semisolid enfleurage of tuberose (*Polianthes tuberosa*, an agave relative native to Mexico), you'd need 150 kilograms to make one kilogram of semisolid enfleurage. At the absolute stage, one estimate I read suggested nine hundred kilograms might yield about two hundred grams of absolute.[188] How much land and time would it take to grow those nine hundred kilos of tuberose? In India, one hectare and one year.[189]

Historically, France has been an epicenter of the perfume industry, but flower production has declined as plants can be grown more cheaply abroad. Production of jasmine (*J. grandiflorum*) around the French perfume capital of Grasse peaked in 1930 at 1,800 tons of flowers; today that number is down to about twenty-seven tons. India grows more than fifty varieties of jasmine, and the farming of flowers is big business there. In the Madurai region, ten thousand acres are devoted to jasmine bushes; however, the plants need irrigation to survive increasing droughts. Exports vary according to abundance; India has a vast domestic market for jasmine itself. Legend has it that over ten thousand jasmine blossoms were required to produce a single ounce of Joy perfume.

Oh, how we love (and hate) scents. My personal bugbear: chemically scented incense sticks and candles. I have walked out of restaurants (what do florals have to do with food at places that do not serve edible flowers?). I have tried to change hotel rooms, opened windows, gagged, raged, and spun on a heel and run from scented shops. All that and I'm not even allergic; I'm just sensually appalled.

But what about those who are allergic? Synthetic fragrances disrupt hormones, contain known carcinogens, respiratory toxicants, and chemicals that affect reproduction. Why do we put up with them? We don't even know what they are. If you look at a scent stick package or shampoo bottle, you'll often see the word fragrance standing alone in a sea of ingredients. Why don't we get to know what the fragrance actually is? In the United States, a loophole in labeling legislation exempts fragrance.[190] California only just recently passed a bill to lift the veil.

In the European Union, a furor erupted a few years ago when plant extracts used in perfumes and cosmetics like oak moss and citral were slated to be banned. These compounds (and many other synthetic ones) were hidden under the words parfum or aroma on labels. In 2023, in lieu of an outright ban (one angry perfumer argued that orange juice should be banned if citral was to be), the EU upped the number of fragrance allergens that must be labeled from twenty-six to over two hundred. Lilial, a trade name for a lily aldehyde used to impart lily-of-the-valley notes in everything from laundry soap to shampoo, was banned outright in 2022 as a reprotoxin. What is a reprotoxin? Compounds that can damage the reproductive process.

With more than five billion people on the planet—washing, lotioning, deodorizing, laundering, sanitizing, grooming—the market of scented personal care and household products has exploded. So much so, fragrance is on the frontier of emerging pollutants.

3

5

4

6

1 Rose production at Kelâat M'Gouna in Morocco's High Atlas. Oils are used locally and exported to Grasse, France, for the perfume industry.

2 Common gardenia, *Gardenia jasminoides*, known as kiele in Hawaii, is native to China.

3 Tuberose (*Agave amica*), native to Mexico, photographed at the home of Christina Hartman on Maui.

4 Filtering Monoï oil made from tiare flowers (*Gardenia taitensis*) in Tahiti.

5 A Punjabi man sniffs a mature rose; roses deliver the most scent at the point they would like to be pollinated—when they're about half open.

6. Mr. Harris with ylang-ylang on Nevis.

Seasonality

What's in Bloom

Phenology is a biological term that refers to timing, namely the cyclical patterns of events in the natural world—as evidenced by migration, bud breaking, egg laying, leaf eruption, leaf falling, flower blooming, hibernation ending, song singing, nest building, fruit ripening, and so on.[191] Living things respond to environmental cues like day length, temperature, and rainfall and set their schedules to have the greatest chance of success. This is true of humans too, and horticulturists have long followed signs to signal sowing and harvesting, among other tasks.

Sadly, today it's often hard to know when flowers are in season because our globalized world often mashes together plants and holidays for marketing purposes (like roses in February) and throws the word season around liberally. Thus protea season might fall in New York's autumn when it is spring in the southern hemisphere. Similarly, mimosa hits the UK market in January, once African trees begin to (or can be forced to) bloom, making an early spring flower in the south of France into a winter flower. In economic terms, the flowers are in season in both places at once, but ecologically they are only in season where they grow.

This impasse in understanding is fostered at the commercial level by wholesaler availability lists, which may not list the provenance of the plants. So how is a florist to know? Floral design schools are beginning to integrate local farms into their curricula, but traditionally students have largely visited wholesale markets importing flowers from around the world. If a florist doesn't realize their work is out of season, we can't expect much more from a customer.

Jack Goody wrote of seasonality and the psychic friction caused by innovations in horticulture as far back as 33 BCE in China. He references Shah Xinchen, the minister of natural resources revenues, who "declared that products such as hothouse plants were all untimely things, whether flowers or not, and would be injurious to men and inauspicious as offerings."[192]

The word for this dissonance is contraseasonal, which basically means against the seasons.

Timing is everything in nature, and "to everything there is a season" reminds us that knowing when a plant is locally in season is key to becoming a strong designer. Flowers perform best when fresh.

Lunar cycles have been used by many cultures to time planting and harvest. While we know that the earth's gravity can influence plant growth (i.e., if you tip a potted plant on its side it will bend to right itself), there's little evidence that the moon's force affects plant growth. The force the moon exerts on us is three hundred thousand times weaker than the earth's gravity.[193] What about the moon's luminance? The glow of moonlight? Can plants use it to grow? Not to photosynthesize but perhaps for other forms of regulation, in response to electromagnetic forces. It could be the rhythms that matter.

Write about winter in the summer.

—ANNIE DILLARD

2

3

1 Madrid Flower School students with instructor Ana Belén Rodríguez at La Oficial Cerámica.

2 *Acacia*, by Rose Fiveash, who devoted her life to illustrating the flora of South Australia. She continued painting until age eighty, completing a book on orchids and a comprehensive collection of botanical illustrations of the state's trees, flowers, and plants.

3 Mimosa harvest, France. *Acacia dealbata* was introduced to Cannes in 1864 from Australia. *Acacia farnesiana*—the source of cassis valuable to the perfume industry—and *Acacia retinodes* followed. Historically, plantings of *Acacias* in France have responded to the demand either from the perfume industry or for cut flowers.

Speciation

Nature and Nurture

An artist cannot speak about his art any more than a plant can discuss horticulture.

—JEAN COCTEAU

Recall Charles Darwin's finches? In 1837, after his return from the Galapagos, Darwin handed over a collection of birds to John Gould, an ornithologist in London. He needed help. He wanted to know what birds he had, and how they were related to one another and to the land. After Gould differentiated a wide array of species, Darwin articulated his idea of independent creation, that new species had developed as a result of natural selection for certain traits, traits that developed in response to the environment.

This is speciation in the classical sense. Today, thanks to genetics, we understand that plants speciate continually, radiating out of geographical regions, and Darwin's ideas, while still generally true, lack the nuance that modern phylogenetics provides about the origin of species.

Citrus, given its economic importance and ancient history of cultivation, is one subject that has fascinated scholars for hundreds of years. Art, artifacts, and fossilized pollen have helped solve some mysteries about speciation—the process by which populations evolve into distinctly separate species.

Recent genomic analyses reveal the center of origin for citrus is the southeastern foothills of the Himalayas. The story begins with ancestral fruits, some of which we eat today, such as citrons and pomelos, and the ancient lime-like *Citrus micrantha*, a distant ancestor of mandarins and kumquats.

Kumquats are still kumquats, more or less. Grapefruits are descendants of pomelos. Oranges came from ancient mandarins and pomelos. *Citrus micrantha* later became known as papeda, whose descendants include makrut limes and yuzu. Lemons are a cross of citron and sour oranges, which themselves were born from a cross of pomelos and ancestral mandarins. Confused yet? Don't be, because the history of citrus involves an interesting term that's salient to plant breeding: introgression.

Technically, introgression means backcrossing a hybrid with a parent or an individual who is genetically similar to a parent. To put this in human terms: long ago when our ancestors walked out of Africa, some hominids migrated north and became Neanderthals in Europe and Denisovans in Asia. When later migrations of early peoples traveled to these regions and copulated, they bred with an ancient version of themselves. They introgressed.

Speciation generally occurs when a group separates from its own species and over time develops new characteristics. In the case of citrus, a changing climate over seven million years ago led to what is called a sudden speciation event. When a change in the environment makes new habitats and resources available, niches open, and plants and animals fill them. This is called adaptive radiation.

Various citrus species have formed through adaptive radiation, but humans also had a heavy hand in creating the fruit we love today. With thousands of years of citrus cultivation, the origins of species are difficult to determine. Consider the citrus bergamot of Calabria in southern Italy, the oil of which is used in Earl Grey tea, orange juice, sweets, perfumes, and cosmetics.[194] Did it travel via the Silk Road or by sea to Italy? And from where? The name is believed to have come from the Turkish *beg-a-mudi*, which means "pears of the prince." Research has shown that by 200 BCE, citrons were spreading around Italy and not long after began to appear in art. Folk tales say the bergamot reached Calabria in the 1300s, while other suggest Christopher Columbus brought it from the Canary Islands. While no one truly knows, botanists do know its parentage: on the maternal side is a sour orange and on the paternal side a citron.

Citrus are a special class of berries known as hesperidiums. The thicker the rind or peel (aka the pericarp), the longer the fruit will last, so if you want longevity for design work, look to the ancient varieties: pomelos, citron, and its wonderfully aromatic and evocative relative, the Buddha's hand.

1 Palo verde (*Parkinsonia florida*) with ranunculus, citrus, and golden columbines (*Aquilegia chrysantha*).

Subtropical

Favored Climes

If you're feeling sad about the state of the world, get to San Diego's beautiful Balboa Park, stroll around the Spanish Colonial Revival architecture, and find the San Diego Botanical Garden Foundation. You'll know you've arrived when you see a black felt bulletin board listing the monthly public meetings held on-site: rare fruit growers, master gardeners, carnivorous plants, shells, florals, turtles, orchids, camellias, arthropods, roses, native plants, geraniums, dahlias, cacti and succulents, plumerias, herbs and ferns, topped off with beekeeping and nine different ikebana groups.

Faith restored.

As the list suggests, San Diego sits in a subtropical zone, a climatic region that for millennia, many civilizations have considered ideal. From Marrakech to Durban, from Cyprus to Shiraz, from Osaka to Genoa, and from Sydney to Buenos Aries, subtropical climates exist in both hemispheres, giving us both a surfeit of ornamental plants and lessons of how to live on a warming earth.

> What it means to be smart, what genius is, depends on when you're asking about it, where you're asking about it, the context you're asking about it in.
>
> —CHARLES KING

But back to Balboa Park, where I visited the San Diego Floral Association's library and read the writing of Kate Sessions, a plantswoman often called the Mother of Balboa Park.

Sessions is an interesting figure in the history of American horticulture. Born in 1857, she was a plant hunter, florist, horticulturalist, and writer. As a nursery owner for over fifty years, she propagated regional native plants, promoting ceanothus, dendromecon, pride-of-California (*Lathyrus splendens*), and holly-leaf cherry (*Prunus ilicifolia*). She also introduced countless plants to California—traveling back from Hawaii with cuttings, hauling 140 species home from Europe, collecting seeds in Baja California, and trading seeds with Australian and South African growers.

She promoted the use of what we now call climate analogs, in her case, plants that came from other arid subtropical regions that she surmised would succeed in the Southern California climate, enduring periods of drought. She entered into a private-public partnership agreement with the city of San Diego, allowing her to operate a nursery on park land in exchange for developing an experimental garden, planting one hundred trees annually in the park, and providing three hundred trees a year to the city.

Sessions's passion for subtropical plants created whole landscapes—she spread foreign jacaranda trees, eucalyptus, and bauhinias for shade and beauty while encouraging home gardeners to plant grevilleas, pittosporums, bougainvilleas, poinsettias, bird of paradise (*Strelitzia*), and more. While considered responsible for the introduction of numerous invasive species, Sessions also helped save some plants from extinction. Today begonias, lilacs, geraniums, hibiscus, and lychees have been named in her honor.

Sessions was also a florist, advocating the use of locally grown plants. In 1909, she noted that the giant native matilija poppy (*Romneya coulteri*) could be cut in "half-blown buds . . . and ship[ped] as far as San Francisco, and they will open up large and perfect."[195]

She also celebrated the development of the bulb fields in 1933 north of San Diego, where the first commercial freesias, ranunculus, and anemones were grown en masse.

With the benefit of hindsight and a knowledge of invasive species, we might view Sessions's work as problematic, but the desire to alter landscapes isn't just a human trait; almost every creature does to some extent. Still, it does feel we're at a tipping point: one estimate I found suggests there are about 6,500 types of ornamental plants grown in the United States: 29 percent of them are native to Asia, 19 percent are European, and 15 percent come from South America and Mexico. Even today, with an increased awareness of the importance of native plants, only about 27 percent of ornamental plants sold in the United States have North American roots.

2

3

1 Passiflora 'White Wedding' and 'Clear Sky' with pokeberry (*Phytolacca americana*) blossoms.

2 Kate Sessions in the Balboa Park Cactus Garden, 1935.

3 A Sicilian balcony and patio planting near Letojanni, Italy.

4 Tebarek Allah, the Tangier home of Umberto Pasti and Stephan Janson.

Succulent

Crazed Collectors

Succulents suit modern urban living because—you guessed it—they can survive without water for long periods and withstand tough conditions (like sitting on a cafe table in the baking sun). When plastic succulents appeared in spas and restaurants, the party may have been over in terms of fashion but the hangover was acute: everyone wanted succulents. In 2018, the floral foam company Smithers-Oasis began offering tips for using succulents in floral design. In 2019, the Royal Horticultural Society in the UK followed suit. The *Guardian* reported that between 2012 and 2017 the global market for succulents surged 64 percent.[196] And that was before the plant parents of the pandemic.

> Luxury is not really a matter of how much you have, but how much you don't need.
>
> —PICO IYER

Take the diminutive dudleya, a greyish-green rosette-shaped succulent very much like the ubiquitous plastic version. Its common name of live-forever isn't particularly charming, but apt—succulents exude waxy substances they use as a kind of dry sunscreen. This gives their green that special dusky look (which pairs beautifully with millennial pink). As for living forever, some dudleyas can reach the age of fifty, which isn't long in the succulent world but is long if you think of living with very little water.

Dudleyas have shallow roots that spread laterally so they can take advantage of whatever rain falls. Such small, shallow-rooted succulents like dudleyas and living pebbles, aka conophytum, are incredibly easy to collect from the wild. You don't need even need a shovel. Sadly, this makes succulents and cacti ideal plants to poach—pop one off a cliff, scrape it from the soil, pry it from between rocks with a screwdriver, wrap it in newspaper, and tuck it away in the dark, and it will likely survive a trip in the post or a bag, suitcase, car, plane, or cargo ship.

The COVID-19 pandemic only made things worse for succulents. According to Molly Williams, author of *Taming the Potted Beast*, demand during the pandemic saw up to a 4,000 percent increase in the price of some plants. Inflated prices and demand created a boom market for poachers.

So hundreds of *Ariocarpus fissuratus*, the rock cactus, disappeared from the American Southwest.

And truckloads of gorgeous globose *Copiapoa cinerea* left Chile.

And boxes of three-hundred year-old living pebbles left Namibia and South Africa.

And hundreds of the threatened flowering cactus *Lobivia pampana* left Peru.

And all that while, we celebrated plant parenting.

South African enforcement officers seized 1.6 million illegally harvested succulents between 2019 and 2024.[197] Doing the math, that's about 6,400 trafficked succulents a week. And those are only the ones found by the authorities. Seven species have been wiped out completely. The trade in succulents is so lucrative, organized crime syndicates are involved. Ultimately, the plants are sold over the internet.

A campaign in China to cut trade in conophytum has resulted in fewer online advertisements in that country. Still, education is needed globally to stop the trade, so here we are.

The Convention on International Trade in Endangered Species of Wild Fauna and Flora (CITES) serves to protect living things—be they rhinos killed for their horns, sharks for fins, or orchids collected from high in a tree canopy. But plants are far from pandas (that is, charismatic megafauna) and thus are often overlooked. (The term for this disregard in conservation circles is plant blindness.) It's one thing to try steal a towering two-hundred-year-old saguaro cactus under cover of night (some saguaros now have RFID—radio frequency identification chips in them to help the authorities to track poachers), but it's entirely another to snatch a few forty-year-old dudleyas from a park, pop them in your pack, and sell them on Etsy. According to the International Union for Conservation of Nature (IUCN), more types of cacti are at greater risk of extinction than birds. Tweet.

1 *Argyroderma delaetii* in bloom. *Argyrodermas* are also known as *bababoudjies*. According to photographer Ana-Filipa Domingues, these plants, like other members of the *Mesembryanthemaceae* only release seeds when wet and when a raindrop hits the seed capsule at specific velocity. *Argyrodermas* occur only in the northwestern part of the Western Cape, a region known as the Knersvlakte (literally meaning "grinding flats," for the grinding noise the quartz makes when walked upon).

Sustainable

Greenwashing

1

George Orwell, in his seminal essay "Politics and the English Language," warned against the use of abstract nouns. What's an abstract noun? A quick definition is a noun you can't see, touch, hear, feel, or taste. Sustainability is one example, economics another. "Can you draw a picture of that?" is often a good question to ask of your nouns.

I bring this up here because the language around sustainability in floriculture is baffling. Flower producers have wised up to consumer demands, so many tout environmental sustainability and social responsibility. They obtain certification to those ends. But finding out who's doing what is rather like peeling an onion: you literally tear up from the repetition of greenish-sounding phrases and corporate doublespeak. For example, the Floriculture

Sustainability Initiative (FSI) has what they call a basket of standards, containing about fourteen certifiers focused on sustainability. These include familiar outfits like Rainforest Alliance or Fairtrade International, but also national operations like the Kenya Flower Council and Floraverde from Colombia. Many of these names will be familiar to wholesale shoppers; plastic flower sleeves often sport these logos. I myself have often reached for these bunches despite knowing the flowers are not local or small-farm, but I reasoned, "At least they're trying," though I never really bothered to check what the companies were actually "trying" to do.

No snowflake in an avalanche ever feels responsible.

—STANISŁAW J. LEC

There's an old expression that goes, "Anyone who gives you a simple answer to a complicated problem is either a liar or a fool," and I would prefer to be neither. Nor is it easy on the side of the grower or on the consumer trying to navigate the array of sustainable options before them.

Each certifier in the FSI's basket has different criteria—the words sound good, but are often intangible. What precisely does stewardship mean in the context of an industrial-scale flower farm? I've learned: many things to many different people. In effect, companies shop for the FSI certification that best fits their operation.

How did we get here, where it's hard to know what's happening on farms and the true cost of flowers? Businesses understood it was important to consumers for them to go beyond simply measuring profit, aka the bottom line, and factor in the environmental and social costs of business. This is known triple bottom line accounting, the three Ps of which are people, planet, and profit.

Today the International Trade Centre (ITC) reviews each certification. That sounds reassuring until you recognize that the ITC is a trade commission, not an environmental group or a humanitarian one.

Most environmental certifications focus on self-reporting: how much pesticide was used? What type? Any banned ones? What's happening with water on the farm? Use levels? Where does the wastewater go? Other certifications focus on health care for workers: do people have access to personal protective equipment when they spray pesticides? (Is that then socially responsible?) Is a fair wage a true living wage? And what are positive working conditions? Being able to eat on the job?

I sound cynical, I know, but my investigation into this level of the industry became more opaque the deeper I delved. A grower or designer might emphasize the sustainable part of their business without mentioning the unsustainable part; they may use vague language or use ill-defined terms like green or eco-friendly, or ally themselves with sustainable organizations to deflect attention away from unsustainable practices.

As Rita Feldmann of the Sustainable Floristry Network noted, the issue of sustainability isn't unsolvable. "Many florists already have a deep appreciation of nature and an understanding of what business practices are problematic, but they're missing the tools and knowledge to change."[198]

She recounted the story of Smithers-Oasis's 2025 release of a floral foam called Renewal. Marketing it as "now sustainable," the company was touting the fact they'd swapped petrochemicals for a plant-based product, which according to Rita "is one step on a potential journey toward a sustainable product," but the product still is destined to a landfill or incineration after use. As she said, "Marketing like this just tricks those desperate for a panacea. From there, the greenwashing just flows downstream."[199]

Many florists call themselves sustainable if they use local flowers or eschew floral foam. The Sustainable Floristry Network doesn't believe those criteria alone can define a business and encourages people to think about sustainability as a practice which may not be perfect but is intentional. To borrow from Orwell, it behooves us to consider that "there are no reliable words." But ask growers and designers: "What precisely do you mean by sustainable?"

2

3

4

BODEGA DE XATE
RECORTE
EMPAQUE
TRANSPORTE
TURBO
CUARTO FRIO
5

6

1 Quince and camellia by Kasumi Teshigahara, 1979.

2 Rattan coffin-making in Transan, Indonesia. Exports increased 40 percent during the COVID pandemic.

3 Jamaica Market in Mexico City. It's estimated that women are responsible for about 60 percent of flower production in Mexico.

4 Bayley Marion with marigolds from my garden.

5 A *xaté* (*Chamaedorea* spp.) processing facility in Uaxactun, Guatemala. The palms are wild harvested from forests for export, providing valuable income to communities who steward the forests and protect an array of associated species. Other plants harvested include chicle (*Manilkara zapota*), used in chewing gum) and pepper (*Pimenta dioica*). Uaxactun lies within the Maya Biosphere Reserve.

6 Designer Luis Felipe Rojas Molina in Mexico City.

Texture

Savanna Style

Zita Elze hails from Brazil, specifically a high tropical savanna region known as the Cerrado, where crystals emerge from the earth, jaguars hunt, and grasslands sway. I might have known texture would be one of the first things she mentioned when we met because her work is always intricate, detailed, and surprising; a tuft of moss might host a sprig of aromatic dried heather, a delicate dried bloom of a paper daisy (*Rhodanthe*), a seed pod, or the cone of a mysterious tree.

Elze studied interior design, garden design, and floral design in Paris before opening her landmark shop near Kew Gardens in London. The flower boutique was meant to be a front for her garden design business, a place where she'd "sell a few bouquets" while getting on with her design business at a desk in the back. But flowers took over the shop, and she now runs the business with her daughter Laura.

> With the gifts nature offers us why should white man want to destroy it all and then instead plant just one single crop?
>
> —SEBASTIANA CAPER KRAHO

When I asked her to chat about tropicals, she initially demurred. "Oh, I don't use them much." Was she thinking of large structural plants, the leaves and flowers of the humid tropics? I pushed her: no, the textural plants, the details. And as we chatted what emerged was a love of texture born from the Cerrado.

The Cerrado is technically tropical; it spans 23 percent of central Brazil (an area about the size of Italy, France, Spain, and Britain combined) and is home to 5 percent of the world's animals and plants. It contains more than eleven thousand plant species (45 percent endemic) and is one the most biologically rich savannas in the world.

I've not been to Brazil, but through my research I found Marcelo Kuhlmann, who holds a PhD in Botany from the University of Brasília and is the author of ten books on the biodiversity and flora of the Cerrado biome. He described the Cerrado to me "as a vast garden, orchard, and natural pharmacy, yet still little known to most Brazilians. Known as the 'cradle of Brazil's waters,' the Cerrado is home to the headwaters of three major river basins in South America," including the Amazon.

Recently more than half of the Cerrado has been converted to cattle farming and croplands—soy farming can be blamed for much of the devastation.[200] Brazil supplies about a quarter of the world's soy, much of it used to feed cattle in the United States. The Cerrado is home to eighty-three distinct Indigenous groups, who are increasingly being pushed out of their territory by intimidation, murder, and the wholesale appropriation of their land. According to the World Wildlife Fund, 98 percent of the deforestation and habitat destruction in the Cerrado is illegal. The situation is bleak with a strong need for international attention, which is another reason why I'm mentioning it here. As Kuhlmann said, "Without proper care, it could vanish in the blink of an eye."[201]

Thinking about his words and Elze's, a more personal question arose: do we all carry a sense of place with us? An artistic imprint of the landscape of home no matter where we are? I think we do. And if we lack the plants that carry our stories, how do we create new meanings and associations?

When Elze first opened her shop, the English floral style of the time was "packed tight. All these big peonies and other dominant flowers," she recollects, "and you could hardly buy any foliage." Now her shop contains elegant grasses, feathery foliage, bright mimosa, dried flowers, nuts, seeds, and airy vines, which she mixes in loose bouquets that have movement but never look unstructured. Her work is intuitive, yet sensitively detailed. "Living embroidery," she calls it.

2

The idea of a mosaic is one Kuhlmann speaks of in our correspondence. The interplay of forest, savanna, and grasslands in the Cerrado "is closely tied to variations in soil types, which differ in texture, depth, fertility, and water saturation. The complex interplay between soil, climate, and fire has shaped the Cerrado's vegetation over thousands of years, creating an extraordinary biodiversity of plants and animals."

What can we do to protect this land and the people who call it home? According to Kuhlmann, "the first step toward conservation is to spark people's interest . . . foster genuine connections and a sense of belonging to the biome."

Looking at images of the Cerrado—its grasslands, marshes, parrots, primates, fruits, hills, and valleys—I see it without seeing it yet myself: a tapestry of life.

1 *Rhynchanthera grandiflora*, a native and ornamental species that occurs in veredas, a type of Cerrado vegetation associated with water-saturated soils.

2 "With all the gifts that nature offers us why should white man want to destroy it all and then plant just one single crop?" Sebastiana Caper Kraho holding a bacuri fruit, also known as the golden fruit of the Cerrado. The fruit is produced by the tree *Platonia insignis* and forms a key component of the Kraho diet.

3 Natural field covered by the plant chuveirinho (*Paepalanthus chiquitensis*) in the Chapada dos Veadeiros, Brazil.

4 Aerial view of the Cerrado vegetation mosaic with forest, savanna, and grassland formations in the Chapada dos Veadeiros, Brazil.

4

Tokenism

Aiming for Equity

The idea behind tokenism is that one person can stand in for many. Tokenism gained traction when companies reactively sought to diversify the gender or racial mix of their employees in order to appear progressive in regards to discrimination. Hiring a BIPOC (Black, Indigenous, or Person of Color) might give the impression of tackling the issue of inequality, but as the *Washington Post* recently pointed out in reference to gender equality, this may be an instance of "twokenism," whereby a company or brand might want to appear woke in order to avoid scrutiny.

> **Tokenism does not change stereotypes or social systems but works to preserve them, since it dulls the revolutionary impulse.**
>
> —MARY DALY

Such was the case recently when a self-proclaimed sustainable flower workshop advocating #nofloralfoam accepted funding from Smithers-Oasis (a leading producer of floral foam) and then offered a BIPOC scholarship. Many floral designers were outraged by the layers of hypocrisy regarding the Oasis money and the potential for the corporation to use the funding for their own greenwashing initiatives, while also recognizing that a destination workshop with students and teachers flying in could in no way be sustainable. People decried the duplicity, false advertising, greenwashing, and tokenism, but in sad testament to our modern age, the backlash led to algorithmic amplification, increasing the metric of engagement on social media, and critique only helped to promote the event.

In the design, floral, and horticultural worlds, it's easy to trip up. Here are some ways to take your blinders off (with thanks to Alexia Fisher and Skye Latimer):

1 Be very wary of diversity shoots. Employ BIPOC professionals in your business, not just as models.

2 Ask yourself if plantations and estates built through slavery are appropriate as places of celebration. Obviously historic homes come loaded with history. It behooves you, whether as a mother of a bride, a gardener, or as a vendor working on-site, to do some research prior to affiliating yourself to a place with a loaded past.

Here's an example: in looking for a venue for my father's memorial, I considered a national historic site. My father studied history and appreciated Canadian heritage. I had a tour, saw the chapel and auditorium, and left with a niggling feeling I should learn more about the history of the site. It was linked to a mission that had been involved in the forced assimilation of Salish and Syilx/Okanagan children.

3 Consider how can you offer representation without tokenism. One of the guiding principles of this book is to highlight plants of the global south and contextualize the work of designers with supporting narratives. This, you could say, was an effort, however limited, toward allyship on my part. In this case, the power was mine to give. By including you, the reader, in my thought process, we can both reflect on who holds power and gets to tell stories. I understand that's a privilege.

4 Recognize that you're likely working with a heteronormative model. Get pronouns right. Try using language that's more inclusive—for example, partners (or any variation of that) as opposed to bride or groom.

5 Consider the symbology of plants before using them. For example, cotton is still deeply problematic for post-plantation families given the legacy of the slave trade and rag trade.

6 Always recognize that different value sets circulate in different communities.

1 I commissioned Ana Myerscough to make this collage to highlight how history should inform aesthetic understanding. The southern magnolia was a common tree on cotton plantation estates in the southern United States. Slave labor was used to create wealth on these properties until the passing of the Thirteenth Amendment, which officially abolished slavery in 1865.

Utilitarianism

The Greater Good

1

Utilitarianism is a moral philosophy that asks how we can do the most good possible for everyone impacted by our activity, including members of other species, nations, and generations.[202] The word itself doesn't sound entirely like its meaning—that is until we see utility in terms of serving others, not just ourselves. As an ethical framework, utilitarianism asks us to consider consequences. Naturally we can't always know the consequences of our actions or decisions, but we can research them, ask questions, and try not to do harm.

> I always wondered why somebody doesn't do something about that. Then I realized I was somebody.
>
> —LILY TOMLIN

For example, it's appealing to support a local grower: you may know them, want to encourage them, and value their contribution to your community. But what happens when we ask whether purchasing their flowers is the right choice in terms of the greater good of humanity?

It depends where you set your moral compass. For a New Yorker who has done their research, the evidence might reveal that a Caribbean ginger bloom has a longer vase life and lower carbon footprint than a local greenhouse-grown anemone. We've learned that when it comes to food, transport only accounts for about 5 percent of emissions. It's what you eat and how it's produced that matters more than how far it traveled to get you.

The environmental reporter Fred Pearce suggested in the *Guardian* that "there's a kind of green imperialism where we are just screwing up a lot of lives for uncertain benefit and a sense of personal virtue." For example, the carbon footprint of flying green beans from Kenya is no greater than that of growing them in a hothouse in the Netherlands.[203]

I asked the owner of Caribbean Cuts, Tom Weiss, in New York how he felt about importing flowers. He looked at me directly and said, "We are the second most eco-friendly business in the whole flower market. Compared to Dutch flowers, Asian flowers, California flowers, we have a lower carbon footprint than any of them."

He added "Plus, we work directly with farmers we know in Puerto Rico. We support people staying on their land, keeping it out of development. These are small farms, they don't use pesticides and grow different things. In my opinion, it's good to have a population earn money off of something easy to produce . . . . Tropical flowers in a tropical climate."

Despite all the benefits, Tom held up his hands in a shrug. "Still, only two percent of the trade on Twenty-eighth Street are tropicals."

Like utilitarianism, effective altruism aims to do the most good possible for others. It means, to quote Shankar Vedantam, looking at "evidence and reason as opposed to doing what feels good or is intuitively appealing."[204]

A recent study in the journal *Nature Cities* notes that backyard gardens often have higher carbon footprints than adjacent farms.[205] How so? For one, infrastructure: raised beds built of timber or metal, hardscaping with concrete, landscape fabric, gravel, transported stone, paving with bricks, installing irrigation, building trellising, installing lighting, buying pots, building greenhouses or plastic tunnels, buying tools, erecting fencing, etc. Then trucking in soil, using potable water for growing, laying turf, cutting grass, and sashaying over to the garden center for vegetable starts, soil amendments, and basket-fillers. I could go on (having done it all).

The study weighed these inputs and looked at the production of food in urban environments in the UK, Germany, United States, France, and Poland and found that urban farms, such as allotments or community gardens, were far more climate friendly than individual backyard gardens. Even better than both were the traditional farms, scaled up, who delivered the most-climate-friendly fruits and vegetables. Cut-flower farming is similar. When next tempted to build a raised bed, go to the farmers market.

We know gardening is good for us, mentally, emotionally, and in the case of collective urban gardens, socially too. Gardening feels good, but when hobby gardens have a carbon cost six times that of conventional agriculture?[206] Utilitarianism reminds us that we should consider the greater good.

1 A work by the New Zealand designer and photographer Emma Bass.

Value

Rip-offs and Restitution

> Our view on what is valuable has been twisted by our sense of what is profitable.
>
> —MARK CARNEY

On Friday the 13th of March 2020, the global floral industry collapsed. I was teaching at the New York Botanical Garden and not thinking of flowers at the time: I was frightened of a new disease sweeping the globe, self-focused, and grieving the loss of the tour for my first book, *Cultivated: The Elements of Floral Style*, including a book party in London and a workshop I was supposed to lead in France. Worse still: I wouldn't be seeing my only child in the UK. Having been told by my prime minister to go home because of a pandemic, I did. My situation at the dawn of the pandemic was challenging but not tragic; I had the means to fly home to Canada.

During the months that followed, we all learned to live with less. Empty store shelves and closed businesses impacted consumption. Supply chains spasmed and contracted, and many recognized the importance of local farms and products. Ursula Gunther describes the impact on her floristry business this way: "In Washington DC, wholesalers closed for six weeks. When they did open, we had one flight a week instead of two or three. The wholesaler couldn't guarantee certain flowers given disruptions to the supply chain. We learned to sell a customer a palette, not a flower."

The pandemic changed what we ate and how we lived as well as also our relationship to flowers. Flowers speak to emotions, and most people report being happier when they're around. Yet while people were trapped at home, flower sales tanked, with houseplants outselling them by far. The oxygenating effect of foliage and the tending of another living thing helped people to get through lonely days.

But what was the impact of the pandemic on the flower growers in countries that had supplied the bouquets once shipped with a click? The cost of shipping plants and flowers initially increased by 400 percent. Flowers were dumped, cut and uncut, because they couldn't reach market. People were laid off.

Immigrant labor explains how tulips are cut and dahlias divided from the smallest boutique farm in Washington State to the vast flower production facilities of Southern California. In the Netherlands, labor isn't as cheaply bought, so flower growers use more machines than humans in flower production and distribution. But in Kenya, it's estimated that thirty thousand people in floriculture lost their jobs due to the pandemic, and forty thousand more were placed on leave.

A Kenyan woman working in floriculture makes about $79 per month, or about $2.60 a day—a poverty-level wage. Some estimates suggest a rose costing £5 in London might earn a Kenyan grower about five cents. The Sustainable Flowers Initiative at Coventry University refers to this discrepancy as "underpayment in the value chain."

Wages matter, but there's a deeper issue here too: the loss of land. Many African (and Colombian, Ecuadorian, and Costa Rican) farmworkers lost their access to land in the move toward industrial floriculture and wage-based plantation work. Land and livelihood are entwined, and the current landlessness of farmworkers in the global south echoes dark periods in history that seem to haunt global agriculture today.

Consider Jamaica in 1865, thirty-two years after the abolition of slave ownership in the British Empire. Jamaican rebels led an uprising to protest land inequality, widespread poverty, and the poll tax that was required to vote. While no longer formally enslaved, most Jamaicans lacked political rights and remained economically exploited. They wanted freedom and basic rights. A lack of freedom when no man owns you anymore? When you are no longer traded as chattel? These are the types of heinous questions the plantation owners might have asked.

To the rebels, freedom didn't mean subsisting as a wage laborer. Freedom meant land. Land to grow food. Land on which to grow one's wealth. So the Jamaican peasants wrote to Queen Victoria asking for land owned by the Crown. Britain's colonial governor of Jamaica, Edward Eyre, imposed martial law. The rebels were denied, they protested, and many were killed.

The current prime minister of Barbados, Mia Mottley, recently traced the connections between land dispossession and colonization: "The underdevelopment of Africa, . . . of the Caribbean, . . . of Latin America, in many instances, is a child of the colonial experiment, and the colonial experiment extracted wealth . . . . We haven't been able to build the kind of domestic enterprises and the domestic foundation that's necessary to sustain our people."[207]

Once slavery was abolished in England, the country continued to use slave-grown American cotton to grow wealth through the textile industry. As David Olusoga notes, "Much of the cotton that was spun, woven, dyed, processed and traded in Manchester was produced by the almost 2 million enslaved Africans who lived, worked and suffered on cotton plantations in the southern United States."[208] It makes you wonder: are flowers so different now?

Today about 30 percent of England is owned by the aristocracy and gentry who, over three hundred years and five thousand inclosure acts, appropriated land that was once held in common by the people of Britain. Many in this aristocracy can trace their ancestry (and wealth) back to foreign plantations and slave ownership. One is Richard Drax, a Conservative MP in England, whose family owns a former plantation in Barbados where sugar is still grown. Drax's family, and that of the former Prime Minister David Cameron, who received funds from British taxpayers through the Slavery Abolition Act. What? Yes, after the abolition of slavery, the slaves were not compensated—their owners were. You read that right: Cameron's great grand-uncle was paid roughly about £3 million in today's money for the 202 slaves he forfeited in Jamaica. The amount of money the government borrowed to pay these slaveowners was so large (about £300 billion in today's currency), it wasn't paid off until 2015. In the words of Kris Manjapra, a professor of history and global studies at Northeastern University, "Generations of Britons have been implicated in a legacy of financial support for one of the world's most egregious crimes against humanity."

Today Caribbean nations are rightfully calling for reparations. As the English MP Dawn Butler recently said in the House of Commons, "There has been precedent for reparation. It has just been paid to the wrong people."[209]

2

1 As our world urbanizes, access to nature diminishes. Flowers represent a connection to the earth.

2 A worker at the Dutch rose farm Afriflora Sher in Naivasha, Kenya.

Wired

Manipulating Flowers

"You must come see the stephanotis," my friend's ninety-year-old mother said. "As soon as you can."

> # Art, like morality, consists in drawing the line somewhere.
>
> —G. K. CHESTERTON

I was grateful for the invitation—a cold and grey day, with not a hint of the tropics in my garden. I knew her stephanotis grew in a room built from three walls of single-paned mullioned glass. A beautiful room overlooking the ocean, it was tacked on to the old basement as a kind of sunroom that she—in every season of the year—used as a bedroom. A child of the Great Depression, my friend's mother knitted hot-water-bottle cozies and reused her bathwater in the washing machine. The scent of the basement was often earthy—bedrock protruded from one corner of the space. The day I visited though, the basement was filled with the sweetness of a hundred white flowers in bloom. Vines wrapped around the ceiling, twenty, no, thirty feet long.

"When I'm old, I want to lie in bed and have them all around me." She pointed up at a stretch of new growth soon to close the circle. "Only a bit more to go."

Recently, I heard Rebecca Stott read an essay she titled "On Not Finishing" in which she writes of visiting an elderly friend who keeps fabric samples about for curtains yet to be made and paint chips for potential redecorations. My friend's mother is the same: for ten years, a slip of Morris wallpaper might hang or a plant stand linger in need of reparation. In the essay, Stott reflects on the sculptures Michelangelo left unfinished, the bodies emerging from marble, and says, "Perhaps Michelangelo wanted to remind us that we are always hauling ourselves into being. That *we* will never be finished."

If you don't know stephanotis, it's a tropical plant also known as Madagascar jasmine (*Marsdenia floribunda*). The scent of hundreds in a small space was intoxicating. My friend said with a smile, "It could explain my cough."

Like many white flowers, the scent is used by the plant as lure for moths. Once popular in wedding bouquets, it is less commonly seen now given that individual blooms require wiring. Jacqueline Kennedy's 1953 bouquet of gardenias and orchids included a small cascade of trailing stephanotis. In 1981, Diana Spencer went all out with her forty-two-inch-long bouquet built from gardenias, roses, freesias, and wired stephanotis.

If you're working with stephanotis flowers, treat them like gardenias and handle delicately. Recut the stems and place in tepid water for half an hour before beginning wiring work. If you've harvested them yourself, sear the stems in a flame for fifteen seconds to seal them and immediately put in cold water to hydrate. Keep them damp in a cooler. They should last about three days.

When working with stephanotis, keep a mister handy and your hands damp while touching the flowers. Stephanotis blossoms are hollow once you separate the calyx from the flower (it easily pops off). You may choose to keep the calyx on as well. Depending on the work you're doing, a 22-gauge wire should suffice, but you can also use a rose wire if you need something lighter-weight for a hairpiece.

Make a loop of wire and place a tiny ball of dampened tissue at the peak of the arc. This will help hydrate the flower, but it will need to be small enough to fit down the neck of the flower. Tape the wires with stretchy floral tape and thread on the blooms.

2

1 An X-ray of stephanotis flowers.

2 Jacqueline Lee Bouvier married John F. Kennedy in 1953. Her bouquet featured wired orchids, gardenias, and stephanotis.

Woke

Do What You Can Do

Do not be overwhelmed.

—WANGARI MAATHAI

Writing this book has exposed me to some hard truths. Compounding the stress, two massive environmental upheavals directly affected my life and no doubt yours: the COVID-19 pandemic and climate change.

Climate change where I live in Canada looks like heat domes, smoke, and fires. These horrors can't all be blamed solely on climate change; poor forestry practices, clear-cutting, road building, and single species plantations have led to increased burns, landslides, and toxic smoke. Seven years ago, we had only a handful apocalyptic days—now, red suns, haze, outdoor masks, air filters, and Air Quality Index (AQI) reports have become a part of summer.

And what does that feel like, to lose the world as you knew it? Devastating, as many Indigenous and displaced people know too well. Terry Tempest Williams had this to say in 1995: "Confronted with the knowledge of dozens of apparently random disasters each day, what can a human heart do but slam its doors? No mortal can grieve that much. We didn't evolve to cope with tragedy on a global scale."[210]

So how do you cope? I'm going to present a few ideas gleaned from an article I read when I was flailing around, trapped in my house on a smoky, sunny day. It's titled "Here's What You Can Do to Cope with Your Anxieties about Climate Change" and was written by Connie Chang, a Californian who migrated east then returned west to a burning state. Here's my take on her piece.

Accept the disorientation, the dread, the psychic torment, the angst, the grief. Don't push thoughts or emotions away, rather give them a set period of time to claim you as their own. As we scroll from one climate horror to the next we reinforce our angst without necessarily feeling it. Stop. Don't just confirm your thoughts; feel your emotions.

Try to process the emotions through art or any creative method that resonates for you. Some people have improved their mindset by grieving with the earth—walking barefoot, swimming, or writing a requiem for a dying glacier. Holding loss in your heart and mind while creating can help you process your emotions, as can breathing exercises or anything that helps you focus on the now.

Those are internal methods, but they lead me to an aside: in a previous life I had a newspaper column titled "Livin' the Life," which was largely a health column. I reviewed spa treatments (a great gig if you can get it), but also botanical wonders, obscure treatments, and books. One of the books I was drawn to review was *Self-Help Inc.: Makeover Culture in American Life* by the cultural critic Micki McGee. She argued the burgeoning self-help movement (this was 2005, three years before Gwyneth Paltrow's Goop) emphasized individual rather than social change. This is a huge topic—individualism—but suffice it to say it plays into climate change insofar as one of the ways you can ameliorate your pain and that of others is through political action. We are best served by serving the world, not ourselves.

As Chang writes, "If you had a neighbor that dumped oil on your property, for example, you'd file a complaint with your city council."[211] Having run for both my city council and my province's legislative assembly, let me tell you that actively doing something about the state of the planet was one of the happiest, most intense, and most energized periods in my life. So show up. The world is run by people who sit through long meetings, so speak up at them, call people to account, advocate, rage, protest, and engage. You can make change. And all the evidence supports the fact you'll feel more empowered if you try.

Still, if you feel frozen by the scale of the tragedies to come, you're not alone. The term for this is psychic numbing. When we ask ourselves, "Can I change the world today?," we'll likely come up with the answer "no." But if we ask ourselves, "Can I change one person's world today?," the answer is more likely to be "yes."

People get demotivated from helping people by the bad feelings they get when they realize there are others that they cannot help. The psychologist Paul Slovic suggests, "You should not be demotivated from doing what you can do by the fact you can't do it all. Do what you can do." Resist compassion fatigue by focusing on one story, one person, one species. Psychologists have proven this: focus not on statistical lives, but identifiable lives. The trick is one of scale.

1 Ruby Pluhar with her work for Slow Research Lab.

Xeric

Drought and Deluge

1

I'm sitting indoors during a squall, the kind that billows, blows, and gushes, delivering rain that erodes as much as flows. It strums at the windows, quieting the wind as if the volume of water it carries is too much for the air to bear.

When rain is in short supply, how it arrives matters. Topography, vegetation, soil structure, and infrastructure determine how water moves across the land. To borrow from my friend Erica Gies, in an age of drought and deluge, water matters more now than ever. We are learning that we control it at our peril.

The term xeric, in reference to habitats, means dry. It has given us the term xeriscaping, which generally refers to landscaping with drought-tolerant plants. This doesn't mean desert plants per se—it means plants that can tolerate periods of drought.

In Mediterranean climates—arid regions around the Mediterranean basin, in California, Western and southern Australia, western South Africa, and central Chile—plants are watered by winter rains. Many go dormant in summer.

Nature's ability to give freely—with little support or protection—is nearing an end. As ecosystems break down, their services do too.

—ERICA GIES

Plants from other arid regions, like parts of Australia, much of the Arabian peninsula and the deserts of Arizona and Mexico, grow in summer, watered by (sometimes scarce) summer rains and prefer (if not require) to be dry and dormant in winter.[212]

In places like San Diego, where xeriscaping is advocated to reduce dependence on imported water, the palette of plants is gradually changing in gardens, but I wondered what the landscape might look like without any imported water at all. I asked Jennifer Jewell from Cultivating Place, based in California, to imagine that future.

She wrote: "72 percent of San Diego's water is being extravagantly and expensively piped from the Colorado River into a region, which naturally receives on average a little over ten inches of rain a year. If you turned off that water what would happen? I imagine we would see two things: the desiccated skeletal remains of centuries of colonial garden plants (think lawn turf, eucalyptus, bougainvillea, mandevilla, agapanthus, citrus trees, even olive trees) skittering off into the surrounding ocean or rolling like tumbleweeds across the Great Basin and southwest."

Poor California. As Jewell said, much of the state is on liquid life support.

As I write this, Los Angeles is burning, again. The twenty-five thousand palms planted before the 1932 Olympics are aged, and the other forty thousand added by the New Deal's Works Progress Administration have been compared to Roman candles they're so volatile.[213] Neighborhoods are burning; hillsides, livelihoods, houses, schools, churches and synagogues. And the palms? Their fronds fly alight in the wind.

Inland in Palm Springs, residents have been advised to convert lawns to xeriscapes while date palms sit in puddles of irrigation water, conjuring the civic myth of a desert oasis. As Gary Paul Nabhan writes of the introduced date palms in California: "They are lucrative commodities in the landscape-nursery industry . . . sold by the foot, hauled by truck, and propped up in yards as if a motion picture studio were making an instant oasis movie right there."[214]

So what would California look like without imported palms?

According to Jewell, there would be a "grand reemergence and expansion of the gorgeous matrix of native coastal scrub chaparral. This ecosystem is characterized by brilliantly colored seasonal displays of ephemeral wildflowers. Communities of silvery salvias and artemisias would shimmer amidst mounding green forms of lilac-blue flowering ceanothus and early flowering manzanitas. Then later flowering coyote bush, and sunny summer encelias, would be interspersed with acid yellow to snow-white flowering buckwheats, among a great host of other biodiversity."

2

3

4

6

1 Olives, rosemary, and plumbago on Paxos, Greece.

2 Life outside Luxor, Egypt.

3 Hailing from Mexico, *Myrtillocactus* produces edible fruits known as *garambullos* in Spanish. Approximately 65 percent of Mexico is composed of dryland ecosystems, and about 50 percent of the plants in these areas are endemic.

4 Saguaro *(Carnegiea gigantea)* flowers generally open for less then twenty-four hours. They are primarily pollinated by lesser long-nosed bats and white-winged doves.

5 A stamp from Bolivia showing *Rebutia kruegeri*.

6 Palo Verde *(Parkinsonia florida)* is the state tree of Arizona. The tree photosynthesizes through its bark.

7 Property surrounded by desert, Rancho Mirage, California.

You

Shifting Baselines

> # If we want things to stay as they are, things will have to change.
>
> —GIUSEPPE DI LAMPEDUSA

My girlfriend has a cat, a big bruiser, who roams outside without a bell. "You shouldn't let him out," I told her. "He'll kill the birds."

"There aren't many birds," she replied.

Go figure. But why didn't she expect more birds? She lives on a beach. It felt like an intellectual impasse I couldn't frame or name until I read Erica Gies's book *Water Always Wins*. She writes, "Humans can't truly grasp how much we have degraded the natural world because our baseline—our concept of what's natural—shifts with every generation."[215]

The idea of shifting baselines comes from the marine biologist Daniel Pauly, who noted a kind of presentism at work in resource management, which skews our sense of what is sustainable. One arresting example I came across showed a series of sport-fishing catches in Key West. In the 1950s, the groupers hung taller than a man. In the '60s and '70s, the biggest fish were half the size. By the 80s, the groupers were gone and small snapper appeared. By the 2000s, the trophy fish were about a foot long.

As the world changes so does our perception of it. My girlfriend had done what many of us do: normalized our normal.

Another example: a small urban park sits at the top of the hill I live on in Canada. It's gorgeous, a wild place with a wide view of the Strait of Juan de Fuca and the Olympic Mountains beyond. Rocky and rugged, it's miraculously iced with soil that holds the finest of our native flora. Each year, between patches of Garry oaks (*Quercus garryana*), the paths widen. Each year, more dogs tear up the earth that homed satinflowers (*Olsynium douglasii*), and each year more people and pets scrape licorice ferns and beautiful purple camas from the rock. And each year I write letters to my local council begging them for a leash law, a dog ban, fencing, reduced parking, any effort whatsoever that might protect what wildflowers are left. Many of the councillors do not know what the park looked like twenty years ago, let alone fifty years ago.

Of course, I don't know what this promontory looked like in 1920 or 1890 either. But I can cobble together an educated guess using historic images, the written records of explorers like David Douglas, and the tales of the Lekwungen people. I see through these lenses in addition to my own eyes. I see eagles and owls circling for a home and mourn for their loss.

Shifting baseline syndrome, aka environmental generational amnesia, has been studied throughout the world and from continent to continent.[216] Questions like, are droughts increasing? Is the climate less predictable? Are there fewer fish? Are your summers hotter? Has your water quality declined? Do you see fewer birds, frogs, or bees? From Africa to Asia, elders have noticed changes. But their grandchildren? Not so much.

So back to the cat. When domestic cats made way their way from Egypt to Europe, then farther afield over thousands of years, they slaughtered birds, mammals, and reptiles as they went. (E. O. Wilson once referred to such invasive species as "biological pollution.")[217] According to the Global Invasive Species Database, cats are in the top one hundred of the worst invasive species ever, contributing to over 25 percent of known extinctions. In Canada alone, it is estimated they kill two hundred million birds per year.

I later saw my cat friend again and didn't mention the birds. We were at a fundraiser for Oxfam, and after the talk and appeal, I sashayed over to the snacks. There I found a member of the local council, who you could say is paid to listen to zealots such as myself, so I started in on the park and the flowers. I pleaded emotionally. I appealed with statistics and reason. Finally, I said, "It's a case of shifting baselines. Soon no one will remember what we had. I'm talking heritage here." And knowing she was a mother, added, "How else can your kids know why this place is special?"

She nodded, perhaps getting it, perhaps not.

Have you no shame? I thought to myself, but I wasn't sure who I was speaking about.

1 Granadilla, *Passiflora quadrangularis.*

Zeitgeist

Ages of Environmentalism

Environmentalism without class struggle is just gardening.

—CHICO MENDES

The term zeitgeist usefully captures the ideas and spirit of a period in history. It's a German word, applicable to almost any cultural domain: a movie might reflect the zeitgeist of a historical moment, much like a garden can embody the beliefs and ideas of the gardener (embedded as they may be in a wider culture).

A quick flip through a gardening magazine today suggests that many of us are wondering how best to engage with the earth. An article on pollinators might be followed by a photo spread of outdoor kitchens, or a feature on bubble-gum pink hydrangeas might follow a piece about no-mow May. The same is true of books on plants: *Bushes for Birds* might be shelved with *Happy Houseplants* and *Ground Covers*.

It's a confusing time. Like gardening, environmentalism has undergone many changes over the course of its history in the West. When industrialization began to threaten ecosystems in the nineteenth century, pollution became a concern, and mass deforestation led to conservation movements that sought to protect natural areas. National parks began to appear—initially in Sweden in 1909, then later the vast networks of national parks in North America.

As an environmental studies undergraduate in the 1990s, I could easily enough define environmentalism at that time: it was a political movement, a philosophy, and ethical framework that put nature first. Students like me bumped up against the fact that the meaning of the word environment implied something out there, thus the environment was not always regarded as intrinsically human. Humans were sometimes included in nature but also treated as a threat to it. This conservation-focused environmentalism led to the removal of Indigenous people from land and lately has led to the tragic situation of approximately twenty-two thousand Maasai, who have been relocated (evicted) from their land by the Tanzanian government to support the conservation of charismatic megafauna for safari tourism despite the fact that Maasai helped shape the very landscape where those lions and giraffes live. Stolen land has been long been called wilderness, a term that too often obscures the people who created and managed landscapes for millennia.

New environmental terminologies have thankfully sprung up (to fit the zeitgeist of our time). One to highlight is eco-imperialism, which refers to the spread of pathogens, plants, and animals during the ages of exploration and colonization. More contemporaneously, it also conveys how some environmentalists impose their views on lower-income countries, for example when people in the global north are appalled that Brazil is destroying diverse ecosystems for cattle and soy production, and yet they continue to create the demand for pet food and leather.

On an economic scale, green imperialism might involve an environmental agenda being imposed upon a country in the global south by the global north. Here's how Mia Mottley, prime minister of Barbados, addressed this issue in the context of climate: "Now when our blood, sweat and tears finances the industrial revolution and the industrial revolution then causes the climate crisis and then I have to pay for the consequences of the climate crisis because of the industrial revolution, which was financed by our blood sweat and tears . . . I think they have no moral authority to tell me anything."[218]

Today we have various schools of thought under the umbrella of environmentalism, including the animal-rights and liberation movements, deep ecology, and ecofeminism to name a few. What these concepts share is a belief in the value of nonhuman nature and our moral obligation to protect species other than our own.

1 *Fockea edulis* is native to the Cape Provinces and KwaZulu-Natal in South Africa. The Khoi call it !Koo, !Ku, or !Kuu. The bulbous base (caudex) is edible.

Afterword

My son posed for me in Zanzibar's Stone Town with a backpack on and a squint in his eyes.

Like a spent journalist, he slumped in a dirty ballcap, world-weary, aged eight, against a limewashed wall in a narrow lane that opened to a market behind him.

"Do we have to?"

His voice had grown thick in the heat, his plea a grunt. Nothing could impress him. Not the Arabesque architecture or ancient doors, not brass genie lamps or animal carvings, not even the fact that he was standing in a UNESCO World Heritage Site. At that point in our trip, if an elephant had trumpeted, he may very well have yawned.

The two of us had been on a safari for a couple of weeks with my future husband's family. I'd reckoned Zanzibar should be on our way home, which it definitively was not, but after two weeks of bouncing around the savanna I wanted more plants—cultivated ones and spices in particular.

"C'mon we need to see the market."

"Not more duka duka . . . " he said. *Duka duka* means "shop" in Swahili. He'd learned the term near the Ngorongoro Crater—a conservation area where giraffes roamed and lions hunted, and the Maasai sold handicrafts on what I now know was once their land.

In Stone Town's Darajani Market, my senses soared at the sight of cloves drying in the sun and stalls piled with cinnamon bark, peppercorn, cardamom, and round nutmeg seeds laced with brilliant orange mace. We bought yellow turmeric roots sliced open by young men, their palms stained gold.

If memory is a hall of mirrors in which we look for glimpses of our past selves, what does that moment in Stone Town mean to me now? How little I knew.

My son's hesitancy might have taught me to pause. I knew the Portuguese had occupied Zanzibar, and I knew the British had made Zanzibar a protectorate. I knew various Arabic groups had been in Zanzibar, and most everyone was Muslim, but beyond that frittering of history, I only thought of the plants.

My son was tired, yes, but I wonder now if he was also uncomfortable with my acquisitiveness, the way I was hungry for experiences. As a parent, desire doubles down: I wanted him to experience things as much as I wanted to experience them myself. We're in Zanzibar! At a spice market! Once in a lifetime!

I yanked on his arm. Sweat beaded his temples. I reasoned he was tiring but not yet not expiring and so like a bitch dragging her puppy, I set out for a white building blackened by time and grime.

I'm making myself sound more adventurous than I was—alone in Zanzibar with a little boy? Truthfully, we had a guide that day, a petite man who had taken us around some farms and now was escorting us through the market.

Writing this today, I wonder about my obsession with plants. Why do people buy rare, poached plants? Desire. Why was Indonesian cinnamon traded in Zanzibar close to two thousand years ago? Because people wanted to taste it. And so I ask myself: if you were a gardener in fourteenth-century Naples and tasted black pepper for the first time, you'd likely try to grow it wouldn't you? If you learned such a thing as silk existed (spun from larvae that eat mulberry leaves, imagine that!), how could you resist it once your fingers had felt it? And what if you could acquire a tree that might feed your family? Breadfruit did just that.

As I marched toward the darkened building, I saw it was smaller inside than it appeared, narrow with a high ceiling and blackened stone stalls. Women wrapped in colorful burqas shopped under hanging rib racks. Tin plates of offal—hearts, kidneys, organ meats—sat on the counters dotted with flies. A dirty dog sniffed a wet spot on the concrete floor then looked up at a man with long knife poised over a goat's leg.

I have to wonder now if my young son had intuited the sufferings of Stone Town. For it wasn't just spices that supported trade in Zanzibar—it was slaves too. Thousands upon thousands of Bantu people were traded for hundreds of years practically where we were standing.

No one quite knows when the slave trade began in Zanzibar it was so long ago. Was it when the Arabs arrived in the seventh century? Likely. How many thousands were taken north by the Omani? How many boys my son's age, girls, women, and men were traded around the Indian Ocean, moved into the Red Sea? Later, when the Europeans came and stayed, and other Europeans came and stayed, how many thousands then? By the 1800s, when the island had been converted to clove and coconut plantations, two-thirds of Zanzibar's population was enslaved.

I did not know this then. Instead I pulled out my camera, my voyeurism almost entirely blind.

Steps from where we stood in Darajani Market is a sculptural installation buried at the site of Zanzibar's slave market. In it, five concrete figures stand buried at the thigh. Four are chained together, linked around the neck with iron collars; their arms unfree, their legs immobile, pillars sunk into the earth. One looks out, none up. The five naked figures stand in a square, a cell, cut into the ground. The piece is by Clara Sörnäs and called *Kumbukumbu Ya Historia Ya Watumwa/Memory for the Slaves*.

We didn't see it.

After the market, my son fell asleep in the van, his face pressed to the window as we traveled up to the northeast coast. I watched the scenery change from shanties to plantations and finally to beach, much of it littered with the blue plastic bags I'd used at the market. Nearing our inn, we bumped along a rough coral road, and he woke to children playing under rows of drying red seaweed, their coral-concrete houses pink in the sun.

Our afternoon blurred with heat, softening both of us. We snorkeled through turquoise water, hot in the shallows, and he could see farther underwater than ever before. He marveled at the fish, spat out exclamation points, "Blue! Did you see that?! Silver!"

Yes, but not with the same eyes.

I recognize that this book has been at times a sharp critique of capitalism and empire and at other times a kind of self-flagellation for all my years of not seeing, not knowing, not connecting the dots between plants and people. Wonder probably didn't feature enough in these pages, but it is what sustains me. We need knowledge, but I wish you wonder most of all.

Most of us open our eyes at some point in our lives and find ourselves in a place we never would have chosen if we'd been paying more attention along the way—a region of unlikeliness all the more disorienting because we have found it on our own, without anyone else to blame, propelled ourselves right into the maw of it by the force of our desires.

—BENJAMIN ANASTAS

Glossary

Abstraction

Popularly, an art movement born in the early twentieth century. The word signifies an artwork that might be complete and yet totally disassociated from an image of the world. Abstraction, like so many art movements, was and is influenced by societal forces such as advances in science and technology.

Abstract artists often put the emphasis on their materials in order to evoke emotion. In floral design, man-made materials or natural ones may be used unrealistically in order to highlight line, form, color, or texture. Similarly, an abstract painter might emphasize the flatness of the canvas rather than conjure an illusion of the world.

Adventitious

This word speaks of growth, of opportunity, of taking advantage of a situation to create roots, gather strength, and lift yourself up. And this, loosely, is the botanical meaning too. An adventitious root is a clever one: snaking out from the base of a stem (on a corn plant or a palm) or hugging a tree's limb (in orchids and monsteras).

Aesthetic

Many Americans might spell this word without the A, but loosely the meaning of aesthetic/esthetic is the same: the words reference a study or philosophy of the nature of beauty. Aesthetics run deep, not only in history, but in terms of culture as well. We might speak of "a certain aesthetic" today, meaning a style or approach, and often add a modifier to denote an association, such as a bohemian aesthetic or modernist aesthetic. To me, the word has greater resonance if you consider its association with the idea of taste, which pivots on the idea of judgment. We look at art, floral design, or a garden and respond critically. This is an aesthetic response; there's no correct answer other than the one we find within ourselves. Biases are rife and our own.

Agroforestry

In the *conuco* gardens of Haiti, castor bean, manioc, maize, and papayas grow above sweet potatoes and beans. Implying a kind of multistory growing of plants, agroforestry alludes to the intercropping of food and flowers with trees and shrubs and is often considered one of the pillars of regenerative agriculture. Java has the highest density of forest gardens, which are known as *pekarangans*. These include everything from tree fruits to perennial spices, annual vegetables, medicinal plants, ornamentals, and occasionally animals. It is estimated that the Javanese eat more than five hundred varieties of plants, with an average village growing about 250 types of plants in neighborhood pekarangans.

Annual

A plant that completes its life cycle in a year.

Anthesis

The period during which a flower is open and functional.

Art Nouveau

A Western art movement that arose in the late 1800s and attempted to blur the distinction between the fine arts and the applied arts. Using glass, metal, ceramics, and textiles, among other things, designers created decorative works with sinuous lines. Plants and flowers, among other organic forms, both guided designs and formed motifs. At the outbreak of World War I, Art Nouveau was usurped by the later decorative and architectural styles of Art Deco and Modernism.

Avant-garde

An art term related to the word vanguard (a military term meaning roughly "in advance"), avant-garde refers to work that questions prevailing values. The term was popularized in France around the time of the Post-Impressionists. Some argue that the term is a bit vacuous now, given its overuse, but in floral design, I think the avant-garde might refer to any work that challenges ideas of beauty and value.

The cultural critic Louis Menand argues that terms like highbrow and avant-garde are designed to distinguish the pleasing and edifying from the mass of cultural products.

Binomial

When plant people say "the binomial is . . . " they are about to say the Latin genus and species. Think: two names.

Biome

A group of ecosystems that share a similar climate and types of organisms.

Bloom

While the flower of a plant can be a referred to as a bloom, this term also refers to a naturally occurring fine, waxy powder coating often found stems, leaves, and fruits.

Bract

A showy modified leaf often shaped like a petal and highly colored to attract pollinators to small flowers. Examples include bougainvillea, poinsettia, achmea, and other bromeliads.

Decoloniality (and other helpful terms)

Decoloniality aims to delink our present structures of knowledge and power in order to create new ones. By contrast, anticolonialism resists colonial structures but does not necessarily strive to create wholly new structures. Neocolonialism is also centered on power but generally refers to processes by which external power in economics, politics, and culture is exercised over former colonies by other nation-states or private actors such as corporations.

Determinate/Indeterminate

In biology, these words speak to growth. For example, we don't grow on indeterminately throughout our lives but rather reach maturity and stop growing. A plant that stops growing once the central stem ends in a flower is determinate. The lateral buds may bloom, such as in jasmine and bougainvillea, but the oldest flower is usually at the end of a branch or the top of the plant. Indeterminate plants keep growing if they have the resources to do so, whether flowering or not. Many people encounter these terms in regards to tomatoes with bush varieties remaining low (determinate) and vining styles indeterminate (and fruiting for a longer period). One easy way to ascertain determinacy is to note the direction of bloom: if the florets open from the top down the flower is determinate; from the bottom up, indeterminate, as in celosia and the royal poinciana.

Dicot/Monocot

Technically dicotyledons and monocotyledons, these words refer to the two classes of flowering plants. Cotyledons are the tiny seed leaves produced by an embryo. Monocots have a single cotyledon and dicots two. Other differentiations exist, such as the number of flower parts. Monocots have flower parts in multiples of three; dicots in multiples of four or five. Palms and arums are monocotyledonous and have roots that arise adventitiously from nodes in the stem. In palms, these roots are called prop roots and are easy to see when clustered near the base of the stem. In dicots and most seed plants, the root emerges from a region called a radicle. Monocots have radicles too, but they are aborted and the plant produces new roots where needed.

Dioecious

A botanical term that refers to species that bear male and female flowers on the same plant, e.g., begonia.

Endemic

In botany, endemic is used to describe a plant whose distribution is limited to a particular geographical region. For example, *Genista stenopetala*, a showy yellow-flowering shrub in the pea family (also known as sweet broom), is endemic to the Canary Islands of Spain. An endemic naturally occurs in an area but is not necessarily confined to it. Brazil and China have the greatest number of endemic plant species in the world.

Enfleurage

A traditional method of capturing the scent of flowers in oil or fat. The process is labor intensive and can be done cold by simply placing and replacing flowers in the fat, or the flowers can be macerated and stirred into melted fat. Levels of saturation can be tweaked depending on how many flowers are used and how often the process is repeated. Enfleurage has been used since ancient times in Tahiti for gardenias and historically in France for jasmine and tuberose.

Epiphyte

Epiphytes make up about 10 percent of all plant species. They are often anchored to other plants and obtain moisture and nutrients from rain, fog, or mist, though some also live on seaweeds, and others obtain nutrients leached from leaves or decaying matter. Unlike parasitic plants, epiphytes don't feed off their host.

Schlumbergera, the ever-popular Christmas cactus, grows on rocks and trees in the Atlantic rainforest region of Brazil as an epiphyte. Other familiar examples include orchids, air plants, and Spanish moss. Epiphytes make good houseplants because they tolerate periods of drought and filtered light given their habitat preference for warm subtropical and tropical forests. There are more than thirty thousand types of epiphytes in the world.

Essentialism

The view that there are certain properties that define what something is. Used today, it might refer to identity or gender, or to ascribing a set of attributes or characteristics to group of people (that are considered essential to their categorization). For example, a cultural essentialist might say all Thai people love flowers. Populists might imagine a mythical national unity based on an essentialized identity linking ethnicity and culture. Essentialism is often reductive.

Ethnobotany

A broad field focusing on the study of the relationships and interactions between plants and cultures. An ethnobotanist might work in archaeology, categorize plants linguistically, study floral displays in graveyards, report on land management practices, or work with Indigenous people. The list of research areas is almost endless and inspiring.

Ethnocentric

When we judge other cultures based upon the mores and values of our own—be they subcultures in our own country or those of foreign places—we center our opinion on perception and risk being biased. For example, one florist may look at the work of another one of a different class or nationality and ask: how could anyone consider that beautiful? Likely such a questioner is looking through an ethnocentric lens.

Eugenics

Did you learn about Gregor Mendel and his peas when you studied genetics in biology class? I did, but sadly, I didn't learn about eugenics—the idea of improving humans through selective breeding. Eugenics became popular at the turn of the twentieth century, when researchers looked for traits to build a superior race of human beings (and concomitantly, when immigration tensions were also high, and racist policies by governments were developed). In the United States, this led to forced sterilizations of those deemed unfit, the Chinese Exclusion Act, and the teaching of Madison Grant's *The Passing of Great Race* on college campuses. While the eugenics movement helped to pave the way for demagogues such as Hitler to undertake the genocide of six million Jews, the ideas linger in various forms and across cultures.

One famous illustrator, Ernst Haeckel, whose images in *Kunstformen der Natur* (1889) formed a kind of ordered catalog of ecological and microscopic wonders, has been called an eager eugenicist and social Darwinist for his belief that systematically killing the disabled would advance human evolution. Taschen made a book of his work, and you can find his illustrations on everything from posters to fabrics to mugs today.

Euphemism

A term developed to replace a harsh or politically difficult one or to obfuscate meaning. For example, in speaking euphemistically, a dump might be renamed a landfill or we may soften death by saying someone passed away. In many parts of the world, the harvesting of trees would be more accurately described as the clear-cutting of forests.

Eco-linguists study how language shapes our understanding of environmental problems. We might try to mitigate the hazards of modern life by using the words climate change instead of climate crisis, or a florist might dispose of plastic sleeves by throwing them away when of course there is no away—there are terrestrial and marine environments where the sleeves will persist before becoming microplastics consumed by animals.

Throughout history you can see how euphemisms reflect politics and cultural change. For example, in Britain, the Council of Foreign Plantations of the seventeenth century transformed into the Colonial Office in the eighteenth century, then later still became the Ministry of Overseas Development. Similarly, the *American Journal of Race Development* became the *Journal International Relations* and finally the journal *Foreign Affairs* in 1922, a name still in use today.

Exonym

In the words of Peter Jordan, who prepared a paper on exonyms for the UN, "Exonyms are all but politically innocent." So why is this important to our understanding of flowers? Place matters to plants. And as you learned about endonyms, local names often reveal uses, locations, characteristics, and relationships.

So what's complicated about exonyms? Consider the term Tonkinese creeper. It reveals nothing about the fact the plant is grown as a vegetable in Thailand known as *ho thien ly*. It tells us there was a creeping vine at the time when the French colonized Vietnam, called that country Tonkin, and that one plant out of countless creepers was considered *the* Tonkinese creeper.

Exonyms, words that were created outside of that place to refer to it, might signal a historical period (e.g., Ceylon, which is the colonial name for Sri Lanka). So don't be afraid to ask questions of names and press on the English exonym—likely there's a story about power embedded in the name of a plant.

Flora

Plants of a defined geographical area, be it a country, region, or habitat. A flora can also refer to a record or publication concerning plants of a certain place. If such a flora is illustrated, it might be referred to as a florilegium.

Floral Colonization

When industrialized countries use the genetic material of wild species from other countries for profit (such as in the horticultural sector or floral trade) with no reimbursement to the country of origin, floral colonization takes place. With 83 percent of the commercial flora in the United States being of foreign origin, the issue is an important if hidden one, dramatically affecting very botanically diverse countries such as South Africa.

Glaucous

Plants with waxy coatings that appear greyish or bluish are often referred to as glaucous. The word is an adjective used to describe the appearance of plants, birds, the sea, or even the eyes. Coming from ancient Greek, at times the word has referred to reflectivity or paleness.

Greenwashing

When companies, businesses, or individuals make claims of being environmentally friendly while cloaking misdeeds or obfuscating their true environmental impact, it's called greenwashing.

Habit

In reference to plants, the manner in which something grows.

Hydration Chamber

Leaves and flowers that lack a water source, or a stem to access one, benefit from hydration prior to design work. A hydration chamber, which can be as simple as a tote or box with damp paper towel inside, creates an airtight and humid environment that allows petals and leaves to rehydrate after harvest and hold before use. Refrigeration is an option for many (but not all) flowers, and just like revitalizing bagged, tired lettuce in the fridge, hydration chambers can work wonders for perking up and storing flowers.

Infructescence

If an inflorescence refers to the arrangement of flowers on a plant, an infructescence is the correct way to describe those flowers once they become berries or fruit. Fruits develop from the ovaries of flowers, and they serve many purposes for plants, including attracting animals who disperse their seeds and adding organic matter to the soil for the plant's growth. What's interesting about this term is it refers to aggregates and makes us think about the array of flowers involved in a bunch of grapes or a pineapple. While we may not use the term often, it's the correct way to speak of a collection of a palm's fruit (such as dates) or the beautiful fruiting structures borne by pandanus.

Kenzan

Japanese devices used to support flowers, *kenzans* may also be known as pin frogs, flower frogs, or needlepoint holders. Made of metal, these heavy, spiked devices can be affixed to the base of a vessel with putty or used with other mechanics. In Japan, kenzans are associated with ikebana, particularly the *moribana* tradition.

Materialism

On first glance, this word conjures up the adjective materialistic, a word we might ascribe to an acquisitive person. And materialism isn't too far off, particularly in the context of early modern science when the objectification of nature led to the collection, extraction, and commodification of plants. This way of understanding obscured other forms of knowledge and understanding.

Meme

Forget social media for a moment. Memes are units of memorable cultural information. They're a culture's building blocks. Unlike genes, they have no biological basis, but are passed on to us by our parents, family, friends, and the people around us. Memes are retained or disappear according to how adaptive they prove to a culture.

Mericlone

Ever wonder why there's an almost identical moth orchid in every office? They're mericlones, grown from meristem culture. Most gardeners understand what a growing tip is, but at the cellular level there are regions of actively dividing cells known as meristems found on a plant's roots and shoots. In researching phalaenopsis cultivation, I came across the term mericlone, which refers to a plant grown from a minute scraping of meristem cells in vitro in a lab. Meristem culture forever changed horticulture in the 1960s. Today mericlones are created and grown inexpensively in labs (usually in Asia) then shipped to Europe and the United States to be "locally grown."

Mise en Valeur

A nineteenth-century term developed in France in order to highlight the benefits of enhancement, aka industrialization, implying the modernization of holdings (be they small French farms or colonies). The idea was to enhance productivity without expanding the scope of the empire.

Monotypic

In botany, a term used to denote that a plant is the only one of a taxonomic group. Some examples include the familiar castor bean, *Ricinus communis*, which is the only species in the genus *Ricinus* (despite there being a number of cultivars). Similarly, *Nandina domestica* is the only species in the genus *Nandina*.

Naïve Art

Artists who lack formal training or education have been said to make naïve art. In 1893, the plant scientist and agroecologist George Washington Carver entered a painting at the Chicago World's Fair titled *Yucca and Cactus*. The work is large-scale, bold, beautiful, and very much in the manner of the French Fauvists (who were contemporaneously painting in that style). Carver, the child of slaves in Missouri, would go on to become the first Black student at Iowa State University and later its first Black faculty member. Later still in Alabama, he would continue to research farming, working with cotton farmers on soil restoration and encouraging Black farmers to grow sweet potatoes and peanuts as a sustainable food source. In between all of this he painted spectacular flowers. (Note: a trained artist who imitates a naïve style is often referred to as a primitivist—see Primitivism.)

Nativar

A native plant which has been tweaked for better garden performance is colloquially known as a nativar. Another way to think of a nativar is as a hybrid with native parentage. A nativar does not offer indigenous wildlife the same benefits as native plants.

Neotropical

Referencing the colonial idea of the New World, this term is used to denote a biogeographic region centered in Mexico and extending north and south into the Americas.

Non-Timber Forest Product (NTFP)

For a long time, many didn't see the forest for the trees, placing more value on the wood or timber extracted from a forest than on the forest as a whole. Timber (often a convenient euphemism for old-growth trees) extraction destroys habitat for plant and animal species and threatens the local lifeways and economies of human communities. Non-timber forest products are as wide-ranging as maple syrup, rubber tree latex, culinary mushrooms, rattan, medicinal barks, tree fruits, cut foliage, and nuts. NTFPs have helped provide economic and social arguments for keeping forests intact in the face of industry and government pressure.

Open- and Closed-Form

These are floral design terms which are used in reference to an arrangement's shape. Closed-form designs have a clean outline and may resemble geometric forms such as triangles or circles, whereas open-form arrangements use negative space or voids in the work.

Parachute Science

When botanists from higher-income countries drop in to lower-income ones and conduct research in communities without consultation, it is known as parachute science.

Patents

What if a plant doesn't have a genus or a species listed on its tag? Many modern plants at the garden center do not. Let's use petunias for an example. Petunia breeding is done in laboratories, allowing technicians to use genes from other genera to bring new characteristics to popular plants. Take *Calibrachoa*, which hails from scrubby South American grasslands. Its trailing habit has helped petunias cover new terrain today, spilling from everything from hanging baskets to window boxes.

In the United States alone more than seven hundred patents have been granted for petunias. Say you see the name SUPERTUNIA VISTA® Snowdrift™ on a tag. What does it mean? Plant breeders' rights have been established. The capitalized name SUPERTUNIA tells us this is a series or a group of plants that have new and shared characteristics, in this case a growth pattern that's suitable for hanging baskets given a low root volume and high flower counts. (The flowers are sterile, so the plant is propagated vegetatively.) The ® symbol signifies the marketing name is also a registered trademark. SUPERTUNIA VISTA® is a series that spreads more than SUPERTUNIA, hence the VISTA. The name Snowdrift is the cultivar, which in this case is trademarked.

Countries vary in terms of systems of oversight for plant breeding, but generally we can look to the criteria set by the International Union for the Protection of New Varieties of Plants (UPOV) for guidance on what is a variety. So what is a variety that might be protected, patented, traded, trademarked, or registered? According to the UPOV:

1. A variety is a plant grouping within a single botanical taxon of the lowest rank.
2. The grouping is defined by the expression of characteristics resulting from a given genotype (i.e., a clone, line, F1 hybrid) or a combination of genotypes (from a complex hybrid or synthetic variety).

3 The plant grouping should be distinguishable from any other plant grouping by the expression of at least one characteristic and be suitable for being propagated unchanged.

It is important to note that most patented seeds can't be saved, replanted, shared, or used for research without permission. By contrast, open-source seeds are free of intellectual property restrictions.

Permaculture

In short, it is a systems-based approach to agriculture and place-based habitation that creates a kind of cultivated ecology. To quote from Bill Mollison, who coined the term: "Permaculture is the conscious design and maintenance of agriculturally productive ecosystems which have the diversity, stability, and resilience of natural ecosystems." Bring it on.

Picotee

A floral term used to describe petals edged with a second color.

Political Ecology

A transdisciplinary academic field developed in the 1970s, political ecology addresses the social, political, and economic ideas and issues that shape environmental problems. For example, an ecologist might look at how algae growth from fertilizer use on flower farms might impact wildlife in African watering holes, whereas a political ecologist might look at that issue in terms of the forces that led to the problem. They might ask: what economic and political relationships led to the development of agriculture in the region? How does agricultural pollution impact not only wildlife but the communities nearby? Who holds the power in such land use decisions? Who is benefiting economically? What communities need to be consulted in order to effect change?

Polyculture

Most natural habitats are polycultures. Prairie and savanna ecosystems, for example, include predators, prey, shrubs, perennials, and grasses. Polycultures are the future. Whereas plowing land releases carbon, polycultures mean reduced water use, reduced nutrient runoff, and reduced pesticide use.

Primitivism

When Paul Gauguin, disenchanted by an increasingly industrialized world, moved to Tahiti in 1891 and Picasso fell under the influence of African art in 1906 (and both sought to paint what they saw—either through Expressionism or Cubism respectively), the art world grappled to find a term for their influences and styles. The term primitivism was created to refer to the fascination (and appropriation) of Western artists with non-Western art, or any art that was considered precivilized—be it prehistoric or tribal. These European artists were responding to globalization (and a restrictive art scene in Paris). A nostalgia arose for "the state of nature." Thus primitivism is associated with the natural as opposed the artificial and with the uninhibited as opposed to the controlled. Because of the derogatory connotations of the word primitive, today the word is often held in quotes.

Salvage

When harvesting plants growing in the wild, salvage refers to the removal of plants from an area that is to be destroyed or developed. One example would be collecting from areas slated for construction. In some jurisdictions, like Australia, approval for salvage must be sought from authorities before collecting plants.

Senescence

The moment your bloom shows a touch of browning it has begun to senesce. So much softer than rot or degrade, the word senescence means to gradually deteriorate in accordance with the biological process of aging.

Series

In reference to flowers, a series is a group of cultivars marketed under one commercial name. For example, the gerbera daisies 'Fireworx Mini', 'Piccolini', and 'Pomponi' are trademarked names developed by breeders to cover a series of related cultivars. In the series 'Piccolini' there are nineteen named cultivars.

Skeletonization

In Victorian times, phantom bouquets were made from skeletonized leaves. Techniques varied depending on the type of leaf. For example, magnolia leaves were left to soak for six weeks outdoors, then rubbed of their flesh until only a tracing of veins remained. Today skeletonized leaves are available, but do consider that they have been bleached with hypochlorite, peroxide, and hydrosulfite, then treated to control yellowing potentially with aluminum sulfate or calcium hydroxide, and treated again with sulfur dioxide to remove the chemical smell, and finally sprayed with a light plastic coating. Better to buy a bucket and soft toothbrush and skeleteonize your own.

Here's a speedier method than the vat rot method as outlined in the 1863 book *The Phantom Bouquet: A Popular Treatise on the Art of Skeletonizing Leaves*. Again, thick, waxy, robust leaves like those of magnolia, sea grape, jackfruit, and gardenia work best. You'll have to experiment with these principles and scale the recipe up as needed.

1. In a large pot, cover a handful of leaves with water and at least a half cup of calcium carbonate (washing soda, not baking soda). The idea here is to disintegrate the soft tissue from the leaf.
2. Boil, then simmer ninety minutes in a well-ventilated space.
3. Let cool and use gloves to extract the leaves.
4. Brush the pulp from the veins using a soft toothbrush or a stiff hog-bristle paintbrush.
5. Set to dry.

Slacktivism

A modern term used to denote a passive form of engagement with a cause in a which a person does very little (e.g., likes a post or uses a hashtag) and delivers very little to that cause in terms of effort or commitment. Slacktivism is linked to virtue signaling in that we gain a reputational benefit through such actions online and also feel good about ourselves despite doing little in real terms.

Spathe/Spadix

In philodendrons and other plants of the *Araceae*, a hoodlike spathe protects the tiny flowers that grow up the spikelike spadix. In anthuriums, breeders have developed colorful spathes and spadices (if you were wondering how to pluralize spadix, this sentence is for you).

Taxonomy

The Greek word *taxis* meaning "order" or "arrangement" gives us this term. For our purposes, taxonomy is a branch of botany interested in the classification and organization of things with shared characteristics. Many of us use Linnaean taxonomy today, citing a plant's family, genus, and species in that order. The system is now regulated by an international committee but was first proposed in 1735 by Carl Linnaeus, a Swedish botanist. Some evolutionary biologists (from the time of Charles Darwin on forward) feel the system is outdated—essentialist and creationist, given its emphasis on ranking and hierarchies. In Indigenous cultures, plants are often named relationally or even kintrinsically—emphasizing relations to other plants, locations, people, and phenomena.

Traditional Ecological Knowledge (TEK)

Perhaps you know what it is to feel at home in the world. To know when the sun rises and sets, the names of local birds, and when to plant seeds. This is ecological knowledge. Traditional ecological knowledge has been recognized by Fikret Berkes as a "knowledge-practice-belief complex." It honors Indigenous knowledge, the sustainable use of resources, and the ecological practices employed by communities with "historical continuity of resource use on a particular land."

Throughout the world, people have shaped landscapes. People have wild harvested, burned, selected, and encouraged plants to grow. In some cultures, the idea of wilderness—as a landscape untouched and unmanaged—is viewed negatively, particularly where humans are considered a part of the natural world.

The US Fish and Wildlife Service honored TEK by transitioning some land management in Montana back to the Confederated Salish and Kootenai tribes.

It's important to note that looking at TEK as a future savior of ecosystems and societies in the face of climate change while still living with (and in) extractive economies and exploitative systems runs the risk of repeating the colonial narrative. It should not be assumed that Indigenous knowledge or land can be used to ensure a stable future for humanity.

Temperate

If you garden between 35 and 66 degrees north or south of the equator, you're a temperate gardener. You experience seasonal variations in climate not as intensely as polar regions but more dramatically than subtropical areas. Your plants will likely experience a killing frost.

Tropism

When environmental factors shape the direction of growth in plants it's called tropism. Plant growth is regulated by hormones, one group of which is known as auxins. When we pinch back a plant to force it to grow laterally, we are eliminating auxins in one area and supporting cell elongation in another. When a plant leans away from darkness or faces east in the morning, it is responding to the environmental factor of light, so the action is called phototropism. When the roots of an upside-down plant head toward the ground or a branch of a tree curves in response to gravity, the term to use is geotropism.

Variegated

Plants that exhibit different colors have long been prized by gardeners. Geraniums with different colored zones on leaves, begonias with silver blistering, or tropical plants with white or yellow areas are often propagated to offer us novelty. Variegation can be inherited through genes or show up randomly (this is referred to as chimeric variegation). Chimeras are often illusory.

Vernacular

Vernacular art refers to work made outside traditional institutions, such as folk art or outsider art made by working-class or underrepresented communities. It may challenge cultures of dominance, reflect cultural heritage, or address questions of identity. Some today feel it includes an implication that vernacular art is made my self-taught artists and is thus not grounded in artistic theory; many decolonial artists reject the term.

Xenophobia

A fear of the "other."

Notes on Flowers & Plants

Conditioning refers to the post-harvest care of flowers. I've chosen to risk English common names in this section. In some cases, the colloquial name is its genus name, as with jacaranda. This is not an exhaustive list of tropical, semitropical, and tender plants useful for arranging, but it is a list of some plants I mentioned in the book and couldn't break out of the narrative to tell you how to use them. Other flowers here I simply lacked the opportunity to mention but learned to love over the course of my research. Below you'll find some conditioning tips on using these plants, flowers, and vines for design work.

Clean water is the most import thing you can offer a cut flower, so change vase water regularly. For professional-level detail, see the wonderfully informative *Cut Flowers of the World: A Complete Reference for Growers and Florists* by Johannes Maree and Ben-Erik van Wyk.

Aloe

I once saw a whole orangey aloe emerging from the base of an elaborate arrangement. The flowers above it didn't matter—transformed into an underwater reef, they became home to an aloe octopus. Set on one side, tentacles curving, that aloe wasn't friend but foe. The serrated edges of the leaves gleamed like teeth. Use potted or bare and replant after use.

Alstroemeria

Alstroemeria is susceptible to stem block, which can occur when air, rather than water, moves into the stem. Cut under water and remove all leaves that might hang below the waterline.

Agapanthus, or Blue Lily.

Agapanthus

Buds open after they are cut and last up to seven days.

Amaranthus

A relative of *Celosia*, the genus *Amaranthus* includes numerous species. Some plants are grown for their edible foliage, others for their high-protein seed, and others for use in ornamental horticulture. Cut inflorescences before they mature seed. Love-lies-bleeding has a russet-red tone, but the creepiest amaranth, in my opinion, is the pale green 'Green Cascade.' I happen to be allergic to this plant so it has an extra ick/itch factor for me, but it's excellent for conjuring moods both steamy and sinister.

Amaryllis (a misnomer) aka Hippeastrum

These popular holiday flowers are native to tropical America. Today in the cut-flower trade, growers use a sugar solution to prevent the splitting and curling of the cut stems. If your amaryllis does this, you can pack cotton wool in the stem and wrap an elastic around it. The flowers last close to ten days and are normally shipped through the cold chain in bud. (PS, if you're confused about the difference between amaryllis and hippeastrum, see entry for Bulb.)

Anthurium

Grown for both flowers and foliage, different varieties of anthuriums are tailored to different uses. While the flowers appear robust, some special handling is required to ensure long vase life (and by long, consider a recorded vase life of forty-four days for one flower!).[219] First, do not refrigerate the leaves or flowers; anthuriums can take heat but not cold and will brown if deeply chilled. If you're unpacking anthuriums (they are often shipped flat to protect the spadix), float them in warm water for a half hour, then recut the stems underwater. You can expect about two weeks from anthurium leaves in water and longer from a well-treated flower in a warm, humid environment. Keep their water clean and refreshed. According to the Mexican designer Leopoldo Gomez, you can judge the age of an anthurium and anticipate vase life. He suggests looking at the condition of the spadix. If it's whitish and has raised bumps on it, the flower will not last as long—in his opinion, vase life will plummet from twenty-one days down to eight. Remove the spadix from a red anthurium and you have beating heart.

Apple-of-Peru aka the Shoofly Plant (*Nicandra physalodes*)

I first encountered this global problem plant at Great Dixter. I later grew it in my garden, and it handily reached six feet in a season, branching into a small tree with a wide canopy of leaves and bell-shaped, pale purple flowers. With black shiny stems, it can be used as a striking cut flower (and the flower buds open in the vase), but the real delight is in the green-and-black calyces surrounding the berries. These waxy lanterns are about an inch long and wide and can be dried on the branch for winter decorations, but do note that *Nicandra* has made its presence felt in some thirty countries, and despite some medicinal uses and a history as a whitefly deterrent (hence the shoofly), the seeds shake free from the dried berries and spread with ease. I now yank up all but one or two plants that appear in my garden every year.

Asparagus Ferns

Not a true fern but a great foliage plant, *Asparagus densiflorus* is a widespread native of South Africa, now naturalized in Australia. The rambling cultivars seen as a houseplant are in the 'Sprengeri' group. The variety that resembles a foxtail is 'Myersii.' *A. setaceus* (often known as plumosa) sprawls up to thirty feet and has spread into gardens around the world given its tolerance for shade and ability to withstand drought. This is the familiar airy asparagus fern used in traditional floristry (see Fernery). Store in high humidity.

Aspidistra

Broad lance-shaped leaves, a high level of environmental tolerance, and a healthy shine have made aspidistra popular houseplants. More than two hundred varieties have emerged from their original Chinese ancestors, with many prominent in the floral trade given their robust vase life of two to three weeks. Leaves can be held in a cooler, either misted and loosely wrapped in bags or upright in water.

Bamboo

Bamboo is the fastest growing land plant in the world, with some species clocking in 0.5 millimeters per minute or about a meter a day. (Giant kelp grows faster in the ocean, so it takes first place for the fastest growing plant.) Bamboos are grasses, and there are more than fifteen hundred species in the world. Bamboo cools, feeds, clothes, houses, delivers, regenerates, protects, shelters, and purifies. In China the plant symbolizes long life and resilience given its ability to bend and maintain its integrity. To tell the story of bamboo would require a book (it can be pulped for paper too), but for our purposes here if you have cut green bamboo, there's no benefit to putting it in water.

Banksia

A diverse group of shrubs and trees in the Protea family, banksias are grown for both foliage and their spectacular flowers. The flowers don't respond to floral preservative or sugars, so clean water is best. Strip leaves from the base of the stem, recut, and keep cool, and you can expect vase life of over two weeks depending on the age of the flower. (Banksias can be stored for up to four weeks in the cold chain before being retailed.) Exported flowers are often picked before the florets open. If picking your own, look for about 20 percent of the florets to be open. Dries well, but note if the leaves dry out, they cannot easily be rehydrated. Use leaf and flower form as a means of identifying your banksia, not just color. According to WildFlowers Australia, in one species, *B. menziesii*, "colour varies from deep burgundy red through to chocolate brown, orange, shades of pink, apricot, bronze and yellow, depending on the selection. Color intensity also varies with seasonal conditions."

The Oblique Leaved Begonia

Begonia

The designer Dafne Tovar adores begonias. She sources whole plants at markets around Mexico City. The effect they have in a space? "Incredible. They're like no other leaf." Tovar chooses to use begonia leaves alone, not complicating her displays with flowers. In her words: "They just aren't needed." After events, Tovar plants the begonias in gardens where they continue to bring joy. She offers light and water to cut *Begonia rex* branches to encourage rooting. In her warm climate, "they last forever. Out of a hundred, I'd say maybe four will be lost."

There are more than two thousand species of *Begonia*, but one year I grew some shriveled tubers that had been wetted and warmed on a heating mat. When they bloomed, I asked myself: why are the flowers different? Begonias are monoecious and often flagrantly so (in my case) with simple male flowers and petticoated females on the same plant. I learned begonia flowers are unisexual, whereas a lily, with all those erect anthers and a sticky stigma, is bisexual.

The name *Begonia* was conjured up by the intrepid seventeenth-century monk-cum-naturalist Charles Plumier (of *Plumeria* name and fame) to honor a French colonial official of Haiti (then called Saint-Domingue), namely a monsieur Bégon who loved plants and made a killing (likely literally and figuratively) on the spice trade. So imperialism was alive and well in my begonias. But did you know Haiti was the first country to abolish slavery, in 1804, and what's more, it is the only state in history created directly from a slave revolt? How I hope for Haiti and how I digress.

Begonias are ranked about number four on top bedding lists, after petunias, geraniums, and pansies. Begonias beguile. The Chinese began cultivating *B. grandis* somewhere around the fifteenth century and the Japanese in the seventeeneth century.

The Missouri Botanical Garden offers this helpful guide to begonia divisions: cane-like, *rex-cultorum*, rhizomatous, semperflorens, tuberous, trailing or scandent, thick-stemmed, and shrub-like. Most modern hybrids mainly descend from three species: *Begonia veitchii* (Veitch funded many plant expeditions to grow his UK nursery business in the nineteenth century), *B. schmidtiana* (collected in Brazil in 1878 by a German firm), and *B. socotrana*, which (and I must quote because I'm so grateful to Judith Taylor for revealing the long arm of bioprospecting that brought plants to our gardens) "was discovered on Socotra, an island in the Indian Ocean about 150 miles off the coast of Somalia . . . [by a] Scottish botanist Isaac Bailey Balfour . . . in 1880. One of its characteristics was the ability to flower in the winter months, giving it immense importance in the hybridizing world."[220]

Our rapaciousness astounds: today more than ten thousand cultivars have been developed, most through traditional hybridization. There's even a *Begonia darthvaderiana*. I kid you not.

According to the American Begonia Society, more than ninety species of *Begonia* are on the IUCN's endangered and threatened species red list. Habitat loss and poaching of rare species for collections present the greatest risks.

If you want to use begonia flowers in an arrangement follow this advice from Worth Brown: "Since moisture is absorbed through the petals, the surface of the flowers should be moistened. This is the method generally recommended by florists: Lay the blossom in the palm of the hand and lower it into a container of clean water until submerged, bring it to the surface, turn it over, and let the excess water run out. Do not shake it. The water which remains down the in the base of the petals will keep the flowers fresh for a long time. Some florists prefer to use a fine spray or syringe on the blossoms, but then a lengthy spraying is necessary."[221]

Berzelia

Looking something like a heather with knobby tops, this plant is also known as button tops and Cape greens. Used as a foliage plant and for texture in bouquets, the plant is wild harvested from the fynbos of South Africa and has a long vase life.

Bird's-nest Fern (*Asplenium* spp.)

Mist and store in plastic bags for only a few days before using.

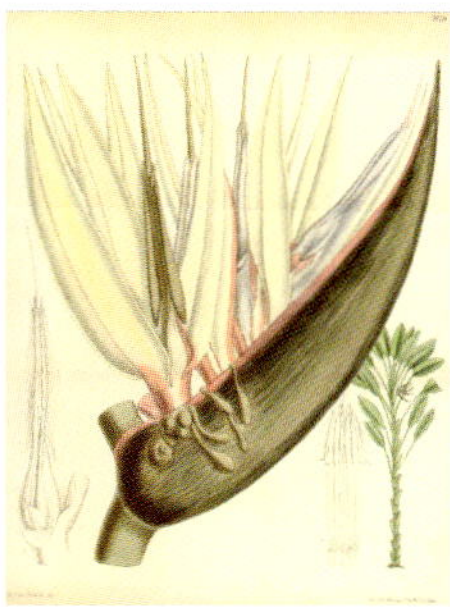

Bird of Paradise (*Strelitzia* spp.)

So many flowers baffle me with the cleverness of their design. Looking at a *Strelitzia*, you can't help but wonder: why those architectural angles, the stiff pointy beak, the sexy spear of blue? At first glance it's hard to figure out where the flower truly is on a bird of paradise, but that desire to know is soon eclipsed by the beauty of the colors themselves—the orange sepals and purplish-blue petals opening out from a dusky sheath.

Strelitzias have hidden nectaries. What pollinator can reach them? Birds. As birds nuzzle their beaks deep, they catch pollen on their feet.

The plant is native to South Africa. Yet from India to Italy, from the Netherlands to Hawaii, from Israel to China, *Strelitzias* have been widely cultivated as a cut flower, garden plant, and house plant. In California, warblers have been known to pollinate *Strelitzia*, raising concerns about seed spreading and invasion in the state.

The main types of *Strelitzia* you'll see in tropical and semitropical gardens include *Strelitzia alba*, which can reach almost thirty feet with distinctive white flowers held in purple sheaths. These beauties hail from South Africa and Madagascar. Another large species, *S. nicolai*, is often grown as a foliage plant indoors, and a related species, *S. caudata*, known as mountain banana, grows wild in the hills of Zimbabwe.

A common species in gardens is *S. juncea*. It has a short stature and distinctive orange and blue blooms. This plant adapts well to indoor growing, as does *S. reginae*, which is one of the most popular birds of paradise, and the one we see most often in cut-flower trade. It takes these *Strelitzias* three to five years to bloom from seed.

When shipped in bud, it's necessary to lift out the feathered wings of the flowers. Soaking the buds in warm water makes the sheath more pliable. Vase life varies between seven and fourteen days. Sugar and citric acid is recommended to extend vase life.

Bitter Melon (*Momordica charantia*)

With names in at least forty-seven languages, bitter melon is a global food plant, growing perennially in the tropics and as an annual in cooler climates. A relative of cucumber, the fruits hang from climbing vines. The wartier version is more appealing for floristry work in my opinion, but the smooth Chinese version is also interesting.

Blushing Bride (*Serruria florida* or *S. rosea* or hybrids)

When cutting blushing bride or shopping for cut stems, ensure half the flowers are open. Only hold the flowers for a few days. *Serruria* is South African. Well-treated blushing bride should hold for about a week. The flower heads dry well.

Boronia

An endemic genus of Australia, these are popular garden plants requiring drainage. Used in the cut-flower industry, *Boronias* need to be cultivated as they are protected from wild harvesting.

Bottlebrush (*Callistemon* spp.)

The vibrant red form looks just like its common name with a mass of red filaments and sometimes red or yellow anthers. This bird-pollinated Australian shrub is drought tolerant, making it a popular garden plant around the world. As foliage, bottlebrush can last up to two weeks; however the flowering stems have a vase life of about a week and resist storage.

Bougainvillea

A love of flowers can mean it's hard to take a break. Some gardeners have a winter, a vast silence of snow I've always longed for, but in temperate and tropical climates things grow on and on.

This fact struck me when I was technically on vacation in Phoenix for a few days. I'd sashayed out of a casita in a gauzy garment, dead set on reading by the pool, and almost instantly stumbled upon a freshly cut pile of purple bougainvillea rising up to my thighs. What coyote trickster had dropped this psychic challenge at my feet?

Instantly I took it all in: the blooms, an adobe wall, my phone in my bag. Dare I build a makeshift arch? Or more realistically, a quasi-arty mass of pure color?

Thankfully, the head gardener saved me from myself. For him that mass of prickly vine had to go and so by inference did I, but we chatted, and I had a lovely tour of the property, gawking at this and that, asking for tips as if one day I'd care for a pepper tree, barrel cactus, or traveler's palm of my own.

Bougainvillea is a true traveler; if any plant has followed me through the writing of this book, it's bougainvillea. Granted it's hard to miss and easy to grow—to the point of rampancy. Native to Brazil, invasive in Cuba and the Philippines, naturalized throughout India, three species—*spectabilis*, *peruviana*, and *glabr*a—have been bred into more than three hundred varieties which have spread throughout the semitropical and tropical regions of the world.

The masses of color we associate with the plant are the result of the papery bracts protecting the tiny flowers inside. Pollinated by bees, moths, flies, and butterflies, bougainvillea drops tiny seeds into cracks and crevices, climbing with arched thorny canes up walls and over buildings.

If you spot a branch of a different color on a bougainvillea, it's a somatic mutation or what might be called in horticulture a bud sport. Snip and root the cutting and it will grow on, though there's a chance of reversion. Still, many new varieties have been raised in this way, and it's easier than directing gamma rays at a plant in a lab to force a mutation (I am not making this up).

The Mexican floral designer Pina Cate uses vast swathes of bougainvillea in her immersive wedding work, positioning elaborately carved Mexican candles in complementary colors alongside the bold shades of bougainvillea. (A fun sidenote: if you've ever had a pink mole sauce in Mexican cuisine, there's a chance it was made with powdered bougainvillea.)

In Hawaii, bougainvillea is used in lei making. Some florists consider the single papery bracts more resistant to wilt than double flowered varieties, but if you're planning to hold the fine bracts for design work follow these steps:

1. Harvest early in the morning or at a point of low transpiration. Wear gloves; there's no such thing as thornless bougainvillea yet.
2. Carry the bracts or sprays home in either paper or cloth bags, not plastic as they will sweat.
3. Heat and humidity can help you, but by that I mean hot-water dipping the stems of sprays, followed by a plunge in cool water. Let the bracts dry off for an hour, then arrange.
4. Mist the sprays to keep them fresh.
5. For lei work, wash and soak the bracts in cold water, then use the hydration chamber method. If you're going rogue and winging it in a tropical climate, you've got about two hours without wilt in the shade for whole sprays of bougainvillea. Worth it.

Bouvardia

A native of Mexico, *Bouvardia* has a sweet scent and has long been used as a garden shrub in warm climates. It's tricky to keep hydrated, particularly if plucked straight from the garden, so take a bucket of water with you. Cut blooms when only a few flowers have opened, and strip the side shoots from the stem. Plunge into water and let the flowers rest. When arranging, ensure all leaves from below the water line have been removed. Commercial growers use preservatives and bactericides to add longevity. If you are picking from the garden and want buds to open, add a little sugar to your water. Use citric acid (available from the pharmacy) to lower pH. If treated well you can expect a vase life of six to twelve days.

Brazilian Peppertree / Florida Holly (*Schinus* spp.)

Once advocated for hedge planting, *Schinus* trees have spread around the world as an ornamental. Used in the floral trade for its long-lasting leaves and pink berries, the trees are invasive in Australia, Bermuda, Florida, Hawaii, New Zealand, Malta, and coastal California. The pink peppercorns are not related to actual pepper, *Piper nigrum*, which is a vine. Consider wearing gloves when working with peppertree as the aromatic sap can burn. And check regulations in your region regarding use.

Buddha's-hand aka the Fingered Citron (*Citrus medica* var. *sarcodactylis*)

Likely traveling from India to China, this temperate-loving lemon relative is valued for its form, complex perfume, and symbolic meaning.

The Buddhist connection centers on the idea of mudras, or hand gestures, made by the Buddha, which teach lessons and are replicated with the hands and fingers in yogic practice. Known as *bushukan* in Japanese, the fruits are often given as gifts at New Year's to bring good luck to a household, and in China are used as offerings on altars.

The Metropolitan Museum of Art in New York holds an eighteenth-century Chinese piece sculpted from carnelian, a type of quartz that interestingly, to this conversation at least, takes its name from flesh. The sculpture shows the fingers of the fruit arched inwards "in an idealized form of the Buddha." As the fruit ripens, it opens and looks like something you'd see trying to eat a teenager in *Stranger Things*.

After using Buddha's hands in displays, use them in the kitchen. The rind is edible, but the fruits lack pulp, so the culinary emphasis lies in capturing the scent from the oils.

Bugle Lily (*Watsonia* spp.)

Native to South Africa, *Watsonia* have been bred into cultivars; however, do your research before using as *W. meriana* is invasive in Australia and California.

Butterfly Bush (*Buddleja madagascariensis*)

The orange-flowering butterfly bush has spread throughout the tropics and is considered one of Hawaii's most invasive plants. Be wary.

Caladium

Also known as angel wings, *Caladium bicolor* has been bred into a range of cultivars featuring their beautiful red, pink, white, and green coloration. The stems of these plants need a hot-water dip and the leaves need a deep soak in cool water before arranging. They don't last long.

Calathea

Commonly grown as houseplants and for the foliage trade, *Calathea* is a diverse genus hailing from the neotropics. Most leaves hold well in water, providing you only submerge the stems. *Calathea* flowers range in form and color from pale blues to popular cultivars like 'Green Ice' to the dazzling 'rattle' varieties. Treat like you would a member of the ginger family.

Calla Lily (*Zantedeschia* spp.)

Callas bruise easily and aren't long-lived in the vase, yet their shapeliness makes them a popular cut flower and potted plant. Large white callas have soft stems that tend to split. Floral preservative can help with this. The whites are more cold hardy than the colored varieties in terms storage, but don't keep either long in a cooler.

Canna

Wild *Canna* grow almost ten feet high. Used as a food plant by Andean peoples for more than 3,500 years, the seeds can be added to tortillas, the young shoots eaten as a vegetable, the leaves and stems used for animal fodder, and most importantly, the starchy nutritious tubers can be eaten baked or made into powder. Today in Colombia, a commercial biscuit is made from the plant known as *achira* (from *Canna edulis*), and in Vietnam, the tubers are used to make noodles. In the 1850s, *Canna* were shortened through breeding into a wide array of bedding plants. The flowers only last a day or two as a cut, but the leaves last longer. Dip the stem in boiling water for a minute, then submerge the whole leaf for a few hours in cool water to condition.

Castor Bean (*Ricinus communis*)

Castor beans have been used as a source of motor oil, a food for silkworms, a fertilizer, a laxative, a detergent, a cotton dye, and an arthritis treatment. The plant traveled from Africa during the Atlantic slave trade and is now invasive in many parts of the world. Also popular in horticulture, the varieties used in floristry include 'Carmencita' and 'Carmencita Bright Red,' 'New Zealand Purple' and 'Red Spire.' As Michael Pollan once wrote, "The castor bean refuses to ingratiate itself, keeping its strange, spiky flower close to the vest, down below the eight-fingered hands of its dark leathery leaves."[222] It's the seed pods and leaves we seem to love (or hate) most.

Cecropia

Invasive in Hawaii, it helps to regenerate forests by growing quickly and shading understory species. Tree sloths in South and Central America eat *Cecropia* leaves, and musical instruments have been made from the hollow trunks, thus the common name trumpet tree. The trees drop leaves as they grow, and these are available dried in the floral trade, either flattened or wavy.

Chinese Violet (*Telosma cordata*)

A vine grown throughout the tropics known variously as pakalana in Hawaii, Tonkin jasmine (a exonym and colonial reference to Vietnam), and cowslip creeper, among many other names.

Edible and prized in Southeast Asia, the immature flower clusters are poached in soups or quickly fried as an accompaniment to meat or seafood. A sun-loving vine, it bears flowers with a delicate citrus scent, although the petals can be a tad delicate, so ensure they're hydrated by either picking them at a period of low transpiration (morning or evening) or wrapping them in damp paper towel then putting them in a hydration chamber in the refrigerator for a number of hours before working into garlands or leis.

Citrus

Gorgeously scented, citrus flowers don't last long. Split the stems into an X and remove unneeded foliage. Do this for fruited branches as well.

Coleus

These brilliantly colored and variegated bedding plants originally hail from Southeast Asia. *Coleus (Plectranthus) scutellarioides*, the species introduced to horticulture from which many cultivars are derived, came into cultivation in 1851 through the Dutch occupation of Indonesia. Heat-tolerant, coleus is now one of the top ten bedding plants, available in combinations of yellow, raspberry, purple, maroon, green, and russet. It's difficult to resist using the wildly colored leaves of coleus as a cut, but it's not reliable (despite the fact that some *Coleus*, like other members of the mint family, will readily root in water!). Choose hardened, mature stems, try a hot-water dip, and rest them in cool water before arranging. This is a plant to date before marrying to a design.

Colocasia/Alocasia

Glossy and waxy varieties last longest in the vase. Taro (*Colocasia esculenta*) was one of the food crops brought by Polynesian settlers to New Zealand and are a starchy dietary staple throughout the region and beyond.[223] The leaves are often used to wrap foods for steaming.

Conebush (*Leucadendron* spp.)

All "Leuks" hail from South Africa. Some of the sixty-odd species are grown (or wild-harvested) for their long-lasting colored foliage, others for their charming flowers, and others for their cones. All last up to three weeks in the vase and are excellent for drying.

Coral Fern (*Gleichenia* spp.)

This Australian native grows up to six feet high. Millions of stems enter the floral trade from South Africa, where the plant is wild harvested from pine plantations (and considered a weed). Also called tangle fern, it can be broken down into smaller pieces for bouquet and boutonniere work. The Floral Design Institute suggests ferns dislike floral preservatives and food, so use only clean water. And as with many other ferns, soaking them in a cool bath before working with them will help them to stay hydrated. A good rule of thumb with ferns is to wait until they are sexually mature to use them—in other words, once the spores are brown.

Cordyline (Ti Plant)

One Nevisian gardener I met called this plant tired lady because despite how colorful and pretty the leaves may be, *Cordyline* always looks a little lax in the *fruticosa* varieties. As Marianne Wilbur once said, "Landscapers have overused rusty-red cultivars of *Cordyline australis* as the ubiquitous 'thriller' plant for container designs for so many years that gardeners can be excused for not realizing that this genus is made up of *truly* thrilling plants." With more than twenty-five species and numerous cultivars, there's a *Cordyline* for almost every occasion and color way—from spiky buff burgundy to luminous fuchsia and variegated pastel pinks. All have a long vase life.

Crinum

A relative of amaryllis, *Crinum* bulbs can weigh up to twenty pounds. Individual flowers don't last long as a cut, but given the stem contains multiple blossoms, one stem might deliver multiple blooms.

Croton *(Codiaeum variegatum)*

The variegated leaves of croton plants feature reds, yellows, and oranges and purples in saturated hues. High impact, tough, glossy, and textural, these leaves last and last. They are sold commercially, but you can also harvest your own. Be careful of the sap if you're sensitive, and let it bleed out in cool water before arranging.

Crown Flower *(Calotropis gigantea)*

Known as *pua kalaunu* in Hawaii, this plant in the milkweed family is found throughout the tropics (having originated in India and Southeast Asia). The flowers are white or pale purple and borne in clusters. What they lack in scent they make up for in abundance and design—crown-shaped, they have a staminal column which appears supported by five intricate icing-like swoops, looking as if they been piped by a pastry chef.

Monarch butterflies have adapted to eating *Calotropis* leaves in Hawaii in addition to the smaller shrub *C. procera* (more common in the Caribbean, where it has been used as a fiber plant).

The latex of these plants has been used as a spear poison in South America, so take heed when harvesting, being sure to wear glasses and not touch your eyes. Some lei makers lotion up their hands before working with the flowers or wear gloves. No matter what, always soak the flowers in water before using to both leach out some of the sap and hydrate the blooms.

Crown flowers can be used whole (without stems) or plucked apart so that the crown alone is removed from the petals and threaded or alternated with whole flowers. Alison Higgins, owner of Grace Flowers Hawaii, budgets about seventy-five of the purple crowns for a simple forty-inch lei.

Crown flower is known as *doc ruk* in Thailand, which translates to "love flower."

Calotropis pods grow into small football shapes, inflated with air (which may explain how they have floated between islands and grow on beaches). Try incorporating branches of pods into short-lived designs.

Cucamelon

Cute as a button these mini-watermelons are, but this vine runs rampant through the American tropics. Do not spread the seeds through use.

Datura aka Angel's Trumpet or Devil's Trumpet

Datura gets its common names for its psychoactive effects. The flowers close at night, and while they can be used in design once cut on the stem, take heed when working with it. The spiky seed capsules have been called witch's apples or thorn apples.

Dead Man's Fingers *(Decaisnea insignis)*

A frost-tolerant tree native to Asia and northeastern India, it's fairly hardy. The fruits of this plant are grey and blue and hang in creepy clusters of three. You can eat the jelly surrounding the seeds.

Dracaena

Known variously as cornstalk plant, dragon tree, Song of Jamaica, and Song of India, dracaenas come in a range of colors with variegated leaves in chartreuse, white, cream, green, yellow, and pinky red. Shiny, waxy, and architectural, dracaena leaves are best washed before use. Cut from the garden and conditioned in cool water, they can easily last two weeks.

Dragon Fruit *(Selenicereus* spp.)

Pink or yellow skinned with white or red flesh and studded with a galaxy of tiny black seeds, dragon fruit also (known as pitaya or pitahaya) are borne from large vining cacti. The plants are trained up posts on farms, and the crowns supported with old tires or metal rings. As they bloom only for one night, workers go out with headlamps and small brushes to hand pollinate the flowers.

Foxtail Lily *(Eremurus* spp.)

Native to western and central Asia and farmed in the cool, dry sagebrush landscapes of Oregon and elsewhere, towering eremurus spikes make a stunning statement in the garden or vase. Cut or purchase when buds just opening at the base. The florets will open up over two weeks.

Eucalyptus

The stem tips can be subject to wilting, so pinch off if required. Use gloves if you find it too sticky. Given the sap, it's best stored on its own in acidified water. Invasive and volatile in many parts of the world, the tree was introduced to Maui in 1870.

Firewheel tree *(Stenocarpus sinuatus)*

In the Protea family, this rainforest tree from Australia can grow to one hundred feet, but in cooler and drier locations, the tree is usually only moderate in size with a low canopy of glossy leaves and striking red inflorescences shaped like spoked wheels. The foliage is long-lasting once well hydrated, and the flowers last a week. The South African designer Coral Shortt advises against using glass vessels with this tree "as they do stain the water like the Protea family do, but more blackish."

Flannel Flower *(Actinotus)*

According to an Australian government document on quality specifications, "Most flannel flowers marketed today come from cultivated plants. In the past they have largely come from bush-picked material, which varied greatly in flower form and quality. Selection of better clones has produced plants with longer stems flowering over longer periods."[224] In Australia, the flowers have a vase life of fourteen to twenty-one days and require an abundance of clean water to hold.

Floss Flower (*Ageratum* spp.)

Hailing from Mexico, these common bedding plants make decent cut flowers but don't last for more than a week in the vase. New varieties with longer stems and better coloration are now grown for the cut-flower trade.

Freesia

Candy-colored cultivars of freesia might make it hard to image that this South African native naturally grows on the shaded edges of woodlands, but think of that when designing with freesia. Undervalued today, freesias have a long vase life and mild scent, though that feature has largely been bred out in favor of color or is lost in transit.

Fuchsia

Give these a boiling-water dip before a long drink of cool water.

Gardenia

Many people are frustrated by how easily gardenia petals bruise, but that's a bit like calling a perfectly ripe raspberry problematic. Gardenias bloom white and fade to cream as they age. The scent too is considered creamy—sweet and velvety. But like many white florals, as they're know in the perfume industry, gardenia contains indole. Now, getting technical, indole is pretty odd: at high concentrations it stinks like feces, but at low concentrations it creates a sultry scent. Chemically, indole is related to tryptophan, the happy post-Thanksgiving-turkey amino acid that releases serotonin. Gardenias really do make people feel good.

When I asked about gardenias over Instagram, people commented from Singapore to Beirut, describing the scent as intoxicating. One woman recounted the story of how her Australian grandfather would snip his *Gardenia magnifica* and place the blooms next to his wife's bed. Another woman said she loved gardenias first through association, recalling how Billie Holiday wore them in her hair and how she went to a florist as a teenager to find one so she could smell the flower for the first time. Decades later, the first plant she grew on her New York balcony? A gardenia.

At the Mercado Jamaica in Mexico City, tight little bunches of glossy gardenias are stacked up for sale as token gifts. Loved the world over, there are more than 140 species of gardenia worldwide, but I'll mention two here as they relate to floral culture.

Gardenia taitensis is the Tahitian gardenia. Gardenias are used for hei, ei, and lei in Tahiti, the Cook Islands, and Hawaii respectively. One estimate I saw suggested one hundred million flowers are harvested every year in French Polynesia. Wearing a gardenia blossom there can signal your romantic availability: over your left ear means you're open to advances, and on the right, the opposite.[225]

Gardenia jasminoides has been grown for over a thousand years in China and is traditionally used to flavor oolong tea; often times the plants are grown next one another in terraced tea gardens. The gardenias are slow-roasted with the tea leaves to impart more flavor. The plant is also native to Japan and Taiwan, where it can reach over forty feet high.

At the end of the eighteenth century, English traders managed to get some plants out of China, but the plant "remained a rarity until the nineteenth-century greenhouse and heating-system revolution enabled nurseries to grow it large-scale. The flowers then became the ultimate floral symbol of luxury for wealthy Americans and Europeans, particularly even more so than orchids."[226]

Gardenias are still special today. Hardy in zones 8 to 10, gardenias love humidity and thus make tricky houseplants. One person told me that when they see buds on the plant, they set a humidifier next to it to coax the flowers open.

Using gardenias in design work poses specific challenges. They need to be held in high humidity. Gardenias are shipped at around 1 to 2 degrees Celsius, so keep them as cool as you can. If you are cutting your own from the garden with hopes of holding them for design work, place them immediately and delicately—holding only the stems—into a hydration chamber (see Glossary) in the fridge. When arranging, try to not touch the petals. Handle with wet hands only. You can expect only a day or two of vase life from gardenias, but for many, even a minute in their presence is worth the fuss.

Ginger

The family Zingiberaceae contains plants both edible and exquisite. Some of them we eat—turmeric, cardamom, galangal, and ginger—others we use as dyes and cures, and others still we ogle for their beauty and complexity. Gingers are a complex group with more than fifty genera and hundreds of species, not to mention cultivars.

Ants love the sticky secretions of ginger blooms. To remove them, rinse the blooms in slightly soapy water, then rinse again under fresh water. Ginger can be rehydrated in a bath, but be sure to recut at least two inches off the stem.

Like many tropical flowers, red ginger resents cold and prefers high humidity. One study out of Bangladesh I found suggested that sugar and ascorbic acid (available at pharmacies) inhibits bacterial growth in vase water. Here are some popular ginger family plants used in design and gardens.

- Alpina (*Alpinia purpurata*): Once cut, the bracts of red ginger (also known as torch ginger and ginger lily) do not continue to open, so this flower is harvested at various stages of development for different looks. Cultivars differ in terms of vase life, but well-handled ginger can last from ten days to three weeks.
- Beehive Ginger, Pagoda Ginger, Honeycomb Ginger (*Zingiber spectabile*): Many gingers hold their flowers under their leaves for protection, and in this species the leaves can be three times the height of the inflorescence. The bracts age from red to yellow (this is a generalization—cultivars abound), while the flowers emerging from those bracts are open-mouthed, deep purple, and rarely seen in the trade as the flower spikes are harvested before they emerge. Vase life ranges from seven to twelve days.
- *Curcurma*: This genus contains turmeric and Siamese tulip. Turmeric has elaborate white flowers held under a canopy of leaves. Most horticultural varieties produce ten to fifteen flowers per season before dormancy in cool climates. Vase life is four weeks. Best not refrigerated.
- Galanga/Galangal: Technically *Alpinia galanga*, I mention it here given its importance in cuisine where it imparts a more peppery, citrusy flavor than pure ginger. The flowers are pretty—not great as a cut, but could be used in a pinch.
- Red Torch Ginger (*Etlingera elatior*) or Malay Rose (*E. venusta*): Fragrant and extravagant, torch ginger has traditionally been added to curries in its home of Malaysia. Its vase life isn't as long as other gingers.
- White Ginger Lily (*Hedychium* spp.): Hailing from India, these ginger relatives are grown for their rhizomes, leaves, and scented flowers. The flowers don't last more than a couple days in the vase.
- *Globba*: With more than a hundred species and countless cultivars, this group of gingers bears flowers that are either pendulous or erect. While many lack the height needed to be cut flowers, their unique bloom deserve more attention. Google the hybrid 'Blue Hawaii' and you'll see what I mean.

Gloriosa Lily (*Gloriosa superba*)

With back-swept petals and elegant long stamens, the flame lily, fire lily, or gloriosa is the national flower of Zimbabwe. It grows up to six feet high. Most in the floral trade are grown in the Netherlands, but the best are grown on Shikoku Island in Japan. According to Hitomi

Gillian, the difference lies in the stems—the Dutch versions having softer stems. Gloriosa lilies are best stored out of water, sealed in a bag or hydration chamber, and kept cool but not cold. If you're trying to get buds to open, use a sugar solution.

Golden Dewdrop or Sky Flower *(Duranta erecta)*

This plant is native to hot limestone soils of the Gulf of Mexico. It is invasive in Africa, Australia, and elsewhere. A common shrub in warm climates, *Duranta* tolerates high temperatures. Its velvety purple clusters of flowers can be used as cut, but given its invasive potential, be wary and wise.

Golden Rain Tree *(Koelreuteria paniculata)*

Gather seed pods as soon as formed. If cut at an early age, the light green fruits need to be conditioned. Later in the season when they dry, they can be used as is. Check locally to see if this is a problem tree in your area.

Grass Tree *(Xanthorrhoea* spp.)

A slow-growing genus endemic to Australia, *Xanthorrhoea* contains about thirty species, some of which only flower after the plant reaches a hundred years old. The flowers are borne on a spectacularly straight spike that might reach up to nine or thirteen feet in height and have long been used by First Nations peoples as throwing spears. Regulations exist around wild harvesting of the flower spikes given their value to wildlife and slow reproductive rate—one may only cut a bloom after the seeds have shed. Consult with local officials before attempting to use this plant.

Grevillea

Also known as spider flower or honeycomb, grevilleas make great cut flowers. More than three hundred species of *Grevillea* hail from Australia with many cultivars in the trade. *G. banksii* grows up to twenty-five feet with striking sculpted inflorescences reminiscent of red bottlebrushes but far more structural, like delicate blown glasswork cones. Planted throughout the world, some grevilleas are considered invasive in Hawaii and Madagascar, where they have colonized forests.

Guzmania

To use guzmanias in floral design, carefully slice the flower spike from the plant with sharp knife. You can peel the bracts off the spike easily to reduce its size. Float in water before arranging. The flowers last upwards of two weeks. Many are epiphytic bromeliads, which generally grow on trees. There are more than 120 species of *Guzmania* and scores of new cultivars developed every year. Perennial, evergreen, with colorful flower bracts that last for months, the plant dies after flowering.

Gymea Lily *(Doryanthes excelsa)*

In western North America, we know well the vicissitudes of global buying power. Sea cucumber meat? We just about wiped out a species through an unregulated fishery. Matsutake or pine mushrooms? People have pulled guns over them. Gymea is an extraordinary endemic with a limited range in eastern Australia. The flowering spikes grow up to twenty feet and the flower head can be up twenty-seven inches across. Thankfully for this species, local interest has led to its protection and propagation.

The leaves of Gymea can reach six feet and are used in floristry. The flowers continue to open once cut but can be held dry and cool for up to two weeks.

Hairy Balls Milkweed *(Gomphocarpus physocarpus)*

Bigger than golf balls, filled with air, the balls of this South African plant can float or be used on the stem in arrangements.

Heliconia

Heliconias are among the showiest of tropical flowers and grow in wet neotropical forests, given most prefer about 40 percent shade. They were once categorized in the banana family for the resemblance of their leaves, but heliconias have three general leaf types: those resembling bananas, those that look ginger-like, and those similar to cannas. Some plants can reach thirty feet.

The flowers of heliconias come in many forms, from pendant to upright, from smooth to fuzzy and the colors are similarly complex thanks to extensive breeding. Provocative, arresting, the flowering structures often grow to four feet in length, but there's so much diversity in this genus it's hard to generalize. A heliconia might look like an elegant, orange Japanese crane or resemble a pine cone or a spear or a scarlet ladder. The proper term for the showy flower covering is a bract, and it's these long-lasting waxy bracts that make the heliconia so popular in designs. Some bracts appear lined up straight and others zigzag, while others appear in a spiral. Heliconias flash out in reds or oranges in order to attract birds. The length of the flowers held in the bracts depends on the bill of the pollinating bird.

Some common species to recognize include:

- ***H. acuminata***: Often used as a landscaping plant. The species name is Latin for "sharpened," and this group of cultivars is among the most delicate.
- ***H. bihai***: These plants grow from four to eight feet and produce bold upright bracts.
- ***H. Rostrata***: Also known as the hanging lobster claw or beaked heliconia, this species can last up to twenty-one days in the vase.

Hibiscus

Pantropical with delicate flowers and woody stems, hibiscus flowers are very short-lived.

Hymenocallis

Originally from the Americas and Caribbean, these elegant white spider lilies or Peruvian daffodils have spread due to their appeal and adaptability. In the Amaryllis family, the stems are hollow, so take care not to smash the ends, which will degrade and shorten the flower's vase life (which isn't long at all). That said, the flowers are both beautiful and often abundant in gardens.

Ixia

A South African flower in the Iris family, ixia flowers open gradually up the length of their stem, but be sure to wait until a few blooms are open before harvesting. You can also snip off the top couple of buds from a stem to encourage the flowers to open, making the flower less of a spike in designs. After harvest, recut stems and condition in cool water to which sugar has been added. This will encourage the remaining blooms to open. Ixia can be stored for a few days in a cooler and have an average vase life of about five to seven days.

Ixora

The ubiquitous landscaping shrub *Ixora coccinea* produces searing orangey-red clusters of flowers. Originating in Sri Lanka and India, the plant now comes in more than four hundred varieties, including pink and white cultivars. The foliage can be used in designs, and the flowering branches will hold about a week.

Jacaranda (*Jacaranda mimosifolia*)

One of the showiest of tropical trees, once loved the world over, jacaranda is native to South America, and now appears in cosmopolitan settings from Pretoria to Calcutta to Coral Gables. It can be invasive, so check on its status in your region before using. The purple flowers don't last long on the tree or in the vase.

Jade Vine (*Strongylodon macrobotrys*)

The spectacular flowering trusses of jade vine can reach up to nine feet. Pollinated by bats, the flowers have hooked cups to hold nectar, luring the bat in to feed. Luminous and unique in color, the plant is a true tropical requiring high rainfall and steamy temperatures. It hails from the Philippines and is robust enough for lei and design work.

Jasmine (*Jasminum* and *Cestrum* spp.)

Jasminum sambac, the national flower of the Philippines, is often used fresh and to make jasmine tea in China. Likely native to India and Southeast Asia, it grows as a sprawling shrub. Star jasmine from India, *Jasminum laurifolium f. nitidum*, holds well on semi-ripe, turgid stems. Avoid cutting woody sprays as they don't hold as well. Hot-water dip if seeking to revive. Note that some jasmine blossoms are shipped preconditioned and if wetted will brown. Do not spray with water! Note that another night-blooming jasmine, *Cestrum nocturnum*, has spread from Cuba and tropical America throughout the tropical Pacific region and naturalizes in moist forests. It's considered a high-risk plant.

Kangaroo Paw (*Anigozanthos flavidus*)

Perennial and long-lived as a cut flower, kangaroo paw is a great choice for striking designs and dries well too. If you're cutting your own, harvest the flowers when a few florets are open. Recut the stems every couple of days once in the vase and they'll last two weeks. The flowers are ethylene sensitive. Traditionally used medicinally, the kangaroo paw started its journey into horticulture when a colonial settler in Western Australia, a woman named Georgiana Molloy, shipped a pressed specimen to the United Kingdom in the early 1800s. Breeders are releasing a blue kangaroo paw soon.[227]

Kalanchoe

One of the best-selling flowering plants in the world, this diminutive succulent hails from Madagascar. Produced in a wide range of colors and flowering forms, the flower clusters can be used in botanical couture work, holding well out of water.

Kniphofia

Thirsty flowers that last up to a week, red hot pokers benefit from having their stems split. You can manipulate red hot pokers by angling them in a conditioning bucket or bending them with warm hands.

Lantana

Lantanas have been cultivated for hundreds of years given their cheery flower heads. Botanists recognize Central America and the West Indies as its true home, but now the plant has traveled far and wide with the help of birds and humans who have used the plant for everything from decorative purposes to erosion control. The Dutch initially brought this plant from the Americas to Europe, where it has become a mainstay of summer bedding displays. In Tanzania the plant has spread like wildfire; a long flowering period and vegetative spread—things that made it popular to gardeners—give it an edge. New Zealand has banned its sale.

You can use lantana flowers in designs (if they aren't invasive in your region); the flowers will continue opening in the vase after being cut and last up to about six days. Cut deeply so you get some of the woody portion of the stem, then split it and dip in boiling water.

Lipstick Tree/Achiote/Bixa *(Bixa orellana)*

Pods are sold in flower markets, but the plant has a richer history as a coloring agent than as an ornamental. Known commercially as annatto, it is found in everything from lipstick to margarine to sauces. Indigenous peoples of South America introduced the plant to the Spanish who carried it to Southeast Asia in the 1600s. Today *Bixa* grows around the world. When fully ripe, the bristly pods open to reveal the red seeds.

Lotus *(Nelumbo nucifera)*

Lotus flowers will not bloom once cut. Shipped in bud with their stems wrapped in cotton wool and plastic, the blooms requires peeling and the manual opening of petals. The petals can be folded inward to reveal the intriguing sexual organs and floated in a bowl or used like a cut flower, but they don't last long—four days at most.

Lychee *(Litchi chinensis)*

Lychee is a member of the Sapindaceae or soapberry family and related to longans, akee, and rambutans. The Cantonese word for longan translates to "dragon eye," likely in reference to the jellied edible aril that surrounds the dark seed of these fruits. Lychees have been cultivated since ancient times in China. Recent genomic evidence has revealed a double domestication, meaning in two separate parts of the country people cultivated and bred the wild trees. There are numerous cultivars of lychee today, but if you're wondering why you see brown-and-red-skinned ones in markets, it's likely the result of refrigeration. All lychees are pink or red when ripe.

Maiden Hair Fern *(Adiantum spp.)*

A delicate and elegant fern, the maiden hair fern thrives in moist conditions (worth noting, as some ferns are known for colonizing lava). My elderly friend who grows huge ones in terra-cotta pots in a bright basement room swears by the trick of emptying her hot-water bottle into the pan every morning. To use in designs, hot-water dip as much of the tough stem as possible, being careful not to steam the leaves. Leave the ferns in the water until it cools, then tie a plastic bag over top. Let sit for at least a day in a cool spot before arranging.

Marigold (*Tageles* spp.)

Marigolds hail from Mexico and Central America. The seeds were brought to the Old World by Spanish missionaries in the fifteenth century and spread. They were introduced to India about 350 years ago. Most cut flowers come from varieties of African marigolds, namely the Inca and Jubilee hybrids. Known as *flor de muerto* in Mexico, marigolds are best harvested when three-quarters open. As they have a hollow stem, use a sharp blade so as not to crush the stem. Plunge into lukewarm, clean water to condition. As with zinnias, hollow stems mean more surface area for bacteria, so change marigold water regularly and recut stems for longer vase life. You can expect about a week from a marigold, however the flower petals themselves keep well past that in a sealed container in the refrigerator. Use these as floral confetti or in salads.

Matilija Poppy (*Romneya coulteri*)

In 1909, the renowned San Diego horticulturalist Kate Sessions claimed that "it is possible to cut half-blown buds and ship as far as San Francisco, and they will open up large and perfect."[228] The flowers last about three days.

Mexican Shrimp Plant (*Justicia brandegeeana*)

A little story: in 2022, I was invited to Houston to speak at the Museum of Fine Arts. My presentation was to be a followed by a workshop. I try to practice what I preach, so I contacted some farms to source local flowers with very little luck, shipped in some roses grown in California by a friend, and arranged with my garden club hosts to forage in a member's garden. In that garden, after I'd crouched under the evergreen magnolias and snipped toad lilies in the shade, I walked into a clearing, bucket and pruning shears in hand, and met a Yayoi Kusama pumpkin. If you don't know what such a pumpkin is, picture a six-foot high fiberglass-reinforced shiny, bright yellow pumpkin painted with black dots. The day only proceeded to get wilder.

Hot, sweaty, and bent over bushes I could not identify, I broke out in a rash and had to make myself known to the manservant so I could get some antihistamine cream. Next came a freeway and a wholesaler. My order of seasonal bronze sunflowers arrived a scorching yellow, the dahlias near dead, and the palette I'd planned usurped by shortages and substitutions. Desperate for blooms, I loaded up a cart with whatever I could pull from the cooler, scanned plastic sleeves for American-grown anything while questioning my career. My hostess, knowing I was disheartened, suggested one last stop—another member's garden, one that had not sculptures but love in it. There running along the length of a bungalow was a bank of sprawling and suckering shrimp plants, some head high. The elderly owner suggested we hack at them and do her a favor.

Sitting between orange and rose, with showy flower bracts (a fine acanthus family feature) that give the plant the common name false hops, the shrimp plants made that vital bridge between the orange of the banksia I'd bought and the pink of ginger I plucked from her garden. The next day, it filled and spilled from the vase.

Justicia comes in other forms and make short-lived but unique cut flowers. Those with woodier stems such as those on the firecracker bush (*Justicia spicigera*) or Brazilian plume (*J. carnea*) will benefit from notching or a hot-water dip to facilitate the uptake of water.

Mimosa (*Acacia* spp.)

What we call mimosa in the floral trade is often a medium-sized Australian tree that goes by the Latin name *Acacia dealbata*, though other species may be used. (Another acacia, the golden wattle, *A. pycnantha*, is the country's national flower.) There are countless varieties of acacia in cultivation and numerous wild species. Many are grown for their feathery leaves and branches of brilliant yellow blooms that resemble tiny pom-poms. Others for perfume, fuel, resin, or dye.

Historically, in the floral trade, budded branches would be forced into bloom by steaming. Today the industry hot-water dips the branches. Sadly, steaming, dipping, and transporting have almost obliterated the scent of mimosa. I've not yet had the pleasure of sauntering down a tree-lined path on the Côte d'Azur, but apparently the scent has been described as a "rich, sweet, warm, green, honey-floral aroma with pronounced powdery and soft cinnamic-balsamic undertones." Mimosa produces what the French call *cassie*, a highly valuable ingredient of floral perfumes. Today much of the production of cassie has moved to North Africa.

The perfume industry continues to use two species: *A. decurrens* var. *dealbata* and *A. farnesiana*. (If the latter species name looks familiar to garden-lovers, good eye! Villa Farnese is a famous Italian Renaissance garden. *Acacia farnesiana* has been in European cultivation since 1611, having been imported from the Caribbean.)

Acacias are tough. As legumes, they fix their own nitrogen or find it with deep roots; this makes them drought tolerant and easy to grow but also invasive, particularly in biodiverse grasslands (wonderful carbon sinks), which acacias convert into stubby, scrubby flammable forest. Spain and Portugal have banned mimosa, and about twenty-three acacias are causing problems around the world. All those puffy flowers we love mean oodles of seeds.

If by chance you're reading this bathed in a yellow glow or are harvesting mimosa yourself, recut the branches before plunging them in to warm water. Ideally, the water should be acidified, but if that's not possible, at the very least try to ensure the branches don't experience a wide range of temperatures. Don't feel poorly if you only get a few days of freshness from mimosa—the flowers quickly dry indoors.

Acacia confusa is considered highly invasive in Hawaii. Note: the native koa trees (*A. koa*) have cream, not yellow, puffball blooms. If cutting your own or purchasing in the store, look for about half the blooms to be open. Once home, submerge the flower heads in water for a few seconds and briefly dip the branch end cuts in boiling water. Condition in warm water.

Monstera

Monstera is a genus with a wide array of species and cultivars—from small climbing vines to large variegated yellow varieties that can tackle tall trees. Monsteras, like tropical figs, have aerial roots. The purpose of these roots are to help the plant climb into the light and to absorb water from rain showers. If you've ever seen a monstera high in a tropical tree you will know why those aerial roots matter: there is often so much vine, so much foliage, that it seems baffling a single root system in the earth might support the plant. It doesn't entirely. Those aerial roots help out. Monstera leaves can last over two weeks in the vase. Store in high humidity either wet or dry.

Mulla Mulla (*Ptilotus* spp.)

Spectacular tufts bloom in a range of purples and pinks from this drought and heat-tolerant Australian plant. Vase life is at least two weeks.

Nipplefruit/Cow's Udder (*Solanum mammosum*)

Native to Southeast Asia, this member of the nightshade family has spread through the Caribbean, Mexico, and Central America. The fruits are poisonous, a dramatic golden orange, looking almost like small, tapered mangoes (some with fingers). Used decoratively in China during New Year's celebrations, the fruits hold well in displays.

Noni Fruit *(Morinda citrifolia)*

Fast-growing, highly adaptive, noni is naturalized throughout the tropics. Some cultures value the leaves for cooking, others the roots for dying, and others the fruits. English-names include monikers like cheese fruit or vomit fruit because while edible, the scent is abhorrent to some. The fruits ripen to a near translucent white resembling a large pocked pod of jelly.

Octopus Tree/Umbrella Tree *(Heptapleurum actinophyllum)*

A world traveler from the tropical forests of Indonesia and Australia, umbrella trees can produce huge racemes holding close to a thousand flowers. Cut in bud or in bloom, the flower is used in large-scale floral displays (the inflorescences can be easily over three feet wide). According to the US National Parks Service in Hawaii, "Improperly disposed octopus tree fruit leis can spread the seed."[229] Planted the world over given its star factor, do some research before using.

Oleander *(Nerium oleander)*

Cultivated since ancient times, this North African shrub is commonly used for hedging. All parts of the plant are poisonous, so use caution: use of the long twigs for barbecuing meat has led to numerous poisonings.[230] If oleander made a great cut flower, you'd know it, but if you're determined to try, cut clusters when they are about half in flower. Split the stems and sear in a flame while you refrain from the breathing the fumes and count to fifteen. Condition overnight in warm water.

Okra *(Abelmoschus esculentus)*

The flowers don't hold, but the edible pods do. The dried pods are available commercially.

Orchid Tree *(Bauhinia spp.)*

In warm climates, bauhinias are near ubiquitous as landscape trees given their tidy form and showy flowers. Invasive in some regions, there are numerous species. In India and Nepal the pods, flowers, and young leaves are eaten. One global ornamental variety is the Hong Kong orchid tree (*Bauhinia* x *blakeana*) with pinky-magenta flowers, but other bauhinias are beautiful as well, including the yellow bell form *B. tomentosa* and the South African orange-flowered shrub *B. galpinii*. Bauhinias have long been world travelers. One was recorded growing in the Royal Botanic Garden at Calcutta at the turn of the nineteenth century.[231] In my experience, the cut flowers only last a couple days.

Orchids

People have so long been obsessed with the dramatic sexual structures of orchids. Michael Pollan once called them the "inflatable love dolls of the floral kingdom."[232] Nearly one plant in every ten species is an orchid. This means there are more species of orchids than mammals, birds, and reptiles combined.

Orchids are used in the Ayurvedic and Chinese traditions as medicine, in cosmetics, and as a food. Dried orchid tubers are ground into a flour called salep used in desserts in Turkey,

Greece, and Iran. Nineteen species are impacted by this practice, though today the gathering and selling of the tubers is banned as many species are threatened. In Africa, terrestrial orchid tubers are ground up with peanuts to make *chikanda*.

The top genera in the trade I've mentioned elsewhere in the book, but include *Dendrobium*, *Cymbidium*, *Vanda*, *Paphiopedilum*, and *Phalaenopsis*. Cut orchids like to be held at consistently cool, but not cold, temperatures. They should not be placed in the sun. Their water should be changed regularly.

Palm

A palm is a monocot, as is a grass. And a palm is as much an idea as it is a plant. Palms are iconic—they appear as brands, in neon, and are printed, painted, and shaped from metal into cellular towers, and lined up along promenades. Palms in northern latitudes are often ill placed. Palms in balmier climes are often the very definition of place.

Palms have been made into sails for canoes, clothes, hats, mats, cups, baskets, coffins, lanterns, tents, ladles, musical instruments, charcoal, brooms, and counting their various parts—root, trunk, seed, bud, shoot, leaf, bloom—they have been thatched, sawn, split, fermented, dried, ground, drunk, eaten, beaten, burned, carved, polished, played, rolled, and written on. In southern India, the Sanskrit name for the coconut palm, *kalpavriksha*, means "the tree that provides all the necessities for life."

There are twenty-five thousand species, ranging from tiny understory plants that might be mistaken for a fern to the tallest monocot in the world, the Indian wax palm. A palm can be a shrub; a palm can be a vine.

Considering how long humans have integrated palms not only into the structure of their homes but also into their lives, it's no wonder dried palms are finding a place in contemporary floral work. Given their size and relative flatness, they make a great choice for wall installations, and their uses are near endless.

A dried palm leaf in a vase can last indoors for months, but humidity can make a difference to their longevity. Unpainted, they make an excellent choice for backdrops, offering a buff teal, sage green, or tan color depending on the variety and how much sun exposure they had in drying.

Palm caps from India are sold in global flower markets as a type of dried flower. The caps are formed where the stem of the drupe meets the exocarp—the green or yellow skin on the exterior of a coconut.

Pandanus

Screw pine, as it's often called, is a plant of seashores and brackish environments. The fruits are great for decor, lasting up to two weeks. This tree offers leaves for basketry and fruits, for eating and arranging. Gorgeous, generous—I'd love to see more designers explore this fine fruit.

Papyrus (*Cyperus papyrus*)

Papyrus loves water, but only up to a point. They are best purchased fresh for the remarkable filaments that spray out from the stalk like a perfect cascading fountain. The plant relaxes into a puff of draping filaments, resembling that science museum gig where a long-haired kid puts a hand on a metal conductor and their hair stands on end. Holds dried for months.

Parlour Palm (*Chamaedorea* spp.)

A friend who worked in Belize told me about Xate.

"You must know it," she said. "The Palm Sunday palm?"

Xate, pronounced SHA-tay, refers to three species of *Chamaedorea—elegans*, *ernesti-augustii*, and *oblongata*—that grow as understory palms in neotropical rainforests from Mexico down to Brazil, with Belize and Guatemala hosting all three species and the latter the epicenter of wild harvesting.[233]

Collected by "xateros" who live in small camps in the forest, the harvest is done by hand, the men slashing through the forest with machetes to find patches of plants, which are then cut, bundled, and hauled back to camp on their backs. Some claim the work is better than agriculture, others that the pay is too low, the work too hard.[234]

The xateros try to ensure a continued harvest, rotating picking locations around their communities. Still, sustainability is an issue. It takes about four years for xate to reach a harvestable size from seed, and of course the harvest requires intact forests. Thousands are employed in the trade. The majority of xate is exported to foreign markets (vase life can be up to forty days).

There has been some concern regarding Guatemalan xateros crossing over into parks and preserves in neighboring Belize to pick xate (as well as to gather what else they can find that may be salable—toucans, say, or tapirs). Poverty is the driver behind these actions.

Passionflower (*Passiflora* spp.)

Hailing from the edges of neotropical forests, this vining plant with famously ornate filaments is sadly not a great cut flower. Legend says it lasts but one day. Cut an open flower bud and condition before arranging, or better yet, untangle the vines and admire their tendrils. The vines have a longer vase life if dipped in boiling water for a few minutes, then submerge the whole vine in cold water for a few hours before arranging.

Peacock Flower (*Caesalpinia pulcherrima*)

This plant has many names around the world: pride of Barbados (it's the national flower), *tabuchin del monte* in Spanish, and *bunga merak* in Malaysian, to name a few. The Latin species name *pulcherrima* means "most beautiful," referencing the flamboyant flowers with showy stamens. Strip the leaves before using as a cut; the flowers won't last too long.

From Kiribati to Haiti, from Iraq to Angola, this member of the legume family succeeds in spreading (like many of its kin) by popping out its seed from pods. Speaking of the seeds, they were used as an abortifacient by enslaved women in the Caribbean. Maria Sibylla Merian, during her time in Suriname, noted in 1726 when describing the peacock flower that "the Indians, who are not treated well by their Dutch Masters, use the seeds to abort their children, so that they will not become slaves themselves."[235]

Pelargonium

Half-hardy and easily grown in terra-cotta pots, scented geraniums are particularly useful in floral design, offering both fragrance and long-lasting interesting foliage. The best selection I've seen was at the San Francisco Flower Market; pelargoniums are native to South Africa and thrive in the Californian climate.

Persimmon (*Diospyros* spp.)

Ripe on the branch, persimmon is a heavy hitter weightwise. Cut a cross in the base of the branch before poking into a heavy-duty pin frog, or wire fruits onto a robust branch or stick.

Petunia

Do not expect petunia buds to open in the vase. Cut stems underwater and leave to rest in cool water before arranging. If your petunias wilt after cutting, they can be revived in a sugar solution.

Philodendron

Large leaves can last out of water for a week once conditioned.

Phormium

Also known as New Zealand flax, Phormiums grow up to twelve feet high, making dramatic appearances in subtropical gardens (and in temperate ones where there's good drainage). While the flower's spikes reach as high as sixteen feet, they aren't used in mainstream floral designs, but the green and purple leaves are used in bold designs and can be split easily for various uses (try stapling them into hoops and curves). You can expect a vase life from three weeks to a month, and water isn't always required for short-lived installations.

Phylica

South Africa is home to a variety of Cape myrtles, my favorite of which is the feathery *P. plumosa*. Many varieties are cultivated and wild harvested around the Cape for local use and export as they make great fillers and last well in the vase.

Pineapple (*Ananas* spp.)

Globally, we eat about thirty million tons of pineapple every year. Thailand grows the most pineapples, but Costa Rica exports 40 percent of the world's supply. The mini pineapples seen in the floral trade are variations of the red pineapple *Ananas bracteatus*. They resent cold dry air, so keep them cool and humidified before arranging.

Striped and variegated pineapple leaves are used in floristry (such as the varieties 'Porteanus' and 'Variegatus'). You can expect a vase life of eight to fourteen days.

Pittosporum (*Pittosporum tenuifolium*)

This plant is endemic to New Zealand, where it is called *kōhūhū*. The branches of kōhūhū have long been important in Maori life ceremonies, such as baptisms, and are still used for welcoming visitors to a marae. Grown throughout the world for its glossy and varied foliage, pittosporums make long-lasting cuts. Note: Cape pittosporum (*P. viridiflorum*) has fragrant flowers but has naturalized and spread beyond gardens outside of its home of South Africa.

Plectranthus

Related to *Coleus*, this genus in the mint family hosts about eighty-five different species, most hailing from southern Africa, Madagascar, and Sri Lanka. Cuban oregano (*P. amboinicus*), used throughout the world as an aromatic herb in cooking, is called *sambarpalli* in India, where it is used to make fresh chutneys. *Plectranthus argenatatus* is a popular silver-leaved species, but a wide range are grown solely for their flowers. Drought-tolerant, striking easily from cuttings, these plants are gaining ground around the world for their great foliage and blooms. Treat like mint when arranging, avoiding young growth and conditioning before using.

Plumeria

Also known as frangipani, melia, and temple tree, plumeria is celebrated around the world for its scent and silken flowers. Originally from Central and South America, these small trees can be easily propagated by cuttings, which also explains their spread—from temples in Southeast Asia to the Caribbean and the Pacific islands, plumerias are highly adaptive given they drop their leaves during periods of drought to enter dormancy. On the Yucatán peninsula, they grow wild in forests and are called *flor de mayo* for their showy spring bloom. Pollinated by sphinx moths, plumerias release their fragrance at night. Store the flowers in a damp paper bag (or hydration box). An adult neck lei will require about fifty-five flowers.

Poinsettia *(Euphorbia pulcherrima)*

The world's most popular potted plants, poinsettias are euphorbias, which means they exude a sticky, white sap (some people are allergic to this plant family). To condition, cut the stems and rinse the sap off, then slice a line up the stem. Promptly dip the stem in boiling water for twenty seconds, shielding the colorful bract from the steam, then leave them to rest in cool water for a few hours. If you treat them this way and if your arrangement is in a cool room, you can expect almost five days of glamour from their showy bracts. Note: the Mexican designer Leopoldo Gomez suggests burning the cut end with an open flame. Can you recut the stem and use it without sealing again? Some florists think so. In my opinion, success depends on the maturity of the stem and how and where it was grown. Tough semitropical poinsettias grown outdoors make more robust cuts. The beautiful flame of Jamaica (*Euphorbia punicea*) bears a strong family resemblance to poinsettia as if that plant's showy bracts had scaled down to the size of bright red bows tied on spare-leaved branches.

Pomegranate *(Punica granatum)*

Pomegranates originated in Iran but are now grow throughout the semitropical world, particularly around the Mediterranean, and in China, Egypt, and the United States. India is the largest producer, planting the drought-tolerant trees in hot regions during the monsoon. Pomegranates are often found in wholesale floral markets, both in their immature form and dried.

Pothos Vine *(Epipremnum aureum)*

This plant is a versatile subject for event work given the range of leaf sizes available on the same vine. If you hold the leaves in a cool, moist environment before installation, they'll last for a wedding without difficulty.

Protea

Popular varieties include 'Pink Ice,' 'King,' and 'Red Ice,' and the species *P. neriifolia* (bearded protea) in pink and white. *Protea repens* is called sugarbush (*suikerbos*) in Dutch, German, and Afrikaans. The vernacular name references the bracts, which are covered in a sticky nectar that can be collected and boiled into syrup (*bossiestroop*).

Conditioning advice for proteas includes a short resting period in acidic water. You can use ascorbic acid (available inexpensively from pharmacies in powder form) with the recommended pH target of 3.5 (you can by pH paper at a pharmacy as well). Store proteas at about 3 degrees Celsius, in high humidity and in water to which commercial flower food (sugar and bactericide) have been added. Well-treated, most proteas can last two to three weeks as a cut flower. The leaves go first, so trim these off, but as the designer Hitomi Gilliam says, "They die well."

Royal Poinciana *(Delonix regia)*

One of the most popular flowering trees in the world given its spectacular red flowers, the royal poinciana is the national flower of the Federation of St. Christopher and Nevis. Also known as the flame tree or flamboyant tree and originally from Madagascar, the name poinciana is said to have come from the first governor of St. Kitts, a Monsieur de Poincy, who introduced it to the island. It is also the official flowering tree of Miami-Dade County. A lovely umbrella-shaped tree, it has fernlike leaves and clusters of bright red flowers. A lesser-known relative from East Africa, *D. elata* has soft, creamy yellow petals with wonderfully flamboyant, deep-orange stamens. The flowers are short-lived and delicate.

Ruscus

Glossy ruscus is grown for the floral trade in places as wide-ranging as Italy, Colombia, and Israel. Growers use shade cloth to promote longer stem length. Prep ruscus for the vase by removing any leaves below the waterline. Vase life is good, with fresh ruscus lasting up to two weeks. If you need to store ruscus, ensure high humidity and low temperatures. Avoid bleached ruscus.

Sago Palm *(Cycas revoluta* and *C. circinalis)*

Sago palms are ancient cycads from southern Japan, not palms. The leaves have an astounding two-to-four-month vase life in water.

Sandersonia

A relatively new introduction to the trade known as Chinese lantern lily or Christmas bells, this South African flower has cute yellow or orange lanterns dangling from its stems. Easy to work with, they can be stored for up to two weeks and last about a week in the vase.

Sansevieria

Commonly known as snake plant or mother-in-law's tongue, these robust spreading plants are useful for adding verticality to gardens and designs. A range of cultivars are grown for the houseplant trade and landscaping, including beautifully variegated types, some with yellow striping and silver banding. Long-lived as a cut. This plant can escape gardens.

Sarracenia

Pitcher plants are carnivorous, grow in boggy ground, and are often wild harvested in the southern United States. Pitcher plants are among the 400 of the 250,000 known angiosperms that feed on insects. Most use elaborate traps involving nectar, color, and modified leaves.

The leaves of sarracenias have evolved into a trap whereby an insect slips down into a pool of digestive juices. Farming sarracenias is possible, but commercial demand puts pressure on wild populations and the fragile wetlands in which they grow. Even if landowners allow unlicensed pickers on their lands, I consider this plant a no-go in floristry. The pitchers people covet for design work can feed the plant for six months. Once cut, they might last a week at best. If you're ever asked, "Hey, where'd you get those gorgeous sarracenias?", you'd best have a better answer than "the wholesaler!"

Sea Grape *(Coccoloba uvifera)*

The leaves of sea grape can be used fresh or dried. I had decent luck making a Christmas tree from sea grape—the leaves held in water for five days in tough conditions. The grapes are used to make jelly in many parts of the world but don't hold well for design work. Use immature clusters or simply the wonderful waxy leaves.

Smilax

Commonly known as greenbrier, smilax is grown for the floral trade in Texas and the American Southeast, where the plant appears naturally. It's a native plant that gardeners throughout the east love to hate as it's highly opportunistic (though the plant has high wildlife value). A genus with cousins throughout the subtropics and tropics of the world, it is used in event work to cover arches and for draping. Sold in bags, it lasts in a cooler for a couple weeks if misted. In an air-conditioned space, out of water, the vine will hold for event work for a couple of days.

Snake Gourd *(Trichosanthes cucumerina* var. *anguina)*

Native to southern and eastern Asia and Australia, and now a pantropical plant, snake gourds can easily reach over three feet in length. I once ate the young vines of this zucchini relative in Sicily, but like luffas, it's best eaten when young. Ripe and hardened snake gourds are made into didgeridoos in Australia.

Spanish Moss *(Tillandsia usneoides)*

What do swamp coolers, those early alternatives to air conditioning, have to do with plants? In the southern United States, they were once stuffed with Spanish moss.

Spanish moss grows throughout the subtropical and tropical Americas and has been introduced everywhere from Hawaii (where it's sometimes called Pele's hair) to Australia (where's it's known as old man's beard). Not a moss but an epiphyte in the pineapple family, the plant doesn't have roots but rather absorbs nutrients from the runoff of water on its host tree. Easy to collect, Spanish moss has been used in car seats, mattresses, and building works. Today you're likely to see it in arts-and-crafts shops.

Happy in warm humid environments, the plant can grow to twenty feet. If you're harvesting it from the wild (check with local authorities if this is permitted), wash it in a soapy bath, rinse, and hang to dry. The color will shift to grey as it dries. (Note that bright green Spanish moss has been dyed). Wreaths stuffed with Spanish moss accept metal floral pins well and can be reused.

Tamarind *(Tamarindus indica)*

A pantropical tree grown for its shade and fruits that look like little brown knobby fingers. The fruits are easily cracked, and the pulp around the seed is both sweet and sour. It is used in sauces, drinks, and desserts the world over. The flowers of the tamarind tree look like tiny delicate orchids.

Tea Tree *(Leptospermum scoparium)*

This plant is now associated with the illustrious manuka honey from New Zealand. (Interestingly, the honey wasn't a thing until the European settlers to New Zealand introduced the European honey bee in the nineteenth century. The Maori had used the small trees to make tools and for firewood.) The term tea tree refers to the fact the leaves can be brewed, not to be confused with the tea tree of essential oil fame. That antibacterial oil is distilled from the leaves of the Australian tree *Melaleuca alternifolia*. A number of horticultural varieties have found their way into gardens the world over, and all can be used as filler flowers. They flower in summer in the southern hemisphere and come in white, pink, and red. Treat like waxflower.

Tillandsia

From minute air plants to large specimens, tillandsias are known for their longevity in designs. Don't be tempted to fill the water receptacle as that can lead to rot in cooler climates or air-conditioned places. Instead dunk the plant or mist it.

Tree Ferns/Monkey Tail

There are many types of ferns that are referred to as monkey tails, but stick with me on this one, because the reason for the allusion isn't just the curlicue of the developing frond that excites floral designers, it's often the russet fur itself.

In tree ferns, this protective layer can be almost pelt-like and has been used for menstrual pads (long ago in Hawaii), as a mattress filler (a brief industry), and today as a substrate for orchid cultivation.

The curls of an immature tree fern frond can be up to six inches across and the stalks are robust. From the catwalks of fashion shows to the vases of the rich and famous, tree ferns are primordial, sexy, and in demand. But that demand comes at a high cost.

In many parts of the tropical world (tree ferns grow the world over from South America to Australasia), tree ferns are either endangered or under threat. In the Philippines, for example, the majority of the twenty-nine species extant are in danger of extinction. In cooler regions such as Tasmania, which is home to about 160 million tree ferns, harvest of whole plants for export are considered sustainably managed. Many of these find their way into English gardens given the climate analogue.

That said, when we see a four-foot fiddlehead in a flower market, we should ask the dealer where it came from. In the United States, the source is likely Hawaii, namely the plant *Cibotium glaucum*, but given the preciousness of the resource, be aware. Also known as hapu'u fern, *C. glaucum* is endemic to Hawaii and has long fronds growing up to nine feet.

A fern frond is technically made up of a stipe and a blade. The blade is divided into sections called pinna, which are attached to the midrib running down the blade. The large pinnae of tree ferns can be easily dried and used in wreath work or for smaller work like boutonnieres.

Tuberose (*Polianthes* spp.)

Tuberose has been cultivated so long by the Maya it's considered a cultigen given no wild species have been found. Ideally, cut it when the spikes are close to the three-quarters open but before the flowers at the bottom of the spike fade. Condition in deep water and the flowers should last seven to twelve days in the vase.

Tweedia *(Oxypetalum coeruleum)*

The first time I saw tweedia was in New York on 28th Street at the flower market. I bought a couple bunches, put them in the ice bucket of my hotel room, and took them off to a flower workshop.

If you've ever been to a flower workshop, you'll know that flowers are the one thing you don't need to bring—it's the equivalent of showing up to a fancy dinner with a brazen baguette in your bag, one you have no intention of sharing.

Tweedia grows best in semitropical zones given its origins in Brazil and Uruguay. In my mind, it is one of the most useful plants for adding zing to other colors. The trick is its blue—so uncommon in plants—skylike, slightly electric, with hints of mauve and white. It's a chilling, icy blue, the perfect contrast to orange. After cutting it can be chilled and held. Be sure to keep tweedia in its own bucket particularly during the conditioning stage as it bleeds milky latex. Vase life averages about a week.

Uluhe Fern/Old World Forked Fern *(Dicranopteris linearis)*

Oh, the folly of fashion! Many years ago, when bleached and dyed plants were just appearing in the trade, I coveted what I thought was a dried fern. I asked a friend in London to look at New Covent Garden. No luck. Then I asked my husband who was in New York to go to the flower market. He found it, and once I got that fern into my hands, I determined first that it was only somewhat real, and second that it was absolutely fabulous, and third that I'd made a big mistake in lusting after it. The fern had been so processed in bleach and dyes and sprayed in plastic I couldn't compost it. And worse: for a while I couldn't name the original plant.

This fern is often seen in fiddlehead form and sold under its Hawaiian name, uluhe. The plant is a keystone species in Hawaiian rainforests (and in other Pacific-adjacent tropical forests) where the mature fern plant can spread to twenty feet in width, making it a strong competitor against invasive species. The purply-black fiddleheads are wild harvested for trade and considered under sustainable management. They're available year-round as is the airy foliage, which can be up to almost three feet in width. A second uluhe fern is in the trade under the name uluhe lau nui and the plant here is *D. pinnatum*. Only available in the winter, you can differentiate this fern from its cousin by the slight edge on the frond, making it appear flatter than the rounded uluhe.

Waratah *(Telopea speciosissima)*

The state flower of New South Wales, waratah makes a wonderful cut flower. The shrubs grow on long stems, last close to two weeks in the vase, and dry well. The genus name *Telopea* comes from the Greek *telopos*, which means "visible from afar" in reference to waratah's showy flowers, some of which reach six inches wide in the wild. All members of the protea family, the five Australian species of *Telopea* grow naturally in damp cool forests on the east coast of the country. Pollinated by birds, they reproduce by seed, but after fire they regenerate from lignotubers, becoming multistemmed after a burn and thus more floriferous. The wild harvest of these plants is strictly controlled in Australia. A number of pink and white cultivars have been developed from the red species for horticulture and the cut-flower trade. In New Zealand the waratah is sometimes called the kiwi rose.

Water Lily *(Nymphaea spp.)*

Water lilies are tricky to work with. The white varieties often bloom at night and refuse to budge a petal in daylight hours. But like a jet-lagged traveler popping out of a chilled plane into tropical air, night-blooming water lilies can be tricked into believing it's time to bloom through a period of refrigeration. This may give you (and the flower) a few daylight hours of enjoyment, but prompt wilt follows. Apparently, water lilies can also be made to open in the cracked bud stage by applying careful pressure from behind the bloom, and I've read that dripping wax between the petals can force the flower to stay open. They benefit from sugar in their water.

Ylang-ylang *(Cananga odorata)*

Often used as a landscape tree positioned next to a window so the scent of flowers might drift on the wind, ylang-ylang has shaggy yellow-green flowers that emerge along the length of branches. One Nevisian gardener I met claimed the scent was "all Chanel No.5," which at the time seemed about right. I love ylang-ylang fresh but not in perfume, proving what we smell is often very different than how something smells on us.

The most fragrant ylang-ylang blooms arrive after rain. The flowers are hand-picked with lamps at night, when the flowers are most redolent. The highest-grade flowers are sexually mature, revealed by red marks on the inside of the petals, signifying the presence of indole.

Historically, France developed small plantations in their Indian Ocean colonies, but today premium ylang-ylang for the aromatherapy industry is grown and distilled in Ecuador.

Branches can be cut from the tree, but the blossoms are best treated as an ephemeral flower, floated in a little water.

Yucca

Designer Bridget Vizoso cuts yucca flowers in the bud stage and claims they last seven days. Split the stems, and condition or leave the stems in a couple inches of boiling water until it cools, then fill the bucket with cool water. The towering flowers of *Y. filamentosa* are too large for most settings, but you can use the smaller shoots. If the buds are reluctant to open, you can manipulate the flowers by soaking and reflexing the petals. Yucca leaves can last three weeks in the vase. Use your pin frog to shred stiff fibrous leaves like those of yuccas or phormiums.

Zanzibar Soapberry *(Majidea zanguebarica)*

A tree with as many names as places it grows (the mgambo, weleweka, Hawaiian pussy willow, black pearl tree, velvet-seed tree, and the Maui mink tree), this plant blooms red then makes spectacular fuzzy seeds, and pods are often used as jewelry, in floral design, and in potpourri.

Zinnia

Cut your zinnias hard (meaning deeply) when growing and they will branch and weave together offering one another support. Remember to pinch the growing tip of zinnias when they reach about ten inches to encourage branching early; this will make a bushier plant and deliver more blooming stems. Like marigolds, zinnia stems are hollow and give bacteria more surface area in which to multiply, but zinnias are worse given their stems are fuzzy. A cut zinnia will usually last only four to seven days (they will last longer if the plants have been watered before the flowers are cut). In a pinch, you can support a floppy zinnia neck by inserting a wire up the stem into the flower head.

Endnotes

1 Christina Nunez, "Why deforestation matters—and what we can do to stop it," *National Geographic*, December 7, 2022. https://www.nationalgeographic.com/environment/article/deforestation.

2 Cal Flyn, *Islands of Abandonment: Nature Rebounding in the Post-Human Landscape*, (Viking, 2021), 222.

3 "Ecological Systems and Future Implications," posted October 30, 2023, posted by Dr. Ariel Lugo, YouTube, private video, https://www.youtube.com/watch?v=wsmOUFyLhog.

4 Coral Madge, "Appreciation or Appropriation?," RAM Blog, Royal Alberta Museum, June 23, 2023, https://royalalbertamuseum.ca/blog/appreciation-or-appropriation.

5 Scott Shepard, host, *The Flower Podcast*, season 12, episode 257, "The Future of Floristry: Rita Feldmann of The Sustainable Floristry Network," April 9, 2024, https://www.theflowerpodcast.com/rita-feldman-sustainable-floristry-network.

6 Email message to the author, February 6, 2025.

7 Michelle Slatalla, "Anthuriums: Rethinking a Hotel Lobby Flower," *Gardenista*, February 17, 2021, https://www.gardenista.com/posts/anthuriums-rethinking-a-hotel-lobby-flower/.

8 Email message to the author, February 6, 2025.

9 *U.S. Floriculture Market Size, Share & Trends Analysis Report By Product (Bedding & Garden Plants, Pott Plants), by Distribution Channel (Offline, Online), by End Use (Commercial, Industrial), and Segment Forecasts, 2024 – 2030* (Grand View Research, August 2024), https://www.researchandmarkets.com/report/united-states-floriculture-market. Kate Olivia Sessions, *The Complete Writings of Kate Sessions in California Garden, 1909–1939*, ed. Barbara Schillreff Jones (San Diego Floral Association, 1998), 59.

10 Judith Taylor, *The Global Migrations of Ornamental Plants: How the World Got into Your Garden* (Missouri Botanic Garden Press, 2009), 10.

11 Taylor, 10.

12 Phyllis Andersen, "Floral Clocks, Carpet Beds, and the Ornamentation of Public Parks," Arnold Arboretum, August 15, 2017, https://arboretum.harvard.edu/arnoldia-stories/floral-clocks-carpet-beds-and-the-ornamentation-of-public-parks/.

13 *Annuals & Biennials: The Best Annual and Biennial Plants and Their Uses in the Garden*. Gertrude Jekyll (Country Life, 1916), 32.

14 Mary Kuhn, *The Garden Politic: Global Plants and Botanical Nationalism in Nineteenth-Century America* (NYU Press, 2023), 10.

15 Taylor, 169.

16 Yoonus Imran et al., "Biopiracy: Abolish Corporate Hijacking of Indigenous Medicinal Entities," https://pmc.ncbi.nlm.nih.gov/articles/PMC7910072.

17 Convention on Biological Diversity, *Case Study 4. Ball Horticulture and the South African National Biodiversity Institute* (United Nations Environmental Programme, 2008), https://www.cbd.int/doc/meetings/abs/abswg-06/other/abswg-06-cs-04-en.pdf.

18 Melanie Gosling, "Flower Report Slams Deal with US Company," *Independent Online*, October 17, 2001, https://iol.co.za/news/south-africa/2001-10-17-flower-report-slams-deal-with-us-company/.

19 Convention on Biological Diversity, *Case Study 4*.

20 Secretariat of the Convention on Biological Diversity, *Nagoya Protocol on Access to Genetic Resources and the Fair and Equitable Sharing of Benefits Arising from Their Utilization to the Convention on Biological Diversity*, (United Nations Environmental Programme, 2011), https://www.cbd.int/abs/doc/protocol/nagoya-protocol-en.pdf.

21 Jamaica Kincaid, *A Small Place* (Farrar, Straus and Giroux, 1988), 19.

22 Edith Young, *Color Scheme: An Irreverent History of Art and Pop Culture in Color Palettes* (Princeton Architectural Press, 2021), 101.

23 Scott Shepherd, host, *The Flower Podcast*, "Learning About Flower Breeding with Dr. Rick Grazzini," October 25, 2021, https://www.theflowerpodcast.com/rick-grazzini.

24 Mike Rimland, "Globetrotting Grower: Europe Versus the U.S. in Floriculture," Greenhouse Grower, April 25, 2011, https://www.greenhousegrower.com/management/finance-operations/globetrotting-grower-europe-versus-the-u-s-in-floriculture/.

25 Andrew G. Hankins, "Sell Cut Flowers from Perennial Summer-flowering Bulbs," *Virginia Cooperative Extension*, January 24, 2019, http://hdl.handle.net/10919/88367.

26 Eric America, “Geophyte Neophyte How to Avoid Having a Nervous Breakdown while Gardening with California’s Native Bulbs & Corms,” LA Native Plant Source, Mar 24, 2024, https://lanativeplantsource.com/geophyte-neophyte/.

27 Halle Marchese and Cody Howard, “Underground Movement: The Secret Lives of Geophytes,” Florida Museum, June 28, 2019, https://www.floridamuseum.ufl.edu/science/the-secret-lives-of-geophytes/.

28 Alexander Theroux, *The Secondary Colors: Three Essays* (Henry Holt & Co, 1996), 9.

29 David Batchelor, *Chromophobia* (Reaktion Books, 2000), 27.

30 Batchelor, 22.

31 Kassia St. Clair, *The Secret Lives of Color* (Penguin Books, 2017), 29.

32 Batchelor, 27.

33 Batchelor, 22.

34 Alexandre Antonelli, “The Evolution and Fate of Tropical Diversity,” lecture, January 11, 2021, The Kew Mutual Improvement Society.

35 Rhett Ayers Butler, “The Top 10 Most Biodiverse Countries,” Mongabay, May 21, 2016, https://news.mongabay.com/2016/05/top-10-biodiverse-countries.

36 University of Copenhagen, “Rwandan Tree Carbon Stock Mapped from Above,” *Phys.org*, December 22, 2022, https://phys.org/news/2022-12-rwandan-tree-carbon-stock.html.

37 Adeola Babalola, Balan Sundarakani, and K. Ganesh, “Cold Chain Logistics in the Floral Industry,” *International Journal of Enterprise Network Management* 4, no. 4 (2011): 400–413, https://doi.org/10.1504/IJENM.2011.043801.

38 Carly Lewis, “We Are Saying It with Flowers. Loudly and Repeatedly,” *New York Times*, February 17, 2021, https://www.nytimes.com/2021/02/17/style/1-800-flowers.html.

39 ROAPE, “Propertied Proletarians? The Kenyan Cut-Flower Industry,” *Review of African Political Economy*, June 21, 2017, https://roape.net/2017/06/21/propertied-proletarians-kenyan-cut-flower-industry/.

40 https://www.wafex.com.au/about-wafex/vert-integration.

41 Sue Shephard, *The Surprising Life of Constance Spry: From Social Reformer to Society Florist*, (Pan Books, 2011), 303.

42 Shephard, 303.

43 Ellen Scott, “Sketches Reveal Hidden Details of Meghan Markle’s Wedding Veil,”*METRO*, May 20, 2018, https://metro.co.uk/2018/05/20/sketches-reveal-hidden-details-meghan-markles-wedding-veil-7562878/.

44 Peter Robertshaw, “Africa’s Earliest Bananas,” *Archaeology Magazine* 59, no. 5, September/October 2006, https://archive.archaeology.org/0609/abstracts/bananas.html.

45 “What Is Happening to Agrobiodiveristy?” in *Building on Gender, Agrobiodiversity and Local Knowledge* (Food and Agriculture Organization of the United Nations, 2004), https://www.fao.org/4/y5609e/y5609e02.htm.

46 David Fairchild, “Our Plant Immigrants,” *National Geographic* XVII, no. 4, April 1906, http://www.virtualherbarium.org/resource/NationalGeographic1906.html.

47 Michael Pollan, “What’s Eating America,” *Michael Pollan website*, June 15, 2006, https://michaelpollan.com/articles-archive/whats-eating-america/.

48 Mark Bittman, Michael Pollan, Ricardo Salvador, and Olivier De Schutter, “How a National Food Policy Could Save Millions of Lives,” *Michael Pollan website*, November 7, 2014, https://michaelpollan.com/articles-archive/how-a-national-food-policy-could-save-millions-of-american-lives/.

49 Jane E. Brody, “The Health Benefits of Knitting,” *New York Times*, January 25, 2016, https://archive.nytimes.com/well.blogs.nytimes.com/2016/01/25/the-health-benefits-of-knitting/.

50 Patrícia Muniz de Medeiros et al., “The Use of Medicinal Plants by Migrant People: Adaptation, Maintenance, and Replacement,” *Evidence-Based Complementary and Alternative Medicine* (2012): 807452, https://doi.org/10.1155/2012/807452.

51 http://www.transcultural-english-studies.de/tag/edouard-glissant.

52 Erin Hale, “Why Colouring Clothes Has a Big Environmental Impact,” BBC, November 4, 2024, https://www.bbc.com/news/articles/c870j92p82wo.

53 William Villa and Juan Houghton, *Violencia política contra los pueblos indígenas en Colombia: 1974-2004*, (IWGIA, CECOIN, 2005), https://iwgia.org/images/publications/0326_ViolenciaColombia.pdf.

54 Mongabay, “How a Rare Colombian Flower Cultivated With Indigenous Knowledge Is Changing Lives,” *EcoWatch*, August 19, 2022, https://www.ecowatch.com/indigenous-agriculture-flowers-colombia.html.

55 Mohamed Osam, “Egyptian Village Struggles to Keep Ancient Papyrus Alive,” *Middle East Eye*, August 13, 2017, https://www.middleeasteye.net/features/egyptian-village-struggles-keep-ancient-papyrus-alive.

56 Elisabetta Bertol et al., “Nymphaea Cults in Ancient Egypt and the New World: A Lesson in Empirical Pharmacology,” *Journal of the Royal Society of Medicine* 97, no. 2 (2004): 84–85, https://doi.org/10.1177/014107680409700214.

57 Manash Pratim Gohain, “The Lotus Can Generate Heat and Regulate Its Temperature like Birds, Mammals: Study,” *Times of India*, May 13, 2013, https://timesofindia.indiatimes.com/home/science/the-lotus-can-generate-heat-and-regulate-its-temperature-like-birds-mammals-study/articleshow/20031896.cms?from=mdr.

58 Jack Goody, *The Culture of Flowers* (Cambridge University Press, 1993), 368.

59 Kincaid, Jamaica, “Flowers of Evil,” *New Yorker*, October 5, 1992, 156.

60 Kincaid, “Flowers of Evil,” 155.

61 Jennifer Jewell, Matt Fidler, hosts, Jamaica Kincaid, guest, *Cultivating Place*, “Cultivating Place: Botany, Geography, History & Power At The Heart Of The Garden, W/ Jamaica Kincaid,” North State Public Radio, July 2, 2020, https://www.mynspr.org/show/cultivating-place-conversations-on-natural-history-and-the-human-impulse-to-garden/2020-07-02/cultivating-place-botany-geography-history-power-at-the-heart-of-the-garden-w-jamaica-kincaid.

62 Kinkaid, “Flowers of Evil,” 159.

63 Personal communication, January 2025.

64 Karen Nero, “Missed Opportunities: American Anthropological Studies of Micronesian Arts” in *American Anthropology in Micronesia: an Assessment*, ed. R. Kiste and M. Marshall (University of Hawai'i Press, 1999), 257.

65 Victoria and Albert Museum, “Chinoiserie – An Introduction,” accessed June 22, 2025, https://www.vam.ac.uk/articles/chinoiserie-an-introduction?srsltid=AfmBOooeAl79fvJw3IZIi4T5-AbqDoZKaU WOOKPKtNDulhgY8onCzw-6.

66 “Kenyan Flower Farm Workers Riot After Mass Sacking,” *Mail & Guardian*, January 31, 2006, https://mg.co.za/article/2006-01-31-kenyan-flower-farm-workers-riot-after-mass-sacking/.

67 Angela Cruz et. al., “Between Cultural Appreciation and Cultural Appropriation: Self-Authorizing the Consumption of Cultural Difference,” *Journal of Consumer Research* 50 (2024): 962–984, https://doi.org/10.1093/jcr/ucad022.

68 Tehila Sasson, *The Solidarity Economy: Nonprofits and the Making of Neoliberalism after Empire* (Princeton University Press, 2024), 9.

69 Gerda Kuiper and Andreas Gemählich, “Sustainability and Depoliticisation: Certifications in the Cut-Flower Industry at Lake Naivasha, Kenya,” *Africa Spectrum* 52, no. 3 (2017): 31-53, https://doi.org/10.1177/000203971705200302.

70 Jana Register, “Leatherleaf Fern — King of the Florida Cut Foliage Industry,” *Produce News*, October 25, 2017, https://theproducenews.com/leatherleaf-fern-king-florida-cut-foliage-industry.

71 Lorna Jean Hagstrom, “Pierson: Fern Capital of the World,” West Volusia Historical Society, accessed June 22. 2025, https://www.delandhouse.com/article_ferneries.

72 Patricio G. Balona, “Volusia Fern Cutters Suffer More Heat-Related Illnesses; How They’re Paid May Be Why,” *Daytona Beach News-Journal*, October 8, 2021, https://www.news-journalonline.com/story/news/2021/10/08/study-volusia-fern-cutters-suffer-more-heat-related-illnesses/5832907001/.

73 Emma Siossian and Meredith Kirton, “Flannel Flowers Burst into ‘Spectacular’ Bloom Near Port Macquarie After Bushfires, Floods,” *ABC News*, September 6, 2021, https://www.abc.net.au/news/2021-09-17/flannel-flowers-burst-into-bloom-after-bushfires/100458610.

74 Besha Rodell, "Australian Floral Designs That, at Long Last, Embrace Australian Flora," *New York Times Style Magazine*, September 23, 2022, https://www.nytimes.com/2022/09/23/t-magazine/australian-florists.html.

75 A. D. Chapman, *Numbers of Living Species in Australia and the World*, 2nd ed. (Australian Biodiversity Information Services, 2009), https://www.dcceew.gov.au/science-research/abrs/publications/other/numbers-living-species/discussion-plants.

76 Peter Beal, "Commercial Production of Australian Wildflowers" SGAP Queensland Region's Bulletin, December 1997, https://anpsa.org.au/APOL10/jun98-3.html.

77 Email message to the author, February 3, 2025.

78 Madeline Stuchbery, "Industry Calls for Inclusion in Biosecurity Levy," *Weekly Times*, May 10, 2023, https://www.flowerindustryaustralia.com.au/news/forgotten-flowers-industry-calls-for-inclusion-in-biosecurity-levy.

79 Nina Wu, "Kilauea Eruption Downsizes One of the Big Island's Largest Orchid Growers," *Star Advertiser*, July 9, 2018, https://www.staradvertiser.com/2018/07/09/hawaii-news/kilauea-eruption-downsizes-one-of-the-big-islands-largest-orchid-growers/.

80 Hitomi Gilliam, interview by Lori Poliski, 2022, transcript emailed to author January 14, 2023.

81 Susan Mcleary, "Mornings with Mayesh: Sue Mcleary & #iloveflorists," livestreamed interview with Yvonne Ashton, host, posted on Jul 19, 2022, by Mayesh Wholesale Florist, YouTube, https://www.youtube.com/watch?v=DdjiAkzMwE4.

82 Jordan Goodman, *Planting the World: Joseph Banks and His Collectors: An Adventurous History of Botany*, narrated by Paul Hilliar (William Collins, 2020).

83 J. H. Coetzee, "Benefit Sharing from Flowering Bulb - Is it Still Possible?" *Acta Horticulture* 570, (2002): 21–27, DOI: 10.17660/ActaHortic.2002.570.1.

84 Mitraja Bais, "Mala: The Floral Garlands of India," *Garland Magazine*, December 1, 2017, https://garlandmag.com/article/mala-the-floral-garlands-of-india/.

85 Sean Wang Zi-Ming, "Plant of the Month: Frangipani," *JSTOR Daily*, February 16, 2023, https://daily.jstor.org/plant-of-the-month-frangipani/.

86 Jen Murphy, "Hawaii Is Rethinking Tourism. Here's What That Means for You," *Bloomberg*, December 30, 2021, https://www.bloomberg.com/news/features/2021-12-30/hawaii-is-rethinking-tourism-here-s-what-that-means-for-you?sref=KD3BmaDL.

87 Manfred Steger, *Globalization: A Very Short Introduction*, (Oxford University Press, 2013), 115.

88 University of Leicester, *Restoring the Ecosystem Services of Lake Naivasha (Kenya) for Globally-Important Exports, Unique Biodiversity and 3/4 Million People* (Research Excellence Framework, 2014), https://impact.ref.ac.uk/casestudies/CaseStudy.aspx?Id=43505.

89 Food and Water Watch and the Council of Canadians, *Lake Naivasha: Withering Under the Assault of International Flower Vendors* (2008), https://www.foodandwatereurope.org/wp-content/uploads/2009/11/FoodandWaterEuropeLakeNavaisha.pdf.

90 Taylor, *The Global Migration*, 165.

91 Kathelijne Bonne, "Plate Tectonics: Caterpillar Tracks of the Planet," *GondwanaTalks*, June 19, 2020, https://www.gondwanatalks.com/l/plate-tectonics/.

92 UC Museum of Paleontology, "Introduction to the Glossopteridales," accessed July 6, 2025, https://ucmp.berkeley.edu/seedplants/pteridosperms/glossopterids.html.

93 Carol Duncan, "Art Institutions: Maybe Feminism Has Just Begun," in *Mobile Fidelities: Conversations on Feminism, History and Visuality*, ed. Martina Pachmanová (KT Press, July 2006), 132, https://www.ktpress.co.uk/pdf/nparadoxaissue19_martina-pachmanova_123-135.pdf.

94 Pierre Bourdieu, *Distinction: A Social Critique of the Judgment of Taste*, trans. Richard Nice (Harvard University Press, 1984) 47.

95 Goody, *The Culture of Flowers*, 233.

96 Victor Margolin, *The Politics of the Artificial: Essays on Design and Design Studies* (University of Chicago Press, 2002), 241.

97 Neil Cummins, Sam Friedman, Sabrina Daniel, hosts, *LSE IQ podcast*, "How Does Class Define Us?," October 31, 2022, https://podcasts.apple.com/si/podcast/how-does-class-define-us/id1223817465?i=1000584649609.

98 *New York Times*, December 11, 1934, 20.

99 Kuhn, 61.

100 Karen Mancl, "China Increasing Agricultural Production on a Sea of Plastic," *New Security Beat*, April 24, 2020, https://www.newsecuritybeat.org/2020/04/china-increasing-agricultural-production-sea-plastic/.

101 Anna Fleck, "Over 112,000 Suicides in India's Farming Industry in 10 Years," *Statista*, May 15, 2024, https://www.statista.com/chart/32258/reported-suicides-of-farmers-farm-laborers-in-india/.

102 Sarah Langford "'Were the Soil a Jungle, the Worm Would Be Its Elephant': Why Everything You Thought About Soil Is Probably Wrong," *Country Life*, January 24, 2025, https://www.countrylife.co.uk/nature/were-the-soil-a-jungle-the-worm-would-be-its-elephant-why-everything-you-thought-about-soil-is-probably-wrong-278668.

103 Vandana Shiva, interview by George Stroumboulopoulo, *George Stroumboulopoulo Tonight*, CBC, posted March 9, 2012, https://www.cbc.ca/strombo/videos/vandana-shiva-full-extended-interview.

104 "E. F. Schumacher," Wikipedia, last edited on May 8, 2025, 17:23 (UTC), https://en.wikipedia.org/wiki/E._F._Schumacher.

105 "Land Governance: Honouring Rights and Responsibilities," The David Suzuki Foundation, April 5, 2021, https://davidsuzuki.org/story/land-governance-honouring-rights-and-responsibilities/.

106 Wade Davis, "The Term 'Indigenous,' in Its Current Use, Might Be Doing Us All a Disservice," *Globe and Mail*, March 25, 2023, https://www.theglobeandmail.com/opinion/article-the-term-indigenous-in-its-current-use-might-be-doing-us-all-a/.

107 "Get to Know: Chloe Rose Quinn on Traditional Balinese Decorations and Creativity," *Elami&Co Productions*, February 14, 2019, https://www.elami.co/blog/2019/2/14/get-to-know-chloe-rose-quinn.

108 "Kapwani Kiwanga, 'Flowers For Africa' - Marcel Duchamp Prize 2020," posted October 21, 2020, by Centre culturel canadien, YouTube, https://www.youtube.com/watch?v=m_eXzRln4Wk.

109 Kapwani Kiwanga, "Flowers for Africa: Rwanda, 2019," Art Basel website, accessed July 13, 2025, https://www.artbasel.com/catalog/artwork/85804/Kapwani-Kiwanga-Flowers-for-Africa-Rwanda.

110 "Installation Art," The Art Story, accessed July 6, 2025, https://www.theartstory.org/movement/installation-art/.

111 "Installation Art" definition, Tate Gallery, accessed July 6, 2025, https://www.tate.org.uk/art/art-terms/i/installation-art.

112 Melissa Ozawa, "10 Questions with Floral Designer Emily Thompson," *Gardenista*, February 9, 2023, https://www.gardenista.com/posts/tk-questions-floral-designer-emily-thompson/.

113 Elizabeth Kolbert, "Where Have All the Insects Gone?," *The New Yorker*, October 25, 2021, https://www.newyorker.com/magazine/2021/11/01/where-have-all-the-insects-gone-e-o-wilson-silent-earth.

114 Richard Porter and Olivia Laing, eds., *A Garden Manifesto* (Pilot Press, 2024), 150.

115 Michael D. Brooks, "Civilizing the Metropole: The Role of the 1889 Parisian Universal Exposition's Colonial Exhibits in Creating Greater France," *The Pegasus Review: UCF Undergraduate Research Journal* 6, issue 2, article 3 (2013): https://stars.library.ucf.edu/cgi/viewcontent.cgi?article=1049&context=urj.

116 Mairead Dundas et. al., "Toxic Cocktail: The Secret Within Your Flowers," France24, July 6, 2019, https://www.france24.com/en/20190607-down-earth-pesticides-toxic-chemicals-slow-flowers-bouquets-agriculture-netherlands.

117 Patrícia C.G. Pereira et. al., "A Review on Pesticides in Flower Production: A Push to Reduce Human Exposure and Environmental Contamination," *Environmental Pollution* 289, (2021): https://doi.org/10.1016/j.envpol.2021.117817.

118 Khaoula Toumi et. al., "Biological Monitoring of Exposure to Pesticide Residues among Belgian Florists," *Human and Ecological Risk Assessment: An International Journal* 26, no. 3 (2019): 636–53, https://doi.org/10.1080/10807039.2018.1528860.

119 "Why Rattan Furniture Is So Expensive | So Expensive," posted

February 19, 2022, by Business Insider, YouTube, https://youtu.be/N88TwF4D2PI?si=pHmlYAYgSnwNvj8o.

120 E. M. Muralidharan, V. B. Sreekumar and R. Kaam, *Establishment of Rattan Plantations*, INBAR Technical Report no. 42 (INBAR, 2020), https://www.inbar.int/wp-content/uploads/2020/09/Establishment-of-Rattan-Plantations_final.pdf.

121 Sam Knight, "The Shipwreck Detective," *New Yorker*, November 4, 2024, https://www.newyorker.com/magazine/2024/11/11/the-shipwreck-detective.

122 Marzena Joseph (@marzena_joseph), "There are many parallels between the principles of Ikebana and those of other art forms. One such parallel is the importance of line, mass, and colour - elements that are as crucial to an Ikebana arrangement as they are to a painting by Kandinsky," Instagram, March 5, 2024, https://www.instagram.com/p/C4JX7DFi5Ez/.

123 American Institute of Floral Designers, *The AIFD Guide to Floral Design* (Schiffer Publishing, 2022), 94.

124 Hui-Lin Li, *Chinese Floral Arrangement* (Dover Publications, 2002), 19.

125 Paul Richard, "Bending to Nature in a Room of Bamboo," *Washington Post*, March 27, 1996, https://www.washingtonpost.com/archive/lifestyle/1996/03/27/bending-to-nature-in-a-room-of-bamboo/a3a5cf50-4ba9-4705-9ed5-1c50699361f3/.

126 Hiroshi Teshigahara, "Bamboo in Sogetsu," accessed, July 13, 2022, originally published in *Bungeishunju*, May 1994, https://www.sogetsu.or.jp/e/about/bamboo.

127 Lori Poliski, "The Final Floral Footprint," *Slow Flowers Journal*, winter 2023, 62.

128 Jules Howard, "Here's What Will Happen When We Run Out of Space to Bury the Dead," *Science Focus*, October 31, 2021, https://www.sciencefocus.com/the-human-body/deal-with-the-dead.

129 Lynn Voskuil "Victorian Orchids and the Forms of Ecological Society," in *Strange Science: Investigating the Limits of Knowledge in the Victorian Age*, eds. Lara Karpenko and Shalyn Claggett (University of Michigan, 2017).

130 "Orchidelirium, the Victorian passion for orchids," Chatsworth, February 3, 2023, https://www.chatsworth.org/news-media/news-blogs-press-releases/orchidelirium-the-victorian-passion-for-orchids/.

131 Taylor, *The Global Migrations*, 191.

132 Mary Noble, "New Way to Propagate Orchids," *New York Times*, December 27, 1964, 94.

133 Noel Kingsbury, *The Story of Flowers: And How They Changed the Way We Live* (Laurence King Publishing, 2023), 129.

134 "Last Chance Tourism," *Under the Influence with Terry O'Reilly*, CBC Listen, January 16, 2025, https://www.cbc.ca/listen/live-radio/1-70-under-the-influence/clip/16121489-last-chance-tourism.

135 "The Age of Plastic: From Parkesine to Pollution," part of Chemistry series, Science Museum, October 11, 2019, https://www.sciencemuseum.org.uk/objects-and-stories/chemistry/age-plastic-parkesine-pollution.

136 Jamie Hailstone, "Paint Is the Largest Source of Plastic in the Ocean, Study Finds," *Forbes: Sustainability*, February 9, 2022.

137 Shepard, Scott, host, *The Flower Podcast*, season 12, episode 257, "The Future of Floristry: Rita Feldmann of The Sustainable Floristry Network." April 9, 2024, https://www.theflowerpodcast.com/rita-feldman-sustainable-floristry-network.

138 "Cristina Romera-Castillo: 'Cleaning the Ocean Out of Plastic Is Like Sweeping in the Desert,'" institut de ciències del mar, September 30, 2022, https://www.icm.csic.es/en/news/cristina-romera-castillo-cleaning-ocean-out-plastic-sweeping-desert.

139 Shepard, "The Future of Floristry."

140 "10 Years of Designing & Building Collective Liberation," *Slow Factory* impact report 2012–2022, https://slowfactory.earth/assets/downloads/Slow-Factory-Decade-Impact-Report-2012-2022.pdf.

141 Richard Hartlage, "Gardens of Roberto Burle Marx," *Garden Design*, accessed July 13, 2025, https://www.gardendesign.com/brazil/burle-marx-rio.html.

142 Georgina Reid, "Roberto Burle Marx: The Modernist Gardener, " *Wonderground*, October 7, 2015, https://wonderground.press/gardens/roberto-burle-marx-the-modernist-gardener/.

143 Reid.

144 Edward Rothstein, "Modern and Postmodern, the Bickering Twins," *New York Times*, October 21, 2000, https://www.nytimes.com/2000/10/21/arts/modern-and-postmodern-the-bickering-twins.html.

145 Lorraine Harrison, *How to Read Gardens: A Crash Course in Garden Appreciation*(A & C Black Publishers Ltd, 2010), 67.

146 Charles Wright, "Clear Night," from *Country Music: Selected Early Poems* (Wesleyan University Press, 1991).

147 Catherine Seavitt Nordenson, "Roberto Burle Marx (1909–1994)," *Architecture Review*, February 3, 2021, https://www.architectural-review.com/essays/reputations/roberto-burle-marx-1909-1994.

148 The Jewish Museum, "Repairing Humanity and Nature: Roberto Burle Marx's Environmentalism," Medium, May 26, 2016, https://stories.thejewishmuseum.org/repairing-humanity-and-nature-roberto-burle-marxs-environmentalism-119e69424c5e.

149 Owen Jones, *The Grammar of Ornament* (Day and Son, 1856; repr., Van Nostrand Reinhold Company, 1972), 6, https://www.google.com/books/edition/The_Grammar_of_Ornament/t1frAAAAMAAJ?hl=en&gbpv=1&printsec=frontcover

150 Jones, 5.

151 Jones, 33.

152 Angela L. Miller, Janet Catherine Berlo, Bryan J. Wolf, and Jennifer L. Roberts, "10.3: Reform and Innovation-Handcraft and Mechanization in the Decorative Arts, 1860–1900" in *American Encounters: Art, History, and Cultural Identity* (LibreText, 2025), https://human.libretexts.org/Bookshelves/Art/American_Encounters%3A_Art_History_and_Cultural_Identity_(Miller_Berlo_Wolf_and_Roberts)/03%3A_Early_Colonial_Arts_1632-1734/10%3A_A_New_Internationalism-_The_Arts_in_an_Expanding_World_1876-1900/10.03%3A_Reform_and_Innovation-_Handcraft_and_Mechanization_in_the_Decorative_Arts_1860-1900.

153 Sara J. Oshinsky, "Christopher Dresser (1834–1904)," The Metropolitan Museum of Art, October 1, 2006, https://www.metmuseum.org/toah/hd/cdrs/hd_cdrs.htm.

154 Vanessa Thorpe, "The Worst Possible Taste: 1852 Design Exhibition Defiantly Revived," *Guardian*, June 29, 2019, https://www.theguardian.com/artanddesign/2019/jun/29/worst-possible-taste-design-exhibition-1852-revived.

155 Olivia Horsfall Turner, *Owen Jones and the V&A: Ornament for a Modern Age* (Lund Humphries Publishers Ltd, 2023), 28.

156 "Wallpaper Design Reform," Victoria and Albert Museum, accessed July 13, 2025, https://www.vam.ac.uk/articles/wallpaper-design-reform.

157 Oshinsky.

158 Jones, 156.

159 Gareth Richards, "Systems of Dominance," *Radicle* Substack, January 14, 2022, https://radicle.substack.com/p/systems-of-dominance.

160 David M. Richardson et. al., "Naturalization and invasion of alien plants: concepts and definitions," *Diversity and Distributions* 6 (2000): 93–107, http://www.ibot.cas.cz/personal/pysek/pdf/naturalization_and_invasion_%20of_alien_plants.pdf.

161 Carine Mardorossian, "'Poetics of Landscape': Édouard Glissant's Creolized Ecologies," *Callaloo* 36, no. 4 (2013): 983–994, https://doi.org/10.1353/cal.2013.0196.

162 Evie Evans, "Cultivating Colonialism: The Musealisation of Natural Objects in the Hortus Botanicus, Amsterdam, and the Royal Botanic Gardens, Kew," (master's thesis, University of Amsterdam, 2021), 53, https://framerframed.nl/wp-content/uploads/2021/05/Thesis-Evie-Evans-Cultivating-Colonialism-2021-LR.pdf.

163 Anny Li, "The World Was Their Garden: Plant Introductions at the US Department of Agriculture, 1898–1984" (master's thesis, Harvard Graduate School of Design, 2022), 43, https://nrs.harvard.edu/URN-3:HUL.INSTREPOS:37372329.

164 Anita Anand and William Dalrymple, hosts, Alex von Tunzelmann, guest, *Empire* podcast, season, 9 episode 25, "The Cuban Revolution," August 5, 2024.

165 Frantz Fanon, *The Wretched of the Earth* (Grove Press, 1963), 36.

166 Rashad Bell and Nuala Caomhánach, "Inside Black Botany: A Conversation with the Curators," posted February 26, 2021, by New York Botanical Garden, https://www.youtube.com/watch?v=cCdefpMRe4s.

167 Eve Tuck and K. Wayne Yang, “Decolonization is Not a Metaphor,” *Decolonization: Indigeneity, Education & Society* 1, no. 1 (2012): 3, https://clas.osu.edu/sites/clas.osu.edu/files/Tuck%20and%20Yang%20 2012%20Decolonization%20is%20not%20a%20metaphor.pdf.

168 Zack Beauchamp, “500 Years of European Colonialism, in One Animated Map,” *Vox*, January 16, 2015, https://www.vox.com/2014/5/8/5691954/colonialism-collapse-gif-imperialism.

169 Robert J. C. Young, *Postcolonialism: A Very Short Introduction* (Oxford University Press, 2003), 32.

170 Bernd Lenzner et. al., “Naturalized Alien Floras Still Carry the Legacy of European Colonialism,” *Nature Ecology & Evolution* 6 (2022): 1723–1732, https://doi.org/10.1038/s41559-022-01865-1.

171 Kincaid, *A Small Place*, 4.

172 Promoting and Protecting Indigenous Arts, “The Parameters and Stakes of Misappropriation and Misuse,” Indigenous Futures Research Centre at Concordia University, accessed August 14, 2025, https://ppia-ppaa.ca/themes/misappropriation-and-misuse/.

173 Richard Sandomir, “Patricia Caulfield, 91, Dies; Battled Warhol Over Use of Her Photograph,” *The New York Times*, September 7, 2023, https://www.nytimes.com/2023/09/07/arts/patricia-caulfield-dead.html.

174 “Peatlands store twice as much carbon as all the world’s forests,” story from United Nations Environment Programme, February 1, 2019, https://www.unep.org/news-and-stories/story/peatlands-store-twice-much-carbon-all-worlds-forests.

175 Dianna Kopansky, Mark Reed, Matt Kaplan, and Jonny Hughes, *Global Peatlands Assessment: The State of the World’s Peatlands* (United Nations Environment Programme, 2022), https://doi.org/10.59117/20.500.11822/41222.

176 Canadian Sphagnum Peat Moss Association, “Peatlands,” accessed July 6, 2025, https://peatmoss.com/peatlands/.

177 “Plastic pots: is there an ethical alternative?” from BBC Gardening Guides, accessed July 13, 2025, https://www.bbc.co.uk/gardening/today_in_your_garden/ethical_plastic.shtml.

178 Porter and Laing, 47.

179 Email to the author, April 15, 2025.

180 Margaret Roach, “Why Gardeners Should Stop Using Peat, and What to Use Instead,” *New York Times*, February 2, 2022, https://www.nytimes.com/2022/02/02/realestate/gardening-peat.html.

181 Henk Westhoek, John Ingram, Siemen van Berkum, Leyla Özay, and Maarten Hajer, *Food Systems and Natural Resources*, (United Nations Environment Programme, 2016) https://www.resourcepanel.org/reports/food-systems-and-natural-resources.

182 Kingsbury, Noel, 181.

183 http://www.hawaiineotropica.com/links/proteas.

184 David Griffiths, “Queer Theory for Lichens,” *UnderCurrents: Journal of Critical Environmental Studies* 19 (October 2016): 36–45, https://doi.org/10.25071/2292-4736/40249.

185 Alex Wilson, “N’tacimowin inna nah,’” *Canadian Woman Studies/ Les Cahiers De La Femme* 26, no. 3-4 (2008): 193–199, https://cws.journals.yorku.ca/index.php/cws/article/view/22131/20785.

186 D. H. McNear Jr., “The Rhizosphere - Roots, Soil and Everything In Between,” *Nature Education Knowledge* 4, no. 3 (2013): 1, https://www.nature.com/scitable/knowledge/library/the-rhizosphere-roots-soil-and-67500617/.

187 Erik Runkle, “Ethylene in Floriculture,” GPNMAG.COM, January 2019, 50, https://www.canr.msu.edu/floriculture/uploads/files/ethylene%20in%20floriculture.pdf.

188 “Tuberose,” Flower. Style, accessed July 13, 2025, https://www.flower.style/flowers-we-love/tuberose.

189 “Tuberose or Rajnigandha,” Venkatramna, January 5, 2023, https://vriaroma.com/blog/89/tuberose-or-rajnigandha.

190 Roddy Scheer and Doug Moss, “Scent of Danger: Are There Toxic Ingredients in Perfumes and Colognes?,” EarthTalk, *Scientific American*, September 29, 2012, https://www.scientificamerican.com/article/toxic-perfumes-and-colognes/.

191 “Why phenology?,” USA National Phenology Network, accessed July 13, 2025, https://www.usanpn.org/about/phenology.

192 Goody, *The Culture of Flowers*, 409.

193 Ryan Pankau, “Lunar Influence on Gardening,” *The Garden Scoop* (blog), College of Agricultural, Consumer & Environmental Sciences, University of Illinois Urbana-Champaign, April 16, 2022, https://extension.illinois.edu/blogs/garden-scoop/2022-04-16-lunar-influence-gardening.

194 Gina Maruca et. al.,“The Fascinating History of Bergamot (*Citrus Bergamia* Risso & Poiteau), the Exclusive Essence of Calabria: A Review” *Journal of Environmental Science and Engineering* A 6 (2017): 22–30, https://www.davidpublisher.com/Public/uploads/Contribute/58ed8a4721c87.pdf.

195 Sessions, 15.

196 Annette McGivney, “‘Yanked from the Ground’: Cactus Theft Is Ravaging the American Desert,” *The Guardian*, February 20, 2019, https://www.theguardian.com/environment/2019/feb/20/to-catch-a-cactus-thief-national-parks-fight-a-thorny-problem.

197 Nomsa Maseko and Rob Wilson, “Illegal Trade Booms in South Africa’s ‘Super-Strange Looking’ Plants,” *BBC News*, December 26, 2024, https://www.bbc.com/news/articles/ced8v60q4x7o.amp.

198 Sustainable Flowers Research Project, About page, accessed July 6, 2025, https://sustainableflowersresearch.org/about/.

199 Email message to author, February 3, 2025.

200 Jack Hurd and Patricia Ellen da Silva, *The Cerrado: Production and Protection* (World Economic Forum, 2024), https://www3.weforum.org/docs/WEF_Sustainable_Transition_Cerrado_2024.pdf.

201 Email message to author, January 24, 2025.

202 Jeff Sebo, “Utilitarianism and Nonhuman Animals,” in *An Introduction to Utilitarianism*, ed. R. Y. Chappell, D. Meissner, and W. MacAskill (2023), accessed July 6, 2025, https://www.utilitarianism.net/guest-essays/utilitarianism-and-nonhuman-animals.

203 Fred Pearce, “Fred Pearce: Land Grabbing Has More of an Impact on the World’s Poor Than Climate Change,” Interview by Tom Templeton, *The Guardian*, May 19, 2012, https://www.theguardian.com/world/2012/may/20/fred-pearce-land-grab-interview.

204 Shankar Vedantam, host, *Hidden Brain* “Playing Favorites: When Kindness Toward Some Means Callousness Towards Others,” NPR, June 8, 2020, https://www.npr.org/transcripts/870352402.

205 Jason K. Hawes et. al., “Comparing the Carbon Footprints of Urban and Conventional Agriculture,” *Nature Cities* 1, (2024): 164–73, https://doi.org/10.1038/s44284-023-00023-3.

206 Leo Bear-McGuinness, “Community Gardens Have Six Times the Carbon Footprint of Agriculture,” *Technology Networks*, January 22, 2024, https://www.technologynetworks.com/applied-sciences/news/community-gardens-have-six-times-the-carbon-footprint-of-agriculture-383009.

207 Tess Lowery, Fadeke Banjo, and Lana Lenfant Al Zouheiri, “8 Mic Drop Moments from Prime Minister of Barbados Mia Mottley,” *Global Citizen*, July 10, 2023, https://www.globalcitizen.org/en/content/prime-minister-barbados-mia-mottley-climate/.

208 David Olusoga, “Slavery and the Guardian: The Ties That Bind Us,” *The Guardian*, March 28, 2023, https://www.theguardian.com/news/ng-interactive/2023/mar/28/slavery-and-the-guardian-the-ties-that-bind-us.

209 Rhiannon James, “UK Must Consider Slavery Reparations as it Is ‘Right Thing to Do’ – Labour MP,” *The Independent*, October 24, 2024, https://www.independent.co.uk/news/uk/dawn-butler-bell-ribeiroaddy-keir-starmer-labour-marsha-de-cordova-b2635016.html.

210 Barbara Kingsolver, *High Tide in Tucson: Essays From Now or Never* (Harper Perennial, 1995), 232–33.

211 Connie Chang, “Here’s What You Can Do to Cope with Your Anxiety About Climate Change,” *The Washington Post*, July 15, 2021, https://www.washingtonpost.com/lifestyle/wellness/climate-change-anxiety-dread-cope/2021/07/14/471eb264-e4d4-11eb-b722-89ea0dde7771_story.html.

212 Johanna Silver, *The Bold Dry Garden: Lessons from the Ruth Bancroft Garden* (Timber Press, 2016), 83.

213 Victoria Namkung, “Conspiracy-Laden, Fire-Prone Icons: What Will Happen to LA’s Palm Trees?,” *The Guardian*, January 23, 2025, https://www.theguardian.com/us-news/2025/jan/23/los-angeles-wildfires-palm-trees.

214 Gary Paul Nabhan, *Gathering the Desert* (University of Arizona Press, 1986), 22.

215 Erica Gies, *Water Always Wins: Thriving in an Age of Drought and Deluge* (University of Chicago Press, 2023), 28.

216 Masashi Soga and Kevin J. Gaston, "Global Synthesis Indicates Widespread Occurrence of Shifting Baseline Syndrome," *BioScience* 74, issue 10, (October 2024): 686–694, https://doi.org/10.1093/biosci/biae068

217 Edward O. Wilson, afterword to *Silent Spring*, by Rachel Carson, (Mariner Books Classics, 2022), 361.

218 "Barbados pm Mia Mottley chews up a swedish journalist," posted October 4, 2023, by LuiSpot, YouTube, https://www.youtube.com/watch?v=gT4Jaa7Z6O8.

219 "Anthurium Species And Cultivars," Anthurium Hawaii, accessed July 6, 2025, http://anthuriumhi.com/tag/anthurium-cultivars/.

220 Judith Taylor, "The Begonia in California, Part 1," Pacific Horticulture, accessed July 13, 2025, https://pacifichorticulture.org/articles/the-begonia-in-california-part-1/.

221 Victoria Kasperski, *How to Make Cut Flowers Last* (M. Barrows and Company, 1956), 54.

222 Jamaica Kincaid, ed., *My Favorite Plant: Writers and Gardeners and the Plants They Love Edited* (Farrar, Straus and Giroux, 1998), 34–35.

223 Louise Furey, *Maori Gardening: An Archaeological Perspective* (Science & Technical Publishing, 2006), https://www.doc.govt.nz/documents/science-and-technical/sap235.pdf

224 Ross Worrall and Bettina Gollnow, *Quality Specifications for Flannel Flower* (Rural industries research & Development Corporation, 2010).

225 "Tahitian Gardenia," Tahiti tourism website, October 3, 2023, https://www.tahititourisme.ca/tahitian-gardenia/.

226 Kingsbury, Noel, 78.

227 FloraCulture International (FCI), "Novel Australian Native Flowers for the World Market," International Association of Horticultural Producers, June 1, 2022, https://aiph.org/floraculture/news/novel-australian-native-flowers-for-the-world-market/.

228 Sessions, 15.

229 Elizabeth Speith and Sky Harrison, *Plant Field Guide by Hawai'i Volcanoes National Park*, accessed July 13, 2025, https://www.643pest.org/fieldguides/NPS_CARDS_HAVO_12112012_final.pdf.

230 Kingsbury, *The Story of Flowers*, 54.

231 Taylor, *The Global Migration*, 99.

232 Scott Simon, host, Michael Pollan, guest, *Short Wave*, "Orchids: 'Inflatable Love Dolls Of The Floral Kingdom" NPR, August 22, 2009, https://www.npr.org/2009/08/22/112124695/orchids-inflatable-love-dolls-of-the-floral-kingdom.

233 Mary Susan Loan, "Xate Survival Story," *Belize Ag Report*, August–September 2013, 9, https://agreport.bz/wp-content/uploads/2022/02/Belize-Ag-Report_Issue-22-Aug-2013.pdf.

234 "Xateros / Proyecto del CIESAS-Sureste y el Centro de Estudios Superiores de México y Centroamérica de la Universidad de Ciencias y Artes de Chiapas. Proyecto Videoastas Indígenas de la Frontera Sur, Spooner Productions," 2004, Archivo Mesoamericano project, video documentary, https://archivomesoamericano.org/media_objects/dz010q056.

235 Kerry Lotzof, "Maria Sibylla Merian: Metamorphosis Unmasked by Art and Science," Natural History Museum, accessed July 6, 2025, https://www.nhm.ac.uk/discover/maria-sibylla-merian-metamorphosis-art-and-science.html.

236 Diana Duff, "Plant of the Month: Mgambo Tree," *West Hawaii Today*, March 6, 2016, https://www.westhawaiitoday.com/2016/03/06/features/plant-of-the-month-mgambo-tree/.

237 Sara Duvisac, *DECOLONIZE! WHAT DOES IT MEAN?* (Oxfam, 2022), 4, https://oxfamilibrary.openrepository.com/bitstream/handle/10546/621456/rr-decolonize-what-does-it-mean-151222-en.pdf;jsessionid=1EE69CFF7FE101E615A737B809179655?sequence=1.

238 Steger, 124.

239 John Kazior, "The Beauty and Violence of Ernst Haeckel's Illustrations," *Eye on Design* by *AIGA*, April 8, 2021, https://eyeondesign.aiga.org/the-beauty-and-violence-of-ernst-haeckels-illustrations/.

240 Kingsbury, *The Story of Flowers*, 193.

Epigraph Citations

AESTHETICS: Charlotte Avery, "25 Jean Piaget Quotes on Psychology, Wisdom and Human Development," Achology, accessed July 17, 2025, https://achology.com/wisdom-for-life/jean-piaget-quotes-on-human-development/.

ANTHROPOCENE: Andrea Malm, "The Anthropocene Myth," *Jacobin*, March 30, 2015, https://jacobin.com/2015/03/anthropocene-capitalism-climate-change/.

APPROPRIATION: Michel de Montaigne, *Essays*, ed. M. Rat (1580, rep. 1958) bk. 1, ch. 25, in *Oxford Essential Quotations*, edited by Susan Ratcliffe. (Oxford University Press, 2016), https://www.oxfordreference.com/display/10.1093/acref/9780191843730.001.0001/q-oro-ed5-00007567.

ARID: Gary Nabhan, "Deserts Are Not For the Faint of Heart; Plants Must Adapt to Various Struggles," *Gary Nabhan*, November 19, 2020, https://www.garynabhan.com/news/2020/11/deserts-are-not-for-the-faint-of-heart-plants-must-adapt-to-various-struggles/.

ARMATURE: Kate Atkinson, *A God in Ruins* (Back Bay Books, 2016).

AROID: Brian Howey, "When a Houseplant Obsession Becomes a Nightmare," *Wired*, October 20, 2022, https://www.wired.com/story/nightmare-houseplant-obsession-nepenthes/.

AUCTION: Kobayashi Issa, "In this World," trans. by Robert Hass, All Poetry (blog), accessed July 17, 2025, https://allpoetry.com/poem/8516785-in-this-world-by-Kobayashi-Issa.

BEDDING: Charlie Chaplin, *My Autobiography* (Simon & Schuster, 1964).

BIOPROSPECTING: Nora Young, host, *Spark*, "The Spark Guide to Civilization, Ep 6–Obsolescence," CBC Radio, February 26, 2021, https://www.cbc.ca/radio/spark/we-re-trapped-in-an-upgrade-cycle-whether-we-like-it-or-not-1.5917265/.

BOTANICAL: Edna St. Vincent Millay, "Never May the Fruit Be Picked," accessed July 17, 2025 https://poets.org/poem/never-may-fruit-be-picked.

BREEDING: Barry Schwartz, *The Paradox of Choice: Why More Is Less* (Harper Perennial, 2005).

BROMELIADS: "Garden of Stories," *Garland Magazine*, https://garlandmag.com/garden/.

BULB: Andy Warhol, *The Philosophy of Andy Warhol (From A to B and Back Again)* (Harcourt, 1975).

CHROMOPHOBIA: Rebecca Mead, "The Intensely Colorful Work of a Painter Obsessed with Anime," *The New Yorker*, November 11, 2024, https://www.newyorker.com/magazine/2024/11/18/the-intensely-colorful-work-of-a-painter-obsessed-with-anime.

CLIMATE: W. S. Merwin, "Place" in *The Rain in the Trees* (Knopf, 1987).

COLD CHAIN: Jack Goody, *The Culture of Flowers*, (Cambridge University Press, 1993).

COLONIAL: Billie Holiday and William Dufty, *Lady Sings the Blues* (Doubleday & Company, 1956).

CORM: Hope Jahren, *Lab Girl* (Alfred A. Knopf, 2016).

CULTIVAR: Noël Kingsbury, *The New Perennial Garden* (Frances Lincoln Ltd, 1991).

CULTIVATED: Jamaica Kincaid, "Flowers of Evil," *New Yorker*, October 5, 1992.

CUTICLE: Loren Eiseley, *The Immense Journey* (Random House, 1957).

DEMONSTRATION: Ruth Reichl, "Ruth Reichl Ditches the Wigs for a New Disguise Fiction," interview by Marnie Hanel, *New York Times Magazine*, May 2, 2014, https://www.nytimes.com/2014/05/04/magazine/ruth-reichl-ditches-the-wigs-for-a-new-disguise-fiction.html.

DESICCATED: Anaïs Nin, *The Diaries of Anaïs Nin Volume 3: 1939–1944* (Mariner Books Classics, 1971).

DEXTERITY: Octavia Butler, *Parable of the Sower* (Four Walls Eight Windows, 1993).

DIASPORA: Édouard Glissant, *Poetics of Relation*, trans. by Betsy Wing (University of Michigan Press, 1997).

DYE: Josef Albers, *Interaction of Color, 50th Anniversary Edition* (Yale University Press, 2013).

ECOLOGICAL: Soraya Kishtwari, "How a Rare Colombian Flower Cultivated with Indigenous Know-How Is Changing Lives," *Mongabay*, August 18, 2022, https://news.mongabay.com/2022/08/how-a-rare-colombian-flower-cultivated-with-indigenous-know-how-is-changing-lives/.

EMERGENT: Andrea Wulf, *The Invention of Nature: Alexander Humboldt's New World* (Vintage, 2016), 6.

ENDONYMS: Banu Subramaniam, *The Botany of Empire: Plant Worlds and the Scientific Legacies of Colonialism* (University of Washington Press, 2024), 59.

EPHEMERAL: Joan Didion, "On Keeping a Notebook," in *Slouching Towards Bethlehem* (Farrar, Straus and Giroux, 1968).

EXOTIC: Thiara Borges, "Miguel Flores-Vianna," *The Velvet Fantastic*, August 4, 2011, https://thevelvetfantastic.wordpress.com/2011/08/04/miguel-flores-vianna/.

FAIR TRADE: Angela M. Eikenberry, "The Hidden Costs of Cause Marketing," *Stanford Social Innovation Review*, Summer 2009, https://ssir.org/articles/entry/the_hidden_costs_of_cause_marketing.

FERNERY: Arianne True, "pandemic: even the nice days, we're inside," *The Madrona Project*, vol. 2, no. 1 (June 2021), https://poets.org/poem/pandemic-even-nice-days-were-inside.

FIX: Austin Kleon, "25 Quotes to Help You Steal Like an Artist," February 10, 2010, https://austinkleon.com/2010/02/10/25-quotes-to-help-you-steal-like-an-artist/

FLORA: Don Bennett and Norma Hall, *The Wattle and the Waratah*, words by Norma Hall, music by Don Bennett, Peters Radio Unit, 1952, https://catalogue.nla.gov.au/catalog/2187601.

FLORICULTURE: Gaylord Nelson, speech at the Woman's Club of Minneapolis, broadcast April 21, 1994, MPR Archive, https://archive.mpr.org/stories/1994/04/21/gaylord-nelson-environmental-speech-followed-by-dean-abrahamson-discussing-earth-day.

FLORISTRY: Alan Bennett, *Talking Heads* (BBC Books, 1988), 34.

FOOTPRINT: Marcel Haedrich, *Coco Chanel: Her Life, Her Secrets*, trans. Charles Lam Markmann (Little, Brown and Company, 1972).

FYNBOS: Anton Crone, "Rising from the Flames in Table Mountain National Park," *Africa Geographic Stories*, March 13, 2015, https://africageographic.com/stories/cape-town-fire-fynbos-table-mountain-life-in-the-ashes/.

GARLAND: Simone LeAmon, "Contemporary Lei and Body Adornment from the Torres Strait Islands" Garland Magazine, December 1, 2017, https://garlandmag.com/article/contemporary-lei-and-body-adornment-from-the-torres-strait-islands/.

GLOBALIZATION: Daniel Chapman, "Land Lovers," *LOOK*, November 4, 1969, 58.

GONDWANA: John McPhee, *Basin and Range* (Farrar, Straus & Giroux, 1981).

HEGEMONY: Dana Arnold, *Art History*, (Oxford University Press, 2004).

HOTHOUSE: Edward Abbey, *Desert Solitaire: A Season in the Wilderness* (Ballantine Books, 1971).

HYBRID: Krishan Rajapakshe, "Male: The Act of Flowers," *Garland Magazine*, January 3, 2019, https://garlandmag.com/male-the-act-of-flowers/.

INDIGENOUS: Lena Khalaf Tuffaha, "To Be Self-Evident" in *Something About Living* (University of Akron Press, 2024), https://poets.org/poem/be-self-evident.

INSTALLATION: Simone LeAmon, "Contemporary Lei and Body Adornment from the Torres Strait Islands," *Garland Magazine*, December 1, 2017, https://garlandmag.com/article/contemporary-lei-and-body-adornment-from-the-torres-strait-islands/.

INVASIVE: Liam Heneghan, "Is There Need for 'The New Wild'?: The New Ecological Quarrels," *Los Angeles Review of Books*, October 15, 2025, https://lareviewofbooks.org/article/is-there-need-for-the-new-wild-the-new-ecological-quarrels/.

JUNGLE: Haley Mellin. Personal communication with the author, January 31, 2025.

KILLERS: Elizabeth Kolbert, *Under a White Sky: The Nature of the Future* (Crown, 2021).

LIANA: Hope Jahren, *Lab Girl* (Alfred A. Knopf, 2016).

LINE: Édouard Manet, "Édouard Manet Quotes," accessed July 17, 2025, https://www.manet.org/quotes.jsp.

MEMORIAL: Diana Vreeland, *Allure* (Doubleday and Company, 1980), 203.

MERISTEM: Prudence Gibson, "Dark Botany," in *Dark Botany: The Herbarium Tales*, ed. Prudence Gibson, Sigi Jöttkandt, Marie Sierra, and Anna Westbrook (Open Humanities Press, 2024), 18, http://openhumanitiespress.org/books/download/Gibson%20and%20all_2024_Dark-Botany.pdf

MICROPLASTICS: "Cristina Romera-Castillo: 'Cleaning the Ocean Out of Plastic Is Like Sweeping in the Desert,'" institut de ciències del mar, September 30, 2022, https://www.icm.csic.es/en/news/cristina-romera-castillo-cleaning-ocean-out-plastic-sweeping-desert.

MODERNISM: Lauro Cavalcanti, Fares el-Dahdah, and Francis Rambert, eds., *Roberto Burle Marx: The Modernity of Landscape*, (Actarbirkhauser, 2011), https://issuu.com/actar/docs/robertoburlemarx.

MOTIF: Jacques Lacan, *The Seminar of Jacques Lacan, Book II: The Ego in Freud's Theory and in the Technique of Psychoanalysis, 1954–1955*, trans. Sylvana Tomaselli, (Cambridge University Press, 1988).

NATURALIZE: Richard Mabey, *Weeds: The Story of Outlaw Plants* (Profile Books, 2012), 5.

OCCUPY: Frantz Fanon, *The Wretched of the Earth* (Grove Press, 1963).

PANTROPICAL: Brandon Withrow, "The Irony of 'Last Chance' Travel in the Age of Climate Change," *Canadian Geographic*, January 17, 2024, https://canadiangeographic.ca/articles/the-irony-of-last-chance-travel-in-the-age-of-climate-change/.

PASTICHE: I. M. Pei, interview by John Tusa, *Architecture on 3*, BBC Radio 3, released on December 8, 2002, https://www.bbc.co.uk/radio3/architecture/pa_impei.shtml.

PEAT: Robert E. Drennan, ed., *The Algonquin Wits* (Citadel Press, 1968).

PERENNIAL: Aldo Leopold, *A Sand County Almanac* (Ballantine Books, 1986).

PHOTOPERIODISM: Charlotte Perkins Gilman, "Coming," 1893, https://poets.org/poem/coming-0.

PROTEA: Daniel Naawenkangua Abukuri, "The Africa They Never See," *The Kalahari Review*, January 28, 2025, https://kalaharireview.com/when-the-earth-let-go-e6ac39c68a36.

QUEER: Loretta Riach, "Inside You Are Two Wolves And They Are Both Nonbinary," *Overcom 9*, February 2023, https://www.bestnewzealandpoems.org.nz/past-issues/2023-contents/loretta-riach/.

REGENERATIVE: Lara Bryant, "Celebrate the International Year of Soils! Some things you never knew..." *NFW Blog*, last updated, December 23, 2015, https://blog.nwf.org/2015/01/celebrate-the-international-year-of-soils-some-things-you-never-knew/.

RIPE: Anaïs Nin, *The Diaries of Anaïs Nin Volume 3: 1939–1944* (Mariner Books Classics, 1971).

SCENT: Dominique Roques, *In Search of Perfumes: A Lifetime Journey to the Sources of Nature's Scents* (HarperVia, 2024), 279.

SEASONALITY: Annie Dillard, *The Writing Life* (Harper & Row, 1989).

SPECIATION: Jean Cocteau, *Newsweek*, May 16, 1955, in *Oxford Essential Quotations*, ed. Susan Ratcliffe, (Oxford University Press, 2016), https://www.oxfordreference.com/display/10.1093/acref/9780191826719.001.0001/q-oro-ed4-00012138.

SUBTROPICAL: Charles King, guest, Ramtin Arablouei, host, *Throughline*, "The Invention of Race," NPR, November 19, 2020, https://www.npr.org/transcripts/936346847.

SUCCULENT: Pico Iyer, "Years ago, writer Pico Iyer lost everything in a wildfire. This is what he learned," interview by Terry Gross, *Fresh Air*, NPR, January 15, 2025, https://www.npr.org/2025/01/15/nx-s1-5259687/pico-iyer-aflame-silent-retreat.

SUSTAINABLE: Stanisław J. Lec, *More Unkempt Thoughts*, trans. Jacek Galazka (Funk & Wagnalls, 1968), 9.

TEXTURE: "Cerrado Savannah—Frontiers & Transformations, Brazil," Peter Canton Photography, accessed August 23, 2025, https://www.petercaton.co.uk/photostory/frontiers-and-transformation/.

TOKENISM: Mary Daly, *Beyond God the Father: Toward a Philosophy of Women's Liberation* (Beacon, 1973).

UTILITARIANISM: MM Writers, "Lily Tomlin Fans Share Favorite One-Liners as 9 to 5 Actress Celebrates Birthday" *MovieMaker*, April 5, 2025, https://www.moviemaker.com/lily-tomlin-celebrated-for-great-one-liners-and-film-roles-as-9-to-5-actress-and-comedian-turns-84/.

VALUE: Nahlah Ayed, host, *Ideas*, "BBC Reith Lectures: Mark Carney, Part One," CBC Radio, July 21, 2021.

WIRED: G. K. Chesterton, Our Note Book, *Illustrated London News*, May 5, 1928, 780.

WOKE: Wangari Maathai, "Prof Wangari Maathai's Keynote Address During the 2nd World Congress of Agroforestry," speech, August 24, 2009, The Green Belt Movement, https://www.greenbeltmovement.org/wangari-maathai/key-speeches-and-articles/2nd-world-congress-of-agroforestry-keynote-address.

XERIC: Erica Gies, "Water Always Wins: 'Quietly radical' book makes case for Slow Water," interview by Gary Wilson, *Great Lakes Now*, May 26, 2022, https://www.greatlakesnow.org/2022/05/water-always-wins-book/.

YOU: Giuseppe di Lampedusa, *The Leopard*, trans. Archibald Colquhoun (Pantheon, 1991).

ZEITGEIST: International Coordination of Revolutionary Parties and Organizations, "ICOR Declaration: Ecology Without Class Struggle Is Just Gardening," June 27, 2024, https://www.icor.info/en/en/2024/ecology-without-class-struggle-is-just-gardening.

AFTERWORD: Benjamin Anastas, *Too Good to Be True: A Memoir* (Little A / New Harvest, 2012).

Acknowledgments

Over the five years I worked on this book, my husband and I lost our three remaining parents, our dog, and two friends. These losses changed our lives in dramatic ways, and we moved through periods of caregiving, grieving, and dislocation. Most authors thank their spouse at the end of their acknowledgments, but I'm putting my husband, Kyle, first because he has unflaggingly supported my work, no matter our challenges and my absences.

I'm also grateful to Dr. Lise Butler, Robbie Honey, Paula Butler, Penny Murray, Leif Skogland, Mara Jernigan, Heidi Schmidt, and Rita Feldmann for not only "getting" this book, but also for buoying me up over the years.

While I was writing I decided to fund a Cultivated Grant to allow others to explore sustainable floristry. Heartfelt thanks to Jennifer Jewell in California and Helen Dyson in London for contributing to the program in 2022 and making it a success. I'm grateful to the grant recipients Rheanna Chen, Lori Poliski, and Thanu Eagelle for giving us all hope for the future.

People around the world assisted me on this project, welcoming me to their gardens, countries and homes. These people include Coral Shortt, Leon Kluge, Johan Nel, Julian Melck, and Freddie Kirsten in South Africa. Thanks to my dear friend Sarah Malm for joining me wildflower hunting, and driving while I stared out the window, agog, and later connecting me to Dr. Mike Rosenberg, chair of the Kampong, who welcomed me in Florida. Thanks to Dr. Christopher Baraloto, who handed me a single scented bloom of *Magnolia champaca*, aka the Joy perfume tree. It was a moment I won't forget at the Kampong.

Thanks to Kato Ryoji in Japan, Eric Tanouhe and David Shiigi on Hawaii, the floral team at the Halekulani on Oahu, Alison Higgins on Hawaii, and Lauren Shearer and Christina Hartman on Maui for your kindness.

On Nevis: Thanks to Richie Lupinacci at the Hermitage for welcoming me over many years while I worked on this book. Thanks to Jill and Ian Pinniger and Mr. Harris for sharing the garden up the hill. Thanks also to Keith Huggins, head gardener at Golden Rock, Christi Douglas of the Botanical Gardens of Nevis, and Chantelle Mayeling Garcia Romero and Tish Brown for your smiles.

Thanks to Barbara Japal of the Antigua and Barbuda Horticultural Society and Pin Affleck and Gordon Watson in Tangier for an illuminating week. Thanks to Emily Fletcher of Peat-Free UK, and in Mexico, thanks to Alicia Reyes and Pili Fuentes for your hospitality.

In my research, I had help from Marcelo Kuhlmann in Brazil, Shoukry Roweis in Toronto, and Craig Scott and Bettina Gollnow in Australia. Thanks to the flower lovers Shawn Shepherd, Sue McCleary, Kelly Norris, Thomas Broom-Hughes, Ursula Gunther, Abigail Sergeant, Eileen Johnson, Kady Dalrymple, Cel Robertson, Dee Hall Goodwin, Anna Svensson, and Hitomi Gilliam for sharing your ideas, empathy and talents. Thanks also to Zita Elze, Tom Weiss, Victoria Clarke, Shane Connolly, Jennifer Morello Fiss, Marzena Joseph, and Dafne Tovar for insightful conversation.

Many thanks to the Garden Club of America and all the institutions that have supported me in my work. I have met so many fantastic plantswomen, seen incredible gardens, and gained insight into the history of horticulture and floral design in the United States through the GCA. I've also made friends. Thank you.

I'm grateful to Sue Donaldson and Sara Stamen for loving my initial lexicon and Tom Fischer and Ryder Wyatt for reading. Many thanks to Ana Myerscough for creatively collaborating on the collages.

This book had so many moving parts and took so long to produce it was a real juggling act for Klaus Kirschbaum, my editor, and Stacee Gravelle Lawrence, photo editor and fixer extraordinaire. Thank you both for your patience, tenacity, and good humor. Evi O: Your creativity with the book design brought my ideas to life and I'm grateful for your vision.

Finally, this book would not have been possible without the photographers, artists, designers, museologists, gallerists, curators, and librarians who create, collect, curate and archive floral images. Thank you for your belief in this project.

Image Credits

Alamy/All Canada Photos: 190 bottom

Alamy/Amoret Tanner: 161

Alamy/Andia: 213 top right

Alamy/anton havelaar: 165 bottom

Alamy/Anna Watson: 78

Alamy/Archive Pics: 79 bottom

Alamy/Avalon.red: 172

Alamy/Carlo Bollo: 102

Alamy/Cavan Images: 137 top

Alamy/Chronicle: 37

Alamy/Classic Image: 174

Alamy/David R. Frazier Photolibrary, Inc.: 190 top

Alamy/De Luan: 265

Alamy/Donatas Dabravolskas: 171

Alamy/Hemis: 210

Alamy/Historic Illustrations: 43

Alamy/IanDagnall Computing: 151

Alamy/Image Source Limited: 119 top right

Alamy/Ivan Vasylyev: 120

Alamy/Jean-Marc Lallemand: 215 bottom

Alamy/Joerg Boethling:101

Alamy/John Robertson: 148 top

Alamy/Jon Arnold Images Ltd: 95

Alamy/Juergen Freund: 112 top

Alamy/Keren Su/China Span: 76 top left

Alamy/M. Kuhlmann: 230, 231

Alamy/Nature Picture Library: 148 bottom

Alamy/NurPhoto SRL: 226 top left

Alamy/PBH: 226 bottom left

Alamy/Ron Giling: 238

Alamy/Science Photo Library: 239

Alamy/Smith Archive: 54

Alamy/steeve-x-art: 168

Alamy/Tom Hanley: 156

Alamy/The Picture Art Collection: 164 lower right

Alamy/ton koene: 49

Alamy/ZUMA Press, Inc: 87

Ayrton Camargo/Tyba: 169

Mandy Barker: 166

Emma Bass: 234

© Burle Marx Institute: 170

Peter Caton: 51, 229

Marco Cedeño-Fonseca: 20

John Lewis Childs, 1898 Catalogue of Bulbs no. Fall, Floral Park NY. Courtesy Smithsonian Libraries: 18

Cornell University Library, Division of Rare and Manuscript Collections: 183 bottom

©Marizilda Cruppe/Greenpeace: 140–41

Ana-Filipa Domingues: 222, 250

Dreamstime.com/ © Ncl: 289

Thanushi Eagalle: 206

Libby Ellis: 128

Courtesy Jenks Farmer: 47 top right

Flickr/James Anderson: 155

© Mateo Fernández Lucero: 82, 83 top, 83 bottom

Courtesy Garden Museum, London, United Kingdom: 27

Boz Gagovski: 47 bottom right

Christin Geall: 6, 13, 14, 16, 17, 21 top, 21 bottom 22, 28, 32, 36, 38, 40, 42 upper left, 42 upper right, 46 top left, 46 bottom left, 47 top left, 47 bottom left, 48, 50, 56, 62, 66, 67, 68, 70, 71, 72 bottom right, 74, 76 bottom right, 77, 79 top, 80, 81, 85, 86, 88, 91, 98, 99, 100, 113, 114, 115, 117, 118 top left, 122, 123, 124, 125 top left, 125 top right, 125 bottom, 132, 135, 136, 142, 143, 146, 149, 153, 154, 160, 165 top right, 178 all, 179, 182, 183 top, 184, 188, 192, 194, 198, 199, 201, 204, 212, 213 top left, 213 bottom right, 216, 220, 221, 226 middle left, 226 top right, 236, 243, 244, 245 top left, 245 top right, 245 bottom right, 248, 254

Getty Images/Evening Standard: 186

Colin Gilliam: 119 top left

Kyle Goetsch: 44–45

Satomi Grim: 119 bottom right

Ken Hermann: 126

Courtesy Hiroshima Municipal Museum of Contemporary Art: 159

Robbie Honey: 64, 162

Mariko Ikeda/The Shirley Sherwood Collection: 209 bottom

Illustrated Adelaide News: 103

Víctor Interiano: 61

Ryoji Kato: 53

Lauren Keith: 75

Kent Flowers: 72 upper left, 73 lower right, 81 lower right, 201 lower right

Joyce Kim: 92

Brandy Kraft: 202

Marcelo Kuhlmann: 228

Jennifer Latour/Open Doors Gallery: 138

Courtesy Library and Archives Canada, Acc. No. 1983-27-368: 57 top

Courtesy Library and Archives Canada, Acc. No. 1983-27-77: 57 bottom left

Courtesy Library and Archives Canada, Acc. No. 1983-27-122: 57 bottom right

Library of Congress/LCCN 00649509: 240

Loza Estudio/Manuel Godoy: 214

Azuma Makoto: 157

Ren MacDonald-Balasia/Renko Floral: 94

Make A Scene! Bali: 144

Lilian Martinez/Ochi Gallery: 209 top

Courtesy Haley Mellin and Dittrich & Schlechtriem, Berlin: 191

© 2016 MoMA, N.Y.: 150

Montreal Museum of Fine Arts/Christine Guest: 134

Courtesy Abelardo Morell and Edwynn Houk Gallery: 52

Ana Myerscough: 13, 132, 232

Courtesy National Gallery of Victoria, Melbourne, Commission 2017: 76 top right

Courtesy National Tropical Botanical Garden: 65
Johan Nel: 72 top

Ngoc Minh Ngo: 176

Marianne North, Royal Botanic Gardens, Kew, London, UK. The Board of Trustees of the Royal Botanic Gardens, Kew/Bridgeman Images: 34

Courtesy Oakes Ames Orchid Library, Harvard University: 164 top

Pamela Pauline: 108

Cindy Pham: 118 top right

Courtesy Hamish Powell and This Humid House: 60

© Queensland Museum/Gary Cranitch: 130

Adeline Rapon: 180

Odilon Redon, courtesy Metropolitan Museum of Art, Bequest of Mabel Choate, in memory of her father, Joseph Hodges Choate,1958: 8

Louise Rietvink/Slow Research Lab: 241

Courtesy Rollins College, Department of College Archives and Special Collections Olin Library, Winter Park, Florida: 39

John A. Salzer, Seed Co. 1896. Catalogue of Plants and Seeds no. Spring 1896, SPRING 1897, SPRING 1898, SPRING 1899, La Crosse, WI. Courtesy Smithsonian Libraries: 26

Courtesy San Diego City Clerk Archives: 219

Marc Sardi: 203

Craig O. Scott: 72 bottom left, 112 bottom left, 112 bottom right

Ned Seidler/*National Geographic* 1968: 30–31

Daniel Shipp: 10, 110–11

State Archives of Florida: 105

State Archives of Florida/Kathleen L. Figgen: 104

Photography by Claire Takacs: 11

Kara Taylor: 196–97

Kasumi Teshigahara/Sogetsu: 224

© This Humid House: 118 bottom, 145

U.S.D.A. Pomological Watercolor Collection/Mary Daisy Arnold: 208

Courtesy U.S. National Park Service, George Washington Carver National Monument: 15

Billy Van Bakker: 58, 84, 218

Vetterle and Reinelt: 24

Victoria & Albert Museum: 175

Virro & Lola: 106

Françoise Weeks: 116

Wellcome Collection/Fernán Federici: 205 bottom

Wikimedia Commons/Francisco Manuel Blanco: 274, 278 bottom

Wikimedia Commons/Bonhams, San Francisco, May 24, 2007, lot 512: 96

Wikimedia Commons/British Museum: 277 top

Wikimedia Commons/Butler University Libraries: 288

Wikimedia Commons/Cooper Hewitt, Smithsonian Design Museum: 263, 264 bottom

Wikimedia Commons/Sarah Ann Drake: 285

Wikimedia Commons/Drkgk: 205 top

Wikimedia Commons/Walter Hood Fitch: 269

Wikimedia Commons/Helen Hewitt: 286

Wikimedia Commons/William Jackson Hooker: 270, 271, 272 top

Wikimedia Commons/Internet Achive Book Images/*The Gardeners' chronicle : a weekly illustrated journal of horticulture and allied subjects*, 1874: 42 bottom

Wikimedia Commons/JAMA030: 213 top right

Wikimedia Commons/John Lindley and Joseph Paxton, drawing by L. A. L. Constans: 265, 276, 278 top, 287

Wikimedia Commons/Pieter Kuipter: 55

Wikimeida Commons/Lena Lowis: 268, 275 bottom, 282, 284 middle

Wikimedia Commons/The LuEsther T Mertz Library, the New York Botanical Garden: 280 bottom

Wikimedia Commons/Liebig Chromos: 164 lower left

Wikimedia Commons/Henrietta Maria Moriarty: 264 top

Wikimedia Commons/National Gallery of Art/Ailsa Mellon Bruce Collection: 279

Wikimedia Commons/nicolai00: 267

Wikimedia Commons/Pierre-Joseph Redouté: 291

Wikimedia Commons/Fyodor Petrovich Tolstoy: 284 bottom

Wikimedia Commons/Post of Bolivia: 245 bottom left

Wikimedia Commons/Post of Congo: 107

Wikimedia Commons/Post of Kenya: 185

Wikimedia Commons/Post of Zanzibar: 253

Wikimedia Commons/PTT Indonesia: 183 top right

Wikimedia Commons/Rezergua: 273

Wikimedia Commons/Rijksmuseum: 277 bottom

Wikimedia Commons/Rosa Fiveash: 215 top

Wikimedia Commons/ Royal Albert Memorial Museum & Art Gallery: 275 top

Wikimedia Commons/Thomas H. Shepherd: 137 bottom

Wikimedia Commons/James Sowerby: 290

Wikimedia Commons/Step, E. & Watson, W.: 280 top

Wikimeida Commons/Sydenham Edwards: 284 top

Wikimedia Commons/Wellcome Collection/L0041678: 89

Wikimedia Commons/Wellcome Collection/L0060786: 152

Wikimedia Commons/Wellcome Collection/L0063385: 90

Wikimedia Commons/wnsstamps.ch: 46 right

Wikimedia Commons/Yale Center for British Art/James Bruce: 283

Wikimedia Commons/Johann Zoffany/Towneley Hall Art Gallery: 133

Wikimedia Commons/Укрпошта, Василь Василенко: 76 bottom left

Damon Winter/The New York Times/Redux: 246–47

Alida Withoos: 272 bottom

Feifei Zhou, Reprinted from *Feral Atlas: The More-Than-Human Anthropocene*, Tsing, Anna L. and Jennifer Deger, Alder Keleman Saxena, Feifei Zhou, http://feralatlas.org/ Courtesy Stanford University Press (c) 2020 by the Board of Trustees of the Leland Stanford Jr. University: 12

Manuel Zuniga: 227

First published in the United States of America in 2026 by

Rizzoli International Publications, Inc.
49 West 27th Street
New York, NY 10001
www.rizzoliusa.com

Publisher: Charles Miers
Editor: Klaus Kirschbaum
Assistant Editor: Emily Ligniti
Photography Editor: Stacee Gravelle Lawrence
Production Manager: Rebecca Ambrose
Managing Editor: Lynn Scrabis
Design: Evi O.Studio

ISBN-13: 978-0-8478-7613-6
Library of Congress Catalog Control Number: 2025942039

Printed in Bosnia and Herzegovina
2026 2027 2028 2029 / 10 9 8 7 6 5 4 3 2 1

The authorized representative in the EU for product safety and compliance is
Mondadori Libri S.p.A., via Gian Battista Vico 42, 20123
Milan, Italy
www.mondadori.it

Visit us online:
Facebook.com/RizzoliNewYork
Instagram.com/RizzoliBooks
Youtube.com/user/RizzoliNY